BUILDING A HOUSE IN HEAVEN

Building a House in Heaven

. . . .

Pious Neoliberalism and Islamic Charity in Egypt

Mona Atia

University of Minnesota Press
Minneapolis
London

QUADRANT

Quadrant, a joint initiative of the University of Minnesota Press and the Institute for Advanced Study at the University of Minnesota, provides support for interdisciplinary scholarship within a new, more collabortive model of research and publication.

Sponsored by Quadrant's Global Cultures group (advisory board: Evelyn Davidheiser, Michael Goldman, Helga Leitner, and Margaret Werry), and by the Institute for Global Studies at the University of Minnesota.

Quadrant is generously funded by the Andrew W. Mellon Foundation. http://quadrant.umn.edu

Portions of chapter 2 were previously published as "'Innocent Victims': An Accounting of Anti-Terrorism in the Egyptian Legal Context," *Journal of Islamic and Near Eastern Law* 9, no. 1 (2011): 1–24. Portions of chapters 3 and 6 were previously published as "A Way to Paradise: Pious Neoliberalism, Islam, and Faith-Based Development," *Annals of the Association of American Geographers* 102, no. 4 (2012): 808–27; reprinted by permission of the publisher.

Published by the University of Minnesota Press
111 Third Avenue South, Suite 290
Minneapolis, MN 55401-2520
http://www.upress.umn.edu

A Cataloging-in-Publication record for this book is available from the Library of Congress.

ISBN 978-0-8166-8915-6 (hc)
ISBN 978-0-8166-8917-0 (pb)

Printed in the United States of America on acid-free paper

The University of Minnesota is an equal-opportunity educator and employer.

20 19 18 17 16 15 14 13   10 9 8 7 6 5 4 3 2 1

To the martyrs,
who gave their lives fighting for a better future for all Egyptians
and the revolutionaries
who continue the struggle.

Contents

Acknowledgments

THIS PROJECT HAS TRAVELED A LONG WAY and I have accrued numerous debts in the process. My thanks go first and foremost to those with whom this research was conducted. Numerous people generously invited me into their offices and worlds; they permitted me to write about their organizations and were generous with their time in speaking to me. The warmth and kindness of too many Egyptians to name individually made my fieldwork not only possible but also immensely enjoyable. Dr. Mohamed Abdel Halim Omar opened numerous doors that would have remained closed, and he warmly welcomed me into the Saleh Kamel Center for Islamic Economics at al-Azhar University, offering frequent stimulating conversations. I thank him and the entire faculty and staff for their guidance and support during my fieldwork. I am also indebted to Mohamed, my research assistant in Cairo, whose presence during interviews facilitated entry into numerous spaces and whose dedication to the project was unyielding.

I would like to thank my entire extended family in Egypt for their generosity, thoughtfulness, and conversation over so many delicious home-cooked meals. I owe special thanks to Wael Hassan Atia for his friendship, benevolence, and humor during my stay in Egypt; to Tamer Elbatesh, who facilitated access on so many occasions; to Tante Rusha and Tante Nadia for their constant care; and to Khalu Nagi for making sure I stayed out of trouble. I am blessed to have had the companionship, intellectual support, and uncompromising friendship of Dina Sherif, as well as the support of the Gerhart Center for Philanthropy and Civic Engagement at the American University in Cairo, especially its director, Barbara Ibrahim. I thank the Bi-national Fulbright Commission in Cairo for funding a full year of this research and providing me with Egyptian research clearance, and in particular Noha El-Gindi for facilitating my entry into government ministries. I am grateful to Egypt's revolutionaries, who planted and fought for the seeds of change in the country and inspired me to rethink and clarify my work years after its completion; and to Ahmed Faheem for sharing his photographs of the uprising.

I am so grateful to my intellectual community on this journey, especially Ananya Roy for inspiring since my first course with her in 1998 and for continuing to provide invaluable support, feedback, friendship, and intellectual challenge. I thank Katharyne Mitchell, Matt Sparke, and Vicky Lawson for asking the right questions, challenging me, and offering their guidance and support; Elvin Wyly for believing in me before anyone else; Arzoo Osanloo for her intellectual stimulation and friendship; and Nezar AlSayyad for his encouragement and feedback on the full manuscript, in the field, and beyond. I am grateful to numerous friends and colleagues who provided generous feedback: Chris Aggour, Wendy Larner, Melani McAlister, Ananya Roy, Inken Wiese, and Jessica Winegar for reading the manuscript in its entirety; Ozan Karaman, Helga Leitner, and Eric Sheppard for guidance during my visit to the University of Minnesota; and the colleagues who offered support for my work in small but greatly appreciated ways: Hiba Bou Akar, Jonathan Benthall, Jennifer Brinkerhoff, Nathan Brown, Marieke de Goede, Katie Herrold, Moustafa Khalil, Daromir Rudnyckyj, Rachel Silvey, and Amy Singer. I would also like to express gratitude for my current intellectual lifeline, the "what is the political" reading group in DC.

I was fortunate to receive financial support for numerous stages of research and writing. I thank the IIE Fulbright fellowship and the Islamic Civilizations Grant for funding my first year of research in Cairo. At the University of Washington, I am indebted to the Department of Geography, the Simpson Center for the Humanities, and the Nancy Bell Evans Center for financial support, and the Graduate School for granting me the Dissertation Fellowship as well as the Universities' Distinguished Dissertation Award. At George Washington University, I thank my colleagues in the Elliott School of International Affairs and the Department of Geography, especially Marie Price and Elizabeth Chacko, as well as Nuala Cowen and Richard Hinton for their excellent cartographic skills. I am especially grateful to the Institute for Middle East Studies for sponsoring my book workshop, which was one of the most satisfying days of my life; for providing me with invaluable research assistants, including Kaylan Grieger, Sarah Jasmine Knight, and Maro Youssef; and finally, for supporting follow-up research trips from 2009 to 2012. Graham Cornwell started work with me as a research assistant but came to play a much larger role over the years and I am indebted to him for his willingness to read numerous drafts. I also thank two anonymous readers for the University of Minnesota Press, Anne Carter and the Global Cultures Quadrant Program, Enass Khansa for reviewing my transliterations, my meticulous copy editor Cherene Holland, and my editor Jason Weidemann, for his enthusiasm for the project and expert guidance in bringing it to completion.

I extend my sincere appreciation to my cherished friends for support throughout the years, especially Abdellah Abat, Basem Abdelmesih, Ehaab Abdou, Johanna Bockman, Anne Bonds, Elliott Colla, Ahmed Shawki Farag, Ilana Feldman, Heather Frost, Doug Grbic, Sherine Hamdy, Hiromi Ishizawa, Manal Jamal, Dina Khoury, Rama Murali, Peter Paproski, Shira Robinson, Nagat El Sanabary, Sara Scalenghe, Sarah Starkweather, Mayssa Sultan, Deborah Watt, Katie Wells, and Andrew Zimmerman.

Last, but certainly not least, I thank my family: my sister, Hoda, and my brother-in-law, Ahmed, for believing in me always; my brother, Walid, for accompanying me into the deep blue with his contagious optimism; and my parents for inspiring my interest in Egypt and supporting me in so many ways.

A Note on Transliteration

I USED A MODIFIED VERSION of the system of transliteration for Arabic set by the *International Journal of Middle East Studies*, except I omitted diacritical marks, with the exception of the ʿayn and the ʾhamza. I used anglicized plurals for Arabic terms found in an unabridged English dictionary (e.g., fatwas). I used the letter *g* instead of *j* to represent the Egyptian dialect. Place names are spelled according to how they are most commonly transliterated, and I use individuals' chosen spellings of their own names when they have appeared in English-language publications (e.g., Ali Gomaa, not Ali Gumaʿa).

Introduction

If it's not meeting a need, turn it into a seed. Remember, we will reap what we sow. When you do good for other people, that's when God is going to make sure that His abundant blessings overtake you. If you want to live your best life now, you must develop a lifestyle of giving: living to give instead of living to get. . . . You can't expect to reap a harvest without first planting your seeds. If you will be faithful and do what God is asking you to do, God will do His part.

These are the words of Joel Osteen, the forty-five-year-old evangelical preacher at America's largest church. He draws twenty-five thousand people to his sermons, 7 million viewers to his weekly television show, and millions of readers to his best-selling book, *Your Best Life Now: Seven Steps to Living at Your Full Potential.* These words, though, might just as likely have come out of the mouth of the wildly popular Islamic preacher Amr Khaled, who before his exile from Cairo drew tens of thousands of Cairenes to a remote suburb to listen to his sermons:

Ever since we started our program, "Life Makers," we began to plant the seeds. The first seed we planted was the seed of positive thinking, and then it was followed by perfection, bearing responsibility, seriousness, and then setting your goal in life. . . . Then, in the second phase we planted the seed of "Let us dream about how we are going to achieve the revival, and what the fields of revival are." Then we planted the seeds of education, agriculture, industry, culture and arts, and technology. . . . Some seeds that we have planted are growing. . . . Because God is Merciful and Generous, He showed us the first indications of these fruits.[1]

In 2008 *Forbes Arabia* magazine produced a "*Da'wa* Stars" list in which they ranked Islamic preachers based on their income. Amr Khaled held the number-one spot, with a 2007 income of $2.5 million.[2] Khaled, no stranger to lists, also attracted the attention of *Time* magazine's top 100 Pioneers and Heroes, *Newsweek*'s top 50 Global Elite, and *Foreign Policy*'s top 20 Public Intellectuals list. In 2010 Khaled took a leading role in the world of Islamic reality television, recruiting participants for his show, *Mujaddidun* (The Reformers), a competition to find the next generation of *da'wa* (preaching) stars to promote an Islamic approach to development. The winner won one hundred thousand euros to start his own development project.[3]

There are astounding similarities between Khaled, "the cool preacher," and Osteen, "the smiling preacher." Both are young, well-groomed, and charismatic leaders of a religious movement. Neither received any formal religious training. Osteen worked as a television producer before becoming a pastor and Khaled was an accountant. The preachers depart from traditional preaching styles, instead blending self-help rhetoric with piety. Critics of both Khaled and Osteen accuse them of serving "religion-light" because their sermons shy away from words like sin or stories of hellfire. Instead, these preachers encourage their followers to plant seeds and reap the fruits of a pious life, which in their narration includes success, happiness, and prosperity.[4] They have been criticized for attaching material wealth to religiosity, yet this is an important component of their appeal. These new religious leaders encourage individuals to be proactive, productive, and entrepreneurial as a way to get closer to God. They represent the opportunity to blend success in the current life (largely monetary) with success in the hereafter.

I draw a parallel between Osteen and Khaled because these preachers are symbols of a much wider phenomenon, the merging of religious and capitalist subjectivity that I call "pious neoliberalism." Pious neoliberalism connotes a transformation in both religious practice and modalities of capitalism. It represents a new compatibility between business and piety that is not specific to any religion, but rather is a result of the ways in which religion and economy interact in the contemporary moment. Pious neoliberalism produces new institutions, systems of knowledge production and subjectivities.

In this book, I explore pious neoliberalism through the lens of Islamic charitable practices. I use Islamic charity as a lens through which to understand the relations between the economy, the state, and broader discourses of religion in Egypt. My approach links questions of governance, authority, economy, and polity with questions of identity, subjectivity, and ways of knowing. In chapter 1, I argue that charity is an economic act and challenge the scripting of the economy and charity as mutually exclusive, instead studying them as coeval cultural productions. Charitable acts are economic interventions, while political economic factors shape charitable practices. An Islamic economic paradigm makes explicit connections between economic prosperity and the well-being of the broader society through the interdependence of charity and financial transactions.[5] Much like the production of conventional finance, the production of Islamic finance required a drastic recalibration of the field to sever finance from charity.[6] Divorcing the economy from social concerns by separating out charity from other aspects of Islamic economics allowed investment and development to occur unabated by rising inequality while perpetuating and accelerating the neoliberalization of the economy.

I discuss pious neoliberalism as a distinct variant of Islamism and neoliberalism that highlights the multiple and sometimes contradictory aspects of their fusion. I employ Cihan Tugal's definition of Islamism as "a project that seeks to shape the state, economy and society along Islamic lines,"[7] and I use the term neoliberalism to connote the extension of market logics into all aspects of life, following Wendy Larner's seminal piece that defined neoliberalism as policy, ideology, and governmentality.[8] Neoliberalism as policy refers to deregulation, privatization, and marketization (inspired by laissez-faire economics) that promoted the advancement of economic growth without regard for social equity. One important consequence of neoliberal policy is the decline of welfare/state-sponsored social services and a shift toward market provision of services, workfare, and entrepreneurialism as the solution to social problems.[9] Neoliberalism as ideology refers to the multiple discourses and political configurations that enabled neoliberalism as a political project. Neoliberalism as ideology does not mean that neoliberalism is a coherent top-down project but, rather, that it attaches to or works through other political projects. Neoliberalism as governmentality refers to the technologies of rule—the subjects, institutions, practices, and spaces associated with marketization. Neoliberal governmentality is about the technologies involved in the governing of subjects, including calculability and technologies of self that hold individuals responsible for their own well-being.[10]

Building on Larner's framework, I consider pious neoliberalism as policy, ideology, and governmentality. Pious neoliberal policies reconfigure religious practices in line with principles of economic rationality, productivity, and privatization. Preachers and leaders present these traits as part of what it means to be religious and apply economic rationality to religious practice. Religious practices are also neoliberalized, as characteristics of faith seen as incompatible with neoliberalism are diluted while new religious practices are formed. Pious neoliberal ideology represents the merging of a market-orientation with faith; it is a productive merger that leads to new institutional forms, like private mosques, private foundations, and an Islamic lifestyle market. Pious neoliberalism generates self-regulating and ethical subjects as faith and the market discipline them simultaneously. The different chapters of the book apply this understanding of pious neoliberalism to examine its associated institutions, practices, spaces, and subjects.

While many scholars examine the project of development through a governmentality lens, charity is usually conceptualized as an act of benevolence.[11] Yet charities have been involved in governance long before the institution of development existed. Charity is also an act of governing because it is one of the apparatuses used to manage the population and organize the social order. It also has the capacity to profoundly shape subjectivities. Since Islamic charities frequently tie aid to religious lessons, personal conduct is linked to the regulation of political or civic conduct.[12] Islamic charities produced pious neoliberal subjects through their poverty alleviation projects while at the same time it was pious neoliberal subjects who introduced business practices into Islamic charities. Pious neoliberalism was not a product of top-down policies imposed upon the public; rather, it was actively produced through the interaction of neoliberalism and Islamism.[13] Pious neoliberal subjectivity is marked by self-regulation and entrepreneurialism, as subjects engage in a moral economy that is inextricably linked with the market, self-government, and faith. Individuals are driven to *khayr* (good deeds) in the form of charity so they can improve themselves and their relationship to God; they are driven to Western neoliberal development in hopes of building an effective and efficient society.

Scholars and practitioners frequently consider Islamic associations as alternatives to a Western aid-dominated development project. However, for years Islamic associations have been adapting discourses of development into their work. Because Islamism and neoliberalism have often been treated as dichotomies, I highlight the space of compatibility between them. I found that Islamic associations had a great deal in common with secular development nongovernmental organizations (NGOs) and Christian faith-based ones alike. Islamic association administrators narrated their work as development and yet emphasized that because of better access to the poor and lower overhead, their organizations were more efficient and effective than Western development organizations. The literature on Evangelism and neoliberalism has been more attuned to faith-based development than the literature on Islamic organizations.[14] The tendency to read anything Islamic as somehow "counter" or "alternative" is deeply problematic. Understanding Islamic charity as part and parcel of the project of development destabilizes Eurocentric development narratives and false dichotomies that read Islamic entities as premodern and development as a solely Western production. The practices that occur under the broad category of Islamic development constitute new cultural productions that combine the "efficiencies" of neoliberalism with the "morality" of an Islamic society. Islamic charitable practices are not *a priori* alternatives to a Western social/economic order; they are fluid, variable practices situated in specific places and times.

Pious neoliberalism is a global phenomenon, but it is also a context-specific one. It is the product of specific histories that facilitated an interface between religion and neoliberalism as a political project.[15] Neoliberalism, while not monolithic, is powerful and transformative precisely because it works through other projects or forces, including religion and authoritarianism. Scholars of Turkey refer to the intersection of market forces and religion as an "Islamic neoliberal" ethic or assemblage.[16] In the Turkish case, pious neoliberalism also produced an "entrepreneurial Islam"[17] as a response to Kemalist-imposed secularism coupled with the rapid neoliberalization of the Turkish economy.[18] In the Gulf, Muslim Indians started businesses that resulted in their "making good and doing good" simultaneously.[19] In Indonesia, Islamic associations democratized the state, while state-owned companies turned to spirituality and management practices to increase the productivity and competitiveness of Indonesian steel.[20] Robert Hefner's "civil Islam" and Daromir Rudnyckyj's "market Islam" convene through the study of Islamic associations as a form of pious neoliberalism.[21]

The Mubarak Era and the Production of Pious Neoliberalism

In the case of Egypt, many factors coalesced to produce a context within which pious neoliberalism emerged. Egypt is an important location to examine the confluence of neoliberalism and Islam, given its historic role as an intellectual center of the Arabic-speaking world, the long-standing presence of international development organizations in Cairo, and the populations' venerable traditions of giving. Historically, Egypt has also been the Muslim-majority country with the strongest relationship to the United States, its largest donor in terms of international aid. The international development project has constituted a large and prosperous industry in Egypt for nearly forty years. As the most populous Arab state, many social trends begin in Egypt, and given its historical position as the Arab world's media provider, it is often considered to be a benchmark for the broader Middle East and North Africa region.[22] Its geographical location makes it an important connector between North Africa and the Arabic-speaking countries that lie to the east. Cairo serves as a regional base for numerous international development NGOs and multinational corporations.

Nearly half of Egypt's 84 million people live below the World Bank–defined poverty line of $2 a day. Whether they are on the more fortunate side of this line as givers or far below this line as recipients, most Egyptians are implicated in the exchange of charitable monies. The majority of charitable giving is bestowed out of a religious inclination. About 90 percent of Egypt's population is Muslim and therefore the majority of religious charities are Islamic. These Islamic associations provide social services and create spaces for community and public engagement. The story of Islamic charity serving such an important role in society is not a new one; the institution of *waqf* (Islamic endowment) governed social care in Egypt until the mid nineteenth century, when Muhammad Ali, considered the founder of modern Egypt, institutionalized, centralized, and bureaucratized social services under a state apparatus.[23] But from the 1952 revolution onward, the state intervened in both the provision of social care and in the management of Islamic institutions. Chapter 2 discusses these state interventions, detailing how the former produced a lucrative international development industry, while the latter led to the rise of Islamic associations.

The Egyptian state under Mubarak was an amalgam of neoliberal and authoritarian "technologies of rule."[24] The state's intervention in social care and religion, an Islamic revival, political economic trends that intensified economic pressures on the poor, and the emergence of the private sector as a key development actor changed the nature of Egyptian charitable practices. Pious neoliberal subjectivity played an important role in both the Egyptian uprising and the political aftermath.

Neoliberal Development

Egypt has a long history of neoliberal rule following on the heels of its brief socialist past. Hosni Mubarak decimated the welfare state, pursued economic growth without regard for escalating inequality, and privatized state-own industries, thus expanding the bourgeois class. After the 1952 revolution, Gamal Abdel Nasser expanded the welfare state to provide free public education, employment for graduates, subsidized housing/food supplies, and universal health care for all Egyptians. His successor, Anwar Sadat, began the process of liberalizing the economy through the *Infitah* (open-door policy), which opened Egypt to foreign aid, trade, and investment, privatized state-owned industries, and kept the welfare-state budget flat despite rapid population growth. In 1986 Mubarak instituted structural adjustment policies, including the devaluing of currency, the lowering of deficits, the privatization of state industries, the elimination of subsidies, and the shrinking of the welfare state.[25] Egypt's neoliberal economy was pro-business, consumption driven, and a vastly unequal environment. Mubarak sought to attract international investment, promoted unregulated markets and unfettered competition, and extended market logics into all components of social life. As the state reorganized social care along economic lines, the majority of Egyptians' lives were negatively affected by the rising cost of living, decreased funding for nationalized health care, education, and subsidies, and the privatization of social care.[26] A shift in the scale of responsibility away from the state and toward individuals (or responsibilization) occurred in tandem with the growth of the third/voluntary or nongovernmental sector.[27]

The creation of the Bretton Woods institutions in 1946 produced an international development industry dominated by multilateral agencies and international aid agencies (like USAID) that became known as the Washington Consensus. The third sector in Egypt grew exponentially as a result of international aid funding. USAID funding to Egypt between 1979 and 2009 was approximately $28 billion, the majority of which went to fund secular and Coptic NGOs.[28] Islamic associations were largely excluded from the lucrative international development stream; international development projects and Islamic charities largely operated in isolation from one another.

The development practices of the Washington Consensus were based on Enlightenment logics and established a linear progress narrative that scripted secularism, economic development, and democracy as insepara-ble.[29] Development interventions graft this linear progress narrative onto non-Western societies.[30] International development ideology, until this day, has a strong secular bias.[31] Yet over the past ten years, the Washington Consensus began to recognize that faith-based organizations (FBOs) were better connected to the poor than their secular counterparts and invited faith-based development organizations (FBDOs) to the table.[32] As develop-ment experts began to realize the role that FBDOs were already playing in development, faith-based groups also engaged with international develop-ment practices. Secular and faith-based organizations began to share some common ground, as Egyptian Islamic association leaders demonstrated the compatibility of Islamic almsgiving with "modern" development practices.

Despite the growth of a development sector, the majority of Egypt's poor and middle classes relied on Islamic associations that provided them with social assistance through cash aid, medical care, and in-kind or subsi-dized social services.[33] In contrast to the secular NGOs, Islamic associa-tions are by and large not supported by Western aid organizations and receive most of their budgets through individual Egyptian donations. Even though these Islamic associations were vital to the stability of the country because of their role in providing social services, the state felt threatened by things that were associated with Islam.

Rising Islamism in an Authoritarian State

The authoritarian state felt that Islamic institutions and groups threat-ened its legitimacy and therefore intervened via an expanding state secu-rity (*amn al-dawla*) apparatus. Egyptians were incredibly disgruntled with their government, having lived under the Emergency Law since 1967.[34] The Emergency Law suspends civil liberties and limits political freedom: it allows for the arrest and detainment of suspects without trial for extended periods; permits the use of military courts for civil suits; prohibits demon-strations, strikes, public meetings, and free media; and perpetuates human-rights abuses, surveillance, and corruption—all in the name of security.[35] While this stringent legal environment affected all groups, the state specif-ically targeted Islamists.[36] The regime used antiterrorism laws not only to undermine the so-called radical Islamists but also to undermine all Islamic groups and institutions.[37] The state's intervention in Islamic institutions precipitated the growth of Islamism in Egypt.

Egyptians are more visibly pious than they were twenty years ago, and this Islamic revival has spatial ramifications.[38] Rising religiosity appeared on the streets of Cairo through a marked increase in the number of women donning the veil and men keeping religious beards; a rise in the number of mosques scattered along the sprawling streetscapes; the public's commitment to attend Friday prayer; the popularity of women's Quranic reading groups; the appearance of stores selling religious attire, Qurans, and recorded sermons; television series, religious satellite channels, and new media sites; and a marked increase in the presence of religious symbolism in homes and shops.[39] Islamic associations also spread piety throughout Cairo by coupling *da'wa* (the call or invitation to Islam, preaching) with charitable giving. Chapter 3 discusses how piety and giving reflect each other and were reflected in space and time. The pious believe they have a responsibility to give charitably and volunteering for an Islamic charity frequently led individuals to become more pious.

Islamic charities moved religion outside the space of the mosque and into unexpected, everyday spaces like shopping malls, sporting clubs, and street corners. During the Mubarak years, Islamic associations and mosques represented some of the most vibrant public spaces in Egypt. In an authoritarian context, these spaces provided numerous Egyptians with a place not only to articulate their values but also to synthesize their own understanding of what it means to be a Muslim in the contemporary era. One way of scripting Islam as modern involved articulating Islam in relation to the market, or what I call "privatizing Islam." In Egypt, privatized Islam produced businesses and institutions that enabled Islam to flourish despite an authoritarian regime that was hostile to Islamic entities. Privatized Islam, discussed in chapter 4, was thus a direct response to statist Islam or the state's co-optation of Islamic institutions. It was expressed through a variety of sites and spaces—privately funded mosques, the replacement of public endowments with private foundations, the development of an Islamic private sector, including Islamic (micro)finance, and finally, the rise of business practices within Islamic charities. Putting Islam into practice in an authoritarian and market-oriented Egypt required new institutions, charitable and developmental practices (and systems of knowledge), and an ethical reconfiguration of subject formation, discussed, respectively, in chapters 4, 5, and 6.

Under pressure from the government and the market, some Islamic charities recalibrated centuries-old practices in an effort to become actors

in the field of "human development."[40] These narratives require a recon-
ceptualization of the relationship between religion and modernity since
religion is often treated as antimodern, while development is decidedly a
modern project.[41] Participating in the project of development as an Islamic
association required a complex negotiation of its perspectives on poverty,
development, and faith. Many associations began complementing cash
transfers, in-kind goods, and social services with the promotion of entrepreneurship and self-sufficiency through development projects. More and
more givers felt the role of associations was to help people help themselves out of poverty, and this translated into integrating the poor into the
global circuits of finance capital or "bottom billion capitalism."[42] Income-
generating projects like entrepreneurship, microfinance, and skill upgrading
could create entrepreneurs out of the poor. Islamic development projects
inculcated neoliberal values as Islamic values, transforming both in subtle
ways.

Cairo's Uneven Development and the
Geography of Islamic Charity

Empirically, I have limited my study to Cairo, primarily because it serves
as the major node for NGO activity across the entire nation. Numerous
associations headquartered in Cairo work in the underserved villages of
Upper Egypt. Cairo houses over one-third of the country's NGOs and a
quarter of Egypt's population. The city is surrounded by a growing number of informal settlements and satellite cities, which, combined, encroach
on the surrounding (and diminishing) agricultural land. The megacity does
not consist of one governorate but includes the governorates of Cairo and
Giza, which meet around the river Nile and parts of Helwan, Qalyoubia,
and the 6th of October governorates. The city can be thought of as a series
of spatially clustered neighborhoods: in the west lie Mohandiseen, Agouza,
Dokki, Zamalek, Imbaba, and al-Haram. Downtown areas include Garden
City, Tahrir, Sayyida Zaynab, al-Bulaq, and al-Manyal and to the east lie
the formerly suburban neighborhoods of Heliopolis and Nasr City. Figure
1 shows Cairo and its environs.

     Many characteristics of Cairo as an urban social space have enabled
pious neoliberalism to flourish. Cairo is a polarized city, with lavish displays
of wealth on the same streets as extreme poverty. The growing disparity is
expressed most visibly in the city's geography, exemplified by the emergence

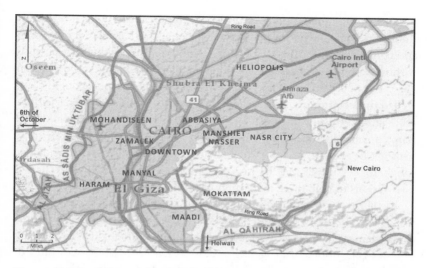

Figure 1. Cairo and environs. Map produced by Richard Hinton using ESRI base source.

of planned gated communities alongside informal squatter settlements.[43] The geography of poverty in Egypt is complex; while rural areas are clearly much worse off than urban ones, official statistics drastically underestimate poverty in Cairo and its environs. Part of the source of this undercounting is from the usual problem of poverty data not being in line with the cost of living, particularly with inflation. However, an equally important source of inaccuracy is the huge number of people living in 'ashwa'iyyat (informal settlements/slums, literally meaning unplanned or haphazard). Estimates in 2006 state that more than 10.6 million people in Greater Cairo live in slums.[44] Islamic charities frequently target these informal settlements, bringing food, blankets, and other supplies to the residents of the narrow alleyways. The landscape is thus equally marked by the development of gated residential communities, upscale shopping malls, and expensive cafés scattered in and around Cairo as by an explosion in the number of mosques and community development associations that serve the poor.[45]

While Cairo has developed a cosmopolitan face, the seven-story shopping malls, the wi-fi cafés, and sparkling display cases are only enjoyed by elites, many of whom made their money during the past three decades of privatization. Privatization increased inequality in Egypt; the richest 20 percent of the population accounts for 43.6 percent of income and consumption, while the poorest 20 percent accounts for 8.6 percent of income and consumption.[46] Millions of people could not obtain their basic needs without some kind of assistance. While many businessmen did quite well as a result of privatization and marketization, many Egyptians did not fare well in this economic climate, a fact that was impossible for even the richest to ignore. Despite impressive economic growth, according to the World Bank, poverty in 2004–5 almost matched the 1995–96 levels.[47] The stark contrast between the classes fueled pious neoliberalism as the wealthy sought to purify their wealth through charity and the poor turned to Islamic associations to help them meet their basic needs.

Rising inequality led to an increase in charitable practices. Islamists saw the gap between rich and poor as an opportunity to build their numbers. Islamic charities responded to this crisis of inequality in Cairo by providing the poor and struggling middle class with social services and aid. Members of the new bourgeois class also played an important role in giving; aside from giving to servants and work staff, they frequently donated to Islamic associations or even started their own charitable foundations. Many of their children volunteered in Islamic associations, particularly during the holy month of Ramadan. Regardless of their wealth, the upper classes were still affected by the presence of poverty in Egypt. Cars and gated communities could not entirely shield individuals from seeing the country's profound poverty. While there are clearly "classed" neighborhoods in Cairo, I was struck by the lack of spatial segregation between rich and poor. For example, Figure 2 shows a shack between two high-end buildings. The shack is built by and for low-wage workers servicing the adjacent buildings. In addition, most buildings have a doorman or *bawwab* that lives on the ground floor or in the garage, so poverty is spread across the city and not limited to low-income neighborhoods. Evolving geographies of poverty and wealth equally have an impact on the geography of Islamic charity.

I define the geography of Islamic charities broadly to include the various patterns that shape the clustering of Islamic charities—their sites, neighborhoods, sources of funding, and broad social networks. Figure 3 depicts the associations I studied in relation to the neighborhoods of Cairo. While there is not a spatial logic to the placement of Islamic charities within the city, there are some clear patterns. Charities are often attached to mosques, and the location of mosques greatly influences where charitable practices

Figure 2. Self-help housing built by workers next to a high-end apartment complex in Nasr City. Photograph by the author.

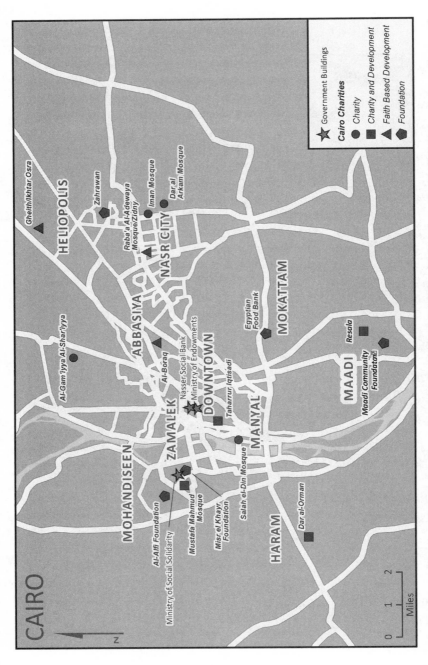

Figure 3. The spatial distribution throughout Cairo of the entities discussed in this book. The organizations are classified as charities, charity and development associations, faith-based development organizations, or foundations. Map produced by Nuala Cowan and Richard Hinton.

develop. Large mosque complexes rely on middle- and upper-middle-class donors and thus tend to be located in wealthy areas. Because the organizations are located in these neighborhoods, the poor have historically had to travel to these neighborhoods to receive aid, making these mosques important transportation landmarks. Mustafa Mahmud and Rabi'a al-'Adawiyya are the two largest mosque complexes in Cairo and charity played a central role in their formation. The neighborhoods of these two mosques, Mohandiseen and Nasr City, respectively, are middle- and upper-middle-class neighborhoods. They are not nodes for poverty, but they are still important social spaces for associations. Large clusters of NGOs congregate around each mosque complex. Likewise, neighborhoods like Shubra, Sayyida Zaynab, and al-Bulaq are not home to many associations but are sometimes targeted by groups such as the Muslim Brotherhood, who distribute goods to the poor residents. Other working-class or informal neighborhoods like Imbaba, al-Haram, Izbat al-Hagana, and al-Higaz are critical sites for Muslim Brotherhood organizing. Suburban sprawl fuels the growth of new large-scale mosques in communities like Sheikh Zayed and New Cairo. Pious neoliberal subjects are building large and impressive mosques in this exurban landscape, and if these desert cities ever fully populate, the space around the mosque is likely to attract NGOs to help the currently unserved population of low-wage workers who service the new gated communities.[48] Examining Islamic charities as a geographical phenomenon contributes to our understanding of the new urban (or exurban) morphology of the city. By forging new spaces for giving throughout the city, charities also changed spatial relations between donors and recipients.

Nasr City is a suburban hub for Islamic charities and was my base during fieldwork. The (now quite urban) suburb neighbors the historic suburb of Heliopolis and consists of ten subdistricts, laid out in a gridlike sprawl. Nasr City's neighborhoods are socioeconomically diverse, with wealthy districts closer to Heliopolis, migrant workers in the more distant 10th district, and factories on the side bordering the informal settlement of Manshiyet Nasser. Since the late 1970s, the neighborhood has been a destination for numerous middle-class Egyptians who made a fair amount of money working in the oil-rich Gulf. Many families spent more than a decade in the Gulf and then used their savings to buy plots of land and settle in the suburbs upon their return to Egypt. The families had private-sector incomes and children who formed transnational identities as a result of the many years they spent living abroad. Perhaps because of the time they spent in the Gulf, the residents had a penchant for shopping malls and Nasr City houses a huge number of malls, including the largest in Egypt, City Stars Centre (Figure 4).[49] Much of Nasr City's land was military land, sold off to its members cheaply and then resold in the secondary real-estate market at several times the price of the initial offering.

Nasr City is an important space for pious neoliberalism because of its socio-spatial segregation, large number of malls and mosques, and diverse population. Home to al-Azhar University, a historic center of Islamic education, the district houses several large mosque complexes, most famous of which is Rabi'a al-'Adawiyya. There are numerous noteworthy mosques throughout Nasr City and the streets are filled with *ma'idat al-rahman* (tables of the merciful) during the holy month of Ramadan.[50] In contrast to the distribution of *zakat* committees all across greater Cairo, a number of the FBDOs discussed in the final chapter are concentrated in or around Nasr City. The concentration of FBDOs in Nasr City is directly related to its core population and the large number of middle-class youth with transnational identities. The Muslim Brotherhood had a strong influence in a few of Nasr City's subdistricts.

Figure 4. City Stars Centre, Egypt's largest shopping mall and an icon of neoliberalism. Photograph by the author.

While the politically oriented organizations tended to focus on the informal squatter settlements (such as Manshiyyat Nasser or Ain Shams) or the crowded inner-city neighborhoods (such as Imbaba or al-Bulaq), I did not come across many social service–oriented organizations that were housed in these areas aside from the largest Islamic association, al-Gam'iyya al-Shar'iyya (discussed in chapter 3). I did not find a systematic explanation for the location of Islamic associations, although the location of particular Islamic entities did have a spatially differentiated logic. Many factors influence the location and size of Islamic charities, including the class composition of a neighborhood and proximity to a mosque and other NGOs, yet a high concentration of recipients or geographically specific need (in a particular community) rarely influenced the location of new associations. The geography of Islamic entities reflects an understated dimension of urban transformation in Cairo.

Mapping the Terrain of Islamic Charity and Development

Drawing upon conceptual frames from geography and anthropology, this project is an "ethnography of encompassment" that takes seriously the spatial relations and on-the-ground practices of Islamic associations in Egypt. Akhil Gupta and James Ferguson define an ethnography of encompassment as "an approach that would take as its central problem the understanding of processes through which governmentality (by state and non-state actors) is both legitimated and undermined by reference to claims of superior spatial reach and vertical height. Indeed, focusing on governmentality calls into question the very distinction insisted on by the term *nongovernmental organization*, emphasizing instead the similarities of technologies of government across domains."[51] I examine Islamic charity as deeply connected to and affected by the state and private-sector actors involved in poverty alleviation. The organizations I studied produced distinct institutions, practices, and subjectivities as they negotiated the relationship between religion, economy, and the state. I studied the sites, neighborhoods, ideology, sources of funding, specific projects, and broad social networks related to Islamic charity work.

I conducted one year of fieldwork with annual follow-up trips during which time I performed participant observation and interviews with the directors of twenty organizations. I also interviewed charity and NGO administrators at several other organizations and interviewed volunteers, ministerial staff, aid recipients, Islamic scholars, bankers, and philanthropists about Islamic charity and development in Egypt.[52] Many of the associations I visited did not self-identify as or want to be labeled as Islamic because of the intense scrutiny and negative connotation that accompanied such a label. Many associations also did not want to be identified as Islamic charities because they believed it detracted from the narration of their work as modern and developmental. Yet the significant role of faith in their work and the importance of critical Islamic tenets like *zakat* (alms), *sadaqa* (charity), and *da'wa* (preaching) were indisputable. Therefore I deploy a purposefully broad definition of Islamic associations. I use the designation "Islamic charity" for organizations I visited for which some component of poverty alleviation was a primary focus and: (a) had Islam in their name or phrases in their name that are derived from the Quran or have symbolic religious meaning, or (b) were attached to a mosque, or (c) were funded primarily through *zakat, sadaqa*, or *waqf* (endowment). I use the term "Islamic development" or the term "faith-based development organization" for entities that met the above criteria and spoke about their work as development (*tanmiya*).

Throughout the book, I map the landscape of charity and development in Egypt, moving back and forth between ethnographic stories of specific organizations and reflections on patterns across the sector. My mapping is both spatial and conceptual, for there were a number of institutional forms that charity took in Egypt and there have henceforth been numerous different players shaping and governing these entities. In order to make sense of this complicated terrain, I created an analytical map that identifies patterns across organizations of charity and development and categorizes the twenty organizations that are the focus of this study (see Figure 5).

I found a set of key issues or traits that constituted major differences between associations. Associations held a variety of positions in relation to nine issues: (1) an adversarial relationship to the state versus supportive of the state; (2) associations with abundant resources and those with limited resources; (3) associations that were focused on returning to Islam's golden past and bringing back "tradition" and those that were interested in narrating their practices as "forward looking" and modern; (4) associations that concentrated their work in a specific location and others whose work was dispersed across Egypt; (5) associations that gave the poor cash aid from charitable donations and associations that worked through development projects; (6) associations driven solely by a desire to please God

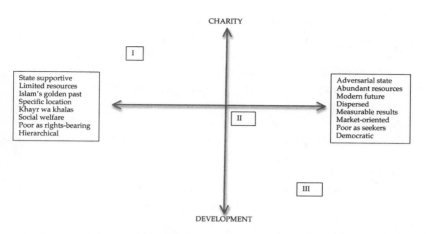

Figure 5. Conceptual mapping of Islamic associations, including clusters as archetypes. Cluster I represents khayr wa-khalas (good deeds and that's it); Cluster II represents samaka wa-sannara (fish and the fishnet); Cluster III represents tanmiya Islamiyya (Islamic development).

(khayr-wa khalas) and others driven by a desire to see measurable, material change; (7) associations with a socialist past and social welfare ethos and associations that believed in the market and capitalism; (8) associations that saw the poor as rights-bearing individuals versus those that saw them as seekers of infinite aid; and finally (9) associations that were hierarchical in terms of their organizational structure and others that were more democratic. This list of positions is defined by the extremes, but in reality most organizations fell somewhere between these poles. Figure 5 encapsulates what I saw as the main defining axes of the aforementioned categories.

Most notably, many of my interlocutors spoke of charity and development as dichotomies.[53] They saw charity as "handouts" to the poor that temporarily increased their income and development as projects that served to improve the long-term living conditions of the poor by "helping the poor help themselves." Associations fell along a continuum spanning from a welfare cash-transfer-based model to a neoliberal development model. I use clusters to represent three different archetypes of organizations I studied. In reality, many organizations have features of more than one cluster and the categories are fluid.[54]

In Cluster I, which I label "*khayr wa-khalas*" (good deeds and that's it), the participants were driven by a desire to please God by doing good deeds and were unworried about the impact of their work on the ground. Chapter 3 mostly describes these associations. Included in this group are five thousand *zakat* committees that report to the Nasser Social Bank, ninety-five thousand government-run mosques, and thousands of quasi-governmental institutions associated with charity and social affairs. They conformed to government protocols and complied with state interventions. These organizations generally followed the status quo and often received financial support from the government. They held a social welfare ethos from a socialist-oriented past, and they had minimal resources. They saw the poor as rights-bearing, tended to concentrate in particular places, and frequently coupled religious lessons with charity.

Cluster II, the "*samaka wa-sannara*" (fish and the fishnet), is based on the Chinese proverb "Don't give a man a fish. Teach him how to fish," which was repeated to me time and time again. This cluster of organizations is mostly presented in chapter 5 and part of chapter 4. Here the line between charity and development is clearly blurred as these associations were simultaneously engaged in charity and development projects. Generally they balanced a social welfare–oriented past with a newfound neoliberal development perspective. The relationships they had with the state ranged from tolerant to adversarial, but these associations tended to have abundant resources from individual donations, the majority made by businessmen. They balanced a desire to please God with aspirations to see measurable change. They tended to work through a diffuse network of organizations and were interested in challenging the status quo. They were able to do so because of their financial independence. The Muslim Brotherhood, although not of central concern in this book, falls into this cluster.

Cluster III is the "*tanmiya Islamiyya*" (Islamic development) cluster. These organizations are faith-driven and results-oriented; they were interested in mobilizing Islam in the name of development goals. I discuss these organizations mostly in chapter 6 but also in chapter 5. They narrated a "modern" Islam, building on the Islamic traditions of *zakat* and *sadaqa* and incorporated them into a neoliberal economic development paradigm. This cluster was also financially independent, often benefiting from the support of larger organizations or large private-sector donations. They tended to see social justice as providing income-generating opportunities to the poor and looked down on groups that gave the poor "handouts." They believed their job was to help the poor help themselves, to turn their quest for "limitless handouts" into an entrepreneurial pursuit of income. They were not satisfied with *khayr wa-khalas* and wanted to see measurable results from their initiatives. They believed that "what works"—effectiveness, efficiency, and accountability—were as important as honesty and good faith in their work. In their self-narration, being productive and efficient was part of being a good Muslim. Within this group, the organizations had different relationships to the state and different degrees of resources to draw upon in their work, but what bound them together was the melding of religion and neoliberal development.

The administrative bureaucracy around Islamic associations is almost as complicated as the overall landscape. I produced the diagram in Figure 6 in order to illustrate the relationship between Islamic charitable practices, Islamic institutions, and the Egyptian government. My mapping highlights the connectivity of charity to other economic activities and therefore begins based on whether a given entity is charitable or profitable. The

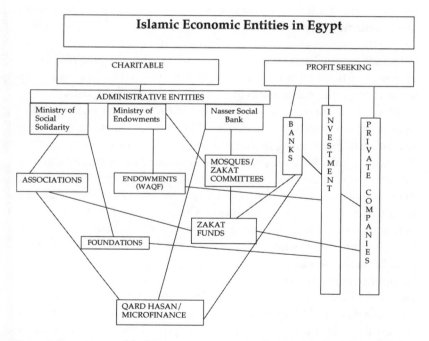

Figure 6. Concept map of the Islamic economic entities in Egypt, including administration.

Ministry of Endowments administers mosques and endowments (*awqaf*). The Ministry of Social Solidarity administers all NGOs (referred to as associations) in addition to foundations, regardless of their aim, religious affiliation, or areas of work. The Nasser Social Bank administers *zakat* committees, which collect alms from the public and which are almost always attached to a mosque. Frequently these *zakat* committees also work closely with associations that are housed inside the same mosque complex. Associations and banks, including the Nasser Social Bank, issue *qard hasan* (interest-free loans) to the poor. Banks, investment companies, and private companies that adhere to Islamic principles also pay *zakat*. They may have their own *zakat* fund or make donations directly to the poor but sometimes work through associations or create a foundation or endowment, much like a corporate social-responsibility program. I conducted research at all of the different administrative bodies mentioned above in addition to my fieldwork with associations, *zakat* committees, and banks.

The book begins with an account of how state interventions produced a historical moment within which pious neoliberalism arose. Chapter 1 places Islamic charity in relation to Islamic economics and introduces the three fundamental Islamic charitable practices of *zakat, sadaqa,* and *waqf*. I argue that Islamic charity is as much an economic act as a social one and demonstrate how Islamic charitable practices are transformed into development practices. Chapter 2 chronicles how the state's intervention in social care (in the name of poverty alleviation) and in managing Islamic institutions (in the name of security) paved the way for Islamic charities to have greater importance in Egypt. Chapter 3 discusses Islamic charity in relation to Egypt's religious revival and the ways in which Islamic charities helped spread Islamic practices outside the space of the mosque and into everyday life spaces. I describe Egypt's culture of giving, especially the mentality of *khayr wa-khalas,* and analyze the month of Ramadan as a heightened space and time for giving. Chapter 4 revisits the state's co-optation of Islam and argues that it had the opposite of the intended effect; instead of quashing Islamic institutions, it fueled the growth of a privatized Islam that was beyond its purview. This chapter focuses on the institutions that constitute a privatized Islam, chiefly the rise of private mosques, private foundations, and an Islamic private sector. One important outcome of a privatized Islam was a growing number of businesspeople becoming involved in the voluntary sector. As private-sector actors became involved in charity work, they scripted their work as development and brought with them private-sector expertise. Chapter 5 analyzes how businesspeople created new forms of knowledge production that quantified and verified neediness through systems of enumeration and evaluation. Their systems produced poverty in a manner that required market-based solutions. A privatized Islam also produced new subjectivities as individuals came to see wealth and religion, private-sector and voluntary-sector work, accountability, and faith as harmonious. They were driven by faith and a belief that their good deeds will be rewarded in the hereafter, but they were also driven by a belief in material benefits for the poor and perhaps indirectly for themselves. Material aspirations, for others or for oneself, are not wholly disconnected from transcendental values, a belief in the afterlife, or a desire to secure for oneself a "house in heaven." These subjects were not victims of neoliberalism; they were actively engaged in making and scripting pious neoliberal subjectivity. Chapter 6 chronicles the expansion of Islamic development or faith-based development organizations in Egypt and the way these organizations promoted market-oriented practices as religious acts. Finally, the Conclusion underscores how pious neoliberalism challenges many of our most basic assumptions and considers how pious neoliberalism played a role in the Egyptian uprising of 2011 and its aftermath.

CHAPTER 1

The Economy of Charity

The objective of Islamic law, though in principle it respects and pro-
tects individual ownership, is to establish justice by preventing wealth
from accumulating in the hands of an oligarchic plutocracy who live
in opulence and luxury, circulating money solely among its mem-
bers, whilst the majority of people exist in hunger, destitution and
contempt. The poor will not be slow, in these circumstances, to form
an army of malcontents capable of threatening the stability of the
community, of weakening and undermining it.

—Mohammad Shujaat, *Social Justice in Islam* p. 303

ISLAMIC CHARITY is of central importance to Islamic economics, and
yet most people equate Islamic economics with Islamic banking, and
finance (IBF). IBF is a segment of Islamic economics, offering a contemporary solution to the problem many Muslims face of how to engage in
financial transactions while avoiding *riba* (usury). *Riba* and *zakat* are the
only two components of Islamic economics that are widely agreed upon;
they, in theory, are "linked together in binary opposition, (therefore) Islamic
finance and Islamic charity are interdependent in forming a circle of seamless discourse."[1] In practice, Islamic finance and Islamic charity are worlds
apart. This divide has multiple dimensions: I wondered how Islamic financiers could underplay the significance of charity to Islamic economics, while
Islamic economists continued to rely on *zakat* as the sole distributive justice component of an Islamic economy. At the same time, I wondered why
the IBF market, which has grown at an exponential pace globally, had
been slow to penetrate the Egyptian marketplace, and why Islamic economics was equated with IBF.

In 2002 Egypt's grand Mufti Sheikh Mohamed Tantawi issued a fatwa
or statement indicating that fixed interest rates, historically deemed forbidden in Islam, were indeed acceptable because the previously held definition of *riba* had been misinterpreted.[2] His declaration was followed in
2003 by the support of al-Azhar Islamic Research Complex (long seen as

the philosophical center of Sunni Muslim scholarship) through a 21–1 vote supporting the legitimacy of fixed interest rates. These statements sparked great controversy in several Muslim-majority countries. The International Fiqh Institute in Abu Dhabi as well as President Musharaf of Pakistan called this declaration erroneous and claimed it was solely the opinion of Sheikh Tantawi. On April 22, 2006, I asked Abdel Hamid Abou Moussa, the head of Faisal Islamic Bank, the largest Islamic Bank in Egypt, his opinion of Tantawi's fatwa. He said:

> You know, in my opinion this decision was a very important part of the banking system in Egypt. Here you have choice, you can choose to use Islamic banks or you can choose to use conventional banking. The fatwa backs this decision. You know if Tantawi had said that these banks are issuing interest and that is *haram* [forbidden], there could have been a huge problem here. A run on the banks. As those conventional banks are not liquid, they are investing that money in other projects as you know. And so there would be a huge liquidity problem if Egyptians en masse went to withdraw their money from conventional banks—which might have very well happened had his decision been otherwise. Second, you'd have a huge increase in demand for Islamic banking, a demand that we are not equipped to deal with in one swoop. So this edict was, in a way, crisis avoidance, and gave the system a great deal of stability.

Tantawi issued his fatwa in support of fixed interest at least in part out of practicality; he was balancing macroeconomic concerns with religious considerations. In fact, Tantawi's fatwa and Abou Moussa's response are not surprising, given that Islamic economics is never fixed but is constantly evolving in relation to what circumscribes it. Despite the widespread belief among Egyptians that fixed interest is in fact not permissible in Islam, there was little outrage against Tantawi's fatwa. In fact, Islamic banking has a very limited market in Egypt, with more than 90 percent of banks continuing to give fixed interest. Most Egyptians keep interest-bearing bank accounts and use non-Islamic banks for everyday transactions like deposits and withdrawals. Sheikh Tantawi's statement that interest is not prohibited in Islam further legitimated the use of conventional banks.

The Egyptian public's lack of interest in Islamic banking is a noteworthy exception to the rising patterns of religious expression in Egypt. This presents another component of the ethnographic puzzle: Why did pious Egyptians not prioritize an Islamic economy? Since the 1980s, Egyptians have become more pious and have expressed that piety through everyday practices, including charity. Yet Egyptian attitudes toward the economy and toward their individual finances remain fairly secular. The economy stands out as one realm where Egyptians did not change their behavior; they kept their money in conventional banks and did not move toward Islamic banking. Sheikh Tantawi's edict is important but not the sole explanation for the weakness of Islamic banking in Egypt. Egyptians also had a tainted experience with Islamic investment companies (IICs) in the 1980s that left them disillusioned.

The IICs were a significant part of a global Islamic finance experiment that proliferated during the 1980s and Egypt was at the heart of these developments. The early 1980s were a period of strong economic growth in Egypt, as remittances sent by Egyptians living in the oil-rich Gulf countries escalated and many middle-class Egyptians found themselves with investment capital for the first time. More than one hundred IICs were offering unprecedented rates of return, far higher than those offered in the conventional market.[3] Many trusted the IICs as a safe investment because of their association with Islam. By the end of the 1980s, it became evident that Islamic investment companies were engaging in capital speculation—buying land but not actually building on it and promising returns that when translated into interest rates were equivalent to 20 percent a month. At the height of the IIC craze, there were 104 institutions with deposits estimated between 5 billion and 8 billion EGP (approximately 1–1.5 billion USD),[4] and 75 percent of accounts were concentrated in the top four IICs: al-Rayan, al-Sherif, al-Hoda Misr, and al-Sa'ad.[5]

In 1988 the government issued a new law (Law 146) requiring public disclosure of investments. Many IICs did not and could not comply without revealing their crony capitalism.[6] As public concern over the sustainability of the IICs widened, investors began to withdraw their money. As more and more investors withdrew their money, it became apparent to the public that the IICs were a Ponzi scheme and had virtually no liquidity. The high interest payments that the IICs were issuing to investors were coming from the principals deposited by other investors. In 1999 the government seized the assets of one of the largest IICs, al-Rayan, and another large IIC, al Sa'ad. By defaulting, these institutions had robbed thousands of Egyptian investors of their money.[7] Despite another law that the investors should redistribute their principal investments, the government confiscated all assets and only approximately 10 percent to 15 percent of people's individual investments were returned to their rightful owners.[8]

Egyptians have a vivid memory of the 1980s IIC debacle, and as a result many Egyptians remain skeptical of IBF. For many, the spread of IICs symbolized the Islamization of the country. Had the IICs lasted, perhaps Islamic banking would have flourished as it has globally. While formal ties between the IICs and the Muslim Brotherhood were limited, the Brotherhood was a staunch supporter of them and saw the government's curtailment of IICs as part of a broader attack on Islamism in Egypt.[9] Since IICs were private-sector Islamic companies, their failures not only hindered the growth of Islamic banking but also slowed down the pace of privatization, which made the Mubarak regime oppose Islamic banking even more vehemently. Thus there were many factors that worked together to slow down the Islamization of the Egyptian economy. The Mubarak regime's preference for conventional banking, Tantawi's edict on *riba,* and the experience of Egyptians with ICCs together formed a shaky foundation for Islamic economics. While Egyptians did not rush to put their money into Islamic banks, they did express their religiosity through the economic act of giving charity.

Despite being considered by the public as social acts, charitable practices like *zakat* and *sadaqa* are economic acts. In fact, Islamic economics is as much about charity as it is about banking. Islamic charity is the most vibrant practice of Islamic economics in Egypt. I discuss the relationship between Islamic charity and Islamic economics and how various interpretations over time changed the meaning of the field. I argue that Islamic charitable practices play a role in poverty alleviation and the various interpretations of how this charity should be mobilized are indicative of the givers' broader economic perspective and interpretation of social justice. The transformation in Islamic charitable practices is an important part of pious neoliberalism.

There are also several compelling reasons to explore Egypt's relationship with Islamic economics. Egypt has never had an Islamic state or Islamic economy, but it does have a long history of Islamic economic practices. Egypt's modern-day rulers pursued both socialist and capitalist economic policies since 1952; thus Islamic economic practices in Egypt were co-constituted with the socialist and capitalist practices of their time. Charitable practices are the most visible markers of Islamic economics in Egypt. Finally, many of my interlocutors engaged in an Islamic discourse of development that drew heavily upon Islamic economic theory.

Islamic Charity as Economics

Islamic economics is a body of knowledge and a set of practices resulting from the application of an Islamic ethical framework to economic concerns. Islamic economic ideology has multiple roots and strands and there is no single authority on the subject, but what ties it together is "an idealized set of principles which would, by definition, safeguard the spiritual and ethical values of the community, protecting its identity as a distinctively Muslim community."[10] While practices that fall under the purview of Islamic economics can be traced back to the seventh century, they were not labeled as such until the 1950s. More than one hundred verses in the Quran deal with the spending of money. They offer guidelines for economic transaction and make numerous references to social classes, trading, and charity.[11] These verses, in addition to *hadith* (pl. *ahadith*), are interpreted by Islamic jurists, who then issue fatwas (religious opinions) on what is permissible or not according to Islamic ethical considerations. This process, known as *ijtihad* (interpretation), results in varying perspectives on what precisely constitutes Islamic economics. The concepts of *amanah* (trusteeship) and *'adala igtima'iyya* (social justice), in tandem with the practices of *zakat, sadaqa,* and *waqf,* constitute an Islamic economic system.[12] The interpretation of these concepts and practices has changed over time.

In the context of the Cold War and the rise of Arab nationalist and socialist movements in the 1950s and 1960s, the Islamic economic system was offered as a "third way" between capitalism and socialism and as a way to manage and distribute finite resources in response to widespread poverty and inequality.[13] Islamic practices of this era had strong anti-Western, anti-colonial, and anti-capitalist undertones and focused on providing social protections for the poor. The meaning of social justice was interpreted as both equity and distributive justice. In the 1970s and 1980s, economic policy in Egypt and many other countries shifted toward economic liberalization. In order to mesh with this shift in economic policy, Islamic economic interpretations shifted toward market efficiency and an emphasis on individual (property) rights and maximum employment rather than on social equity. In the late 1980s and the 1990s, Islamic economics became growth-oriented and the phrase Islamic economics became nearly synonymous with IBF, itself a field defined by financial transactions that avoid *gharar* (excessive risk), *maysir* (speculation/gambling), and *riba* (usury). Over time, Islamic economics has converged with neoliberal economic ideology, moving its distributive justice/equity features to the background in favor of competitive profit margins. IBF has grown into a $1 trillion industry, with hundreds of Islamic financial institutions (IFIs), mutual funds, a Dow Jones Index, a burgeoning Islamic microfinance industry, and dozens of new Islamic financial instruments that mimic conventional finance. IBF is the most visible and fastest-growing component of an Islamic economic system practiced worldwide. Most contemporary discussions of Islamic economics thus tend to focus on the IBF industry and the debates around *riba* and *shari'a* compliance rather than discussions of charity or a holistic and just economic system.[14] A shift away from theorizing Islamic economics as a broad Islamic economic system accompanied the rise of IBF and, as a consequence charity and protection for the poor became relegated to the realm of the social. Yet Islamic charity is an integral part of what it means to participate in an Islamic economy. The type of capitalist production being promoted in the name of Islamic economics is critical to the ways that certain moral codes are enforced or eliminated from the overall landscape of Islamic economics and informs the specific practices of pious neoliberalism.

Surrendering Surplus to God: Trusteeship and the Giving of Charity

The concept of *amanah* (trusteeship) is deeply linked to charitable obligations and differentiates Islamic economics from conventional economics. *Amanah* is a form of trusteeship where all things that belong to God are handed over to human beings for their collective well-being. Humans are not the absolute owners of wealth and property; rather, they are entrusted with resources. Individuals have the right to possess private property and the right to allocate their resources as they see fit, but they also have a moral and spiritual responsibility to use those resources to benefit society.[15] Trusteeship lies at the core of Islamic economic structures and practices: "*Amanah* operating through the institutions of zakat, *infaq,* and *sadaqah,* seeks to promote a culture, a way of living, imbued with the spirit of fellow-feeling, mutual support, sacrifice, co-operation, equity and fair play as opposed to rank individualism, self-centeredness, avarice, competition, injustice and exploitation."[16] Therefore if a person has been endowed with excess wealth, he is instructed to "voluntarily surrender the surplus" to the poor.[17] *Amanah* produces a culture of giving among the pious and in particular drove many wealthy pious businessmen in Egypt to engage in remarkable acts of charity.

Trusteeship places constraints on the rational, self-maximizing homo-economus, generating a *homo-Islamicus*, a differentiated economic subject who considers divine interpretation when making economic decisions.[18] Trusteeship is widely interpreted to mean that individuals have a responsibility to their extended families, neighbors, and broader society. Zubair Hasan argues, "To the extent that people voluntarily observe the Islamic norms, it will resemble the capitalist structure minus its major ills including glaring income inequalities. On the other hand, the more people neglect their *amanah* obligations the greater will be the need for state intervention that will ensure distributional equity by putting socialist-type curbs on individual freedom but falling short of repression."[19] From this perspective, inequality is a result of an imbalance in *amanah*. While trusteeship produces a culture of charity, it does nothing to address income inequality. In fact, most contemporary Islamic economists believe that income inequality is inevitable, and that income equality would amount to excessive restrictions on individuals and create a disincentive to work.[20] Instead they call for an avoidance of extremes in wealth, elimination of exploitative practices, just wages for the poor, a balance between support for the accumulation of wealth and economic growth, on the one hand, and concerns for justice and protections for the poor, on the other. Islamic charity is most concerned with the later, protections for the poor, specifically ensuring that the poor can meet their basic needs. Basic needs are defined as needs for sustenance, including food, water, clothing, housing, supplies for work, and marriage expenses.[21] Trusteeship leads to charitable practices, but the type of charitable practices relies on specific interpretations of what constitutes social justice as well as economic ideas about what is the most effective way to ensure that the poor's basic needs are met.

Social Justice and Social Solidarity ('*Adala and Takaful*)

At the Second International Conference on Islamic Economics held in Islamabad in 1983, scholars concluded that distributive justice in an Islamic system was defined as (a) guaranteed fulfillment of the basic needs of all; (b) equity (not equality) in personal incomes; and (c) the elimination of extreme inequalities in personal income and wealth.[22] Zubair Hasan argued that calling on individual personal responsibility to discourage extremes in inequality will achieve distributive justice; distributive justice in turn will promote mutual love and social cohesion and minimize political disruption from glaring income disparities.[23] Sayyid Qutb historically argued that economic justice is permitting "the claims of the poor upon the wealth of the rich, according to their needs, and according to the best interests of society, so that social life may be balanced, just and productive."[24] These authors offer no concrete definitions or advise on what should be done in the circumstance that the wealthy do not respond to the needs of the poor. At the same time, these scholars do not see income or class equality as desirable because human beings are not equally able; they claim that a system that does not reward individuals based on their achievements will be inefficient and unjust.[25] While numerous scholars in the 1950s and 1960s did argue for income equality as a definitional part of social justice in Islam, Sayyid Qutb, one of the most influential Islamist thinkers defined social justice not as equality but as equal opportunity: "Absolute justice demands that men's rewards be similarly different and that some have more than others—so long as human justice is upheld by the provision of equal opportunity for all."[26] Contemporary interpretations of social justice equate social justice with equal opportunity and equal opportunity with employment opportunities. Employment rights are an important part of the contemporary Islamic social justice agenda.

Guaranteeing the rights of workers is a critical way to ensure that their basic needs are met. Basic economic rights at a minimum include food, shelter, and clothing, but frequently scholars also include health care, education, subsidies for gas/oil, transportation, marriage expenses, and water. These economic rights further extend to the unemployed as well as to non-Muslims living in an Islamic context.[27] Workers rights are discussed in several passages of the Quran, including their right to adequate, fair, and prompt wages and benefits.[28] Many argue that workers have a right to share in the profits of their labor, as a hadith from Musnad Ahmad states, "Let the worker have his share out of the profit gained through his labour for God's agent is not to be deprived."[29] In terms of wages, the Quran supports the notion that the employer should pay a living wage so that the wage earner can provide for his family's basic needs. Despite the emphasis on economic rights in Islamic economic theory, how people actually interpret and deploy these rights are of utmost importance. In practice, Egyptian Islamists did little to advance these economic rights and instead relied on *amanah* and charity to fulfill the rights of the poor.[30]

While early Islamic economists emphasized redistribution as fundamental to social justice and Islam in the 1960s, today the meaning of social justice is equal opportunity instead of economic equality. The dominant interpretation of the meaning of social justice among charity workers in Egypt is to limit inequality by creating employment opportunities so that individuals can be self-sufficient. Many Islamic associations thus focus on job creation as the primary means for achieving economic rights. A survey by the Center for Development Studies in 2007 found, in line with the aforementioned interpretation of social justice in Islam, that Egyptians do not believe that income equality is a necessity of social justice in Islam.[31] Furthermore, Sheikh Khaled el-Guindy reiterated that *zakat* is an important mechanism for social equality (not income equality); it is paid to ensure that "there is security, a low crime rate, and few political and social tensions."[32] Thus, equality is largely interpreted by Egyptian Muslims involved in charitable work as giving people equal opportunity (not equal income). Social justice in this context is about providing people access to capital and jobs, focusing on efficient use of resources through giving with conditionality, and giving equal opportunities rather than equitable resources.[33]

While Islamic economists argue that the Islamic institutions of *zakat*, *sadaqa*, and *waqf* should work in conjunction with one another to avoid the exploitation of the poor, prevent excessive risk taking, and ensure that capital is used for productive projects, in practice these institutions operate in isolation from one another and there is no modern-day example of a holistically integrated Islamic economic system at the nation-state scale. *Waqf*, *sadaqa*, and *zakat* form the foundation of an Islamic economy, with *zakat* at the fore; their historical meanings illuminate how these different kinds of Islamic charity translate into contemporary economic practices.

Waqf

In Arabic, the root *waqf* means to hold, confine, isolate, or preserve certain revenue or property for religious or philanthropic purposes. A *waqf* (pl. *awqaf*) is an Islamic endowment and a form of ongoing charity (*sadaqa gariya*); the terms *waqf* and *sadaqa gariya* are often used interchangeably.

As an endowment or trust, *waqf* is obviously an economic practice, but *waqf* is also frequently created on behalf of those who have passed away, in the form of establishing a public good such as a water fountain or constructing a mosque. *Sadaqa gariya* can take any form—some examples include giving out Quranic tapes and booklets, making educational materials freely available, or planting fruit trees in a public square. Also, unlike other forms of *sadaqa*, *waqf* is usually not anonymous; it is formalized through a contract, and there is an identifiable endower on the logic that a public display of generosity might inspire others to give more. A hadith by Ibn Majah describes the different forms of *awqaf* a person might leave behind and how this is received by God:

> The righteous works that continue to benefit a believer after his death include the knowledge that he taught and spread among others, a righteous son whom he leaves behind, or a copy of the Qur'an that he bequeaths to his inheritors, or a mosque that he builds, or a rest house that he builds for the wayfarers, or a cana of water that he digs for the benefit of others, or a charity that he gives out of his property during his life while he is sound of health. He will continue to receive reward for all these even after his death.

The first documented *waqf* was a well in Medina; the first use of *waqf* by the state dates back to the tenth and eleventh centuries to support *madaris* (Islamic schools).[34] Historically, *awqaf* played a crucial economic and social role. They were an important source of funding for and played a critical role in the provision of public services, including support for the building of mosques, schools, libraries, hospitals, water supply, cemeteries, gardens, windmills, public transport facilities, parks, roads, and the provision of health-care services for the needy and disabled.[35] Often revenue from farms, gardens, buildings, shops, and industrial plants were put toward charitable purposes in the form of *waqf*. There were numerous iterations of *waqf* in Egyptian history before the 1952 revolution.[36]

There are three kinds of *waqf*: charitable, familial (heirs), or a mixture of both purposes. An individual, family, group of individuals, or an entity can agglomerate the capital for *waqf*. Assets including land (usually agricultural), buildings, cars, machinery, books, and money can be used to establish the endowment.[37] The purpose is set by the endower and changed only according to his will.[38] Historically, most *waqf* took the form of real estate; however, there are numerous ways to allocate *waqf* money, whether through direct benefit (such as housing people or building a mosque) or investments (financial or agricultural). Because of Islamic finance, there are now numerous ways of financing *waqf,* including *musharaka* (partnerships), *mudaraba* (partnership where one party provides the capital and the other the labor), *murabaha* (percentage markup), *ijara* (contract of lease and hire), *istisna'* (contract for manufacture and purchase of a specific item), *sukuk* (bonds), and the Islamic stock market and Islamic financial institutions.[39]

Despite the importance of *waqf* historically, the institution lost its preeminence in Egypt over the past forty years as a result of government intervention, including the creation of new laws to regulate *waqf,* the abolition of private-inheritance *waqf,* the deterioration of the sovereignty of the endower over his endowment (*shart-al-waqif*), governmentally appointed endowment supervisors, and the collection of taxes and fees on *waqf.*[40] Most of these changes were instituted under President Gamal Abdel Nasser (1956–70) and were part of the statist project of nation building that extended techniques of governance in the postindependence era. The changes that occurred during this period eventually led to the annihilation of *waqf* as a form of charity in Egypt (see chapter 4). Today there are calls for a *waqf* revival in Egypt and in several other Muslim-majority countries, but dramatic regulatory changes would have to occur before any new *waqf* would be established in Egypt.[41]

Sadaqa

Sadaqa means "benevolence." It is the wider umbrella of charity under which *zakat, waqf, qard hasan* (benevolent loan), and *sadaqa gariya* fall. *Sadaqa* is an economic act because it involves the movement of money, time, or in-kind goods. *Sadaqa* has numerous economic functions, including as a major source of funding for Islamic associations, a form of volunteerism, the distribution of Ramadan food bags, and the funding for numerous other social programs such as health clinics. It is an act of personal devotion and piety; giving purifies the giver when performed with the sole intention of serving God. According to several verses in the Quran, charity should be given for the sake of God and will be repaid bountifully.[42] According to a hadith narrated by Abu Hurayra, "When a person dies all his good deeds cease except for three: a continuous act of charity, beneficial knowledge, and a righteous son who prays for him." The main difference between *zakat* and *sadaqa* is that *zakat* is obligatory, while *sadaqa* usually refers to *sadaqa tatawwu'iyya* (voluntary charity). It has many of the same purposes as *zakat*—mainly to achieve social solidarity, social cohesion, and to strengthen the sense of unity and brotherhood between Muslims.[43] *Sadaqa* can take many different forms, material and nonmaterial. According to hadith, every good deed is a form of *sadaqa*; a kind word and a smile are both considered forms of *sadaqa*.[44] The best form of *sadaqa* is to pass on knowledge (according to hadith from the source ibn Majah 91/1 number 1844). People perform *sadaqa* as voluntary work, in-kind contributions, and providing free services to anyone; there are no specific groups designated as recipients. Volunteerism as a form of *sadaqa* has become a popular way of articulating one's piety, and voluntary charity has experienced a revival among the middle and upper classes. Since *sadaqa* is much more general and open, Islamic associations also increasingly use it as a funding mechanism for development-oriented programming, including microcredit, microenterprise lending, and support for nonpoverty-related policies like art or environmental protection. Voluntary work is an undercountered form of economic activity.[45] Thus, in addition to its role in poverty alleviation, volunteerism makes sadaqa an important economic act.

Zakat

Zakat is the third pillar of Islam, following only a declaration of faith and prayer. *Zakat* is the most prominent feature of and the only widely agreed-upon component of an Islamic economic system.[46] The word *zakat* itself appears in eighty-two verses of the Quran and literally means purity, development, blessings, and praise, but in practice is a form of almsgiving. As a form of redistribution of income, albeit a small one, *zakat* plays an important economic role and provides a source of income for female-headed households and orphans. Given as an act of piety, *zakat* is one way to cleanse oneself spiritually and purify one's wealth.[47] Islamic economists see *zakat* as a tool for limiting the accumulation of wealth, ensuring an equitable distribution of wealth, limiting social conflict, achieving social solidarity, discouraging hoarding, and encouraging the circulation of capital in the economy for the betterment of society.[48]

There are also various forms of *zakat*—a *zakat* on money, on trade, on merchandise, etc. A Muslim is responsible for paying *zakat al-mal* (or alms on money) equivalent to 2.5 percent of his net worth if after meeting his needs he reaches *nisab* (possesses the equivalent of 85 grams of gold or 600 grams of silver) for a period of one year.[49] There is also a compulsory *zakat al-fitr* (alms on feast), in which every Muslim who can afford to pays a *zakat* equal to the amount it costs to feed a person in need for one day. In Egypt, the *zakat al-fitr* is between 5 and 8 LE (slightly more than $1) per person and must be paid before the Eid prayer at the end of the month of Ramadan. *Zakat* is frequently paid directly to the poor that one knows personally, through a donation box in the mosque or through an Islamic association.

In Egypt and other countries where *zakat* is an entirely private matter (in the sense that the state does not collect *zakat* funds), people believe that giving in secrecy amounts to higher Godly rewards *(thawab)*. Giving in secrecy is thought to safeguard the self-esteem of the recipient while reducing conceit and pride in the giver. In support of giving in secret, many of my interlocutors repeated the saying of the prophet that praises he who "gives where his left hand does not know what his right hand is giving." Thus many believe that "special religious merit is gained by giving alms in secret."[50] Giving in secrecy is an important cultural factor in Egypt, as many givers give in secret so as not to flaunt their giving. The belief that giving in secrecy is better makes it very difficult to talk to individuals about their giving practices.

Zakat is not actually a form of charity but a right of recipients, linked to the concept of trusteeship. Since individuals are not the lawful owners but rather the holders of wealth endowed upon them by God, believers give *zakat* obligatorily.[51] In an era of increased income inequality, Timur Kuran argues that framing *zakat* as a right of the poor and as a tool for social stability actually further legitimizes the polarization of income because, "on the one hand, it counsels the rich not to feel obligated to eradicate poverty and never to feel guilty for being well-off. On the other hand, it dampens the resentments of the poor and moderates their demands."[52] Although *zakat* aims to reduce poverty, it does not prevent the creation of a wealthy class, nor does it ensure wealth redistribution.[53] Since economists largely hold that different class positions are acceptable, the rich do not see their wealth as problematic and instead are content to participate in charity. While *zakat* did diffuse mounting tensions in Egypt for decades, economic inequality, class polarization, and injustice eventually led to a massive uprising.

Several economists argue that *zakat*, while an important component of Islamic economics, cannot solve all of societies' problems or act as a substitute for transfer payments as part of distributive economics.[54] Although *zakat* does little to address distributive justice concerns, it does a great deal to help the poor meet their basic needs, and in this sense it has an important economic function. Today *zakat* is also frequently used in IBF as a mechanism through which to make illegitimate (fixed-interest-bearing) funds legitimate, a process that Benthall and Bellion-Jourdan call "halalization." Interest is sometimes siphoned from principal and then turned into *zakat*: "A process of halalization (making *halal* or legitimate) has arisen to religiously launder, as it were, funds deriving from illegitimate transactions. The *zakat* and halalized moneys have provided considerable recurring income for the charitable sector."[55] Thus *zakat* is increasingly used as a way to purify financial transactions for the rich.

Fatwas on *Zakat* and the Definition of Deserving

The issue of who is entitled to receive *zakat* is one of the key debates regarding Islamic charity.[56] In recent years, new fatwas have reconfigured *zakat* in line with the neoliberalization of Islamic economics. The parameters of the "deserving" underlie the organizational structure of charity in Egypt, since charities will only give *zakat* to the eight categories of protected groups mentioned in the Quran, and *sadaqa* tends also to be organized around accounts within these broad categories. *Surat al-Tawba* is the most cited verse in the Quran with respect to *zakat*; inevitably all discussions of *zakat* return to it:

> The offerings given for the sake of God are [meant] only for (1) the poor and the (2) needy, and (3) those who are in charge thereof, and (4) those whose hearts are to be won over, and for (5) the freeing of human beings from bondage, and [for] (6) those who are overburdened with debts, and [for every struggle] in (7) in the cause of God, and [for] (8) the wayfarer: [this is] an ordinance from God—and God is all-knowing, wise. [9:60]

The eight categories of qualified *zakat* recipients are widely interpreted as: the poor, the needy/impoverished, the administrators over *zakat* funds, recent or potential converts, slaves or people in bondage, overburdened debtors, in the cause of God (*fi sabil Allah*), and travelers who have no means of returning home. Widows and orphans are given special protection under the category of the poor and needy and every charitable organization I studied in Egypt served these groups. Widows and orphans are protected and served by Islamic charities because to the givers of charity, they constitute the most clearly identifiable group of the deserving poor.[57] In terms of the administration of *zakat*, organizations can spend up to 12.5 percent of *zakat* donations on administrative expenses. Overburdened debtors is a category that is not as frequently served, although with the rise of microfinance, many poor Egyptians have taken out loans they cannot service or repay. A fatwa was issued by *Dar al-Ifta* in 2009 encouraging Islamic charities to use *zakat* to waive debts and a few Islamic charities I visited had begun to do so.[58] For example, Dar al-Orman Association, discussed in a later section, began a new project in 2010 to relieve the debts of those who could not pay due to an emergency and who otherwise would end up in jail. As of 2012, they had relieved 680 debtors.

As for the seventh category, "in the cause of God," it is the one that is most open to interpretation and it is a contentious area of discussion. Historically, in the cause of God has been interpreted as supporting freedom fighters protecting the religion (*jihad*), as well as for supporting the travel of those who cannot afford to perform the pilgrimage to Mecca (*hajj*). Recently some Islamic scholars and charity administrators have speculated that this rigid interpretation of "in the cause of God" is not entirely accurate:

> In times like we are in today, it is imperative that the scholars, may Allah have mercy on them all, give their fatwas in a manner that caters for the needs of our society to defend against the intellectual onslaught against our values and way of life and aid us in fulfilling our obligation to showcase to the world the beauty of our religion. This cannot be done except by appropriate funding for dawah and community development organisations, Islamic radio and media, Islamic institutes and universities, funding students of knowledge and supporting teachers of goodness—and any project or worthy cause that is directly involved in working in the broader meaning of the path of Allah.[59]

Some Islamic jurists ('ulama') have argued that there are numerous ways of working toward the cause of God (for example, shrouding the dead, building mosques, and funding *da'wa*) and have issued fatwas to support causes relevant to modern social problems (for example, environmental issues, human rights, refugees).[60]

The interpretation of what constitutes "in the cause of God" remains heavily debated, but in general the trend in Islamic jurisprudence has been to issue fatwas providing support for the use of *zakat* to strengthen charitable institutions, environmental organizations, health-care services and cultural institutions.[61] In an interview with Mohamad Abdel Halim Omar, who at the time was the director of the Saleh Kamel Center for Islamic Economics at al-Azhar University, he told me that 80 percent of *'ulama'* prefer a strict/rigid interpretation of "in the cause of God," while 20 percent have argued for its opening. While many *'ulama'* are clearly resistant to changing the meaning of *zakat*, Egypt's Grand Mufti Ali Gomaa issued numerous fatwas opening up *zakat* to new activities.[62]

One important example of Ali Gomaa's expansion in what qualifies for *zakat* spending is a fatwa he issued in support of the Egyptian Food Bank. Food banks, under the logic of the strict interpretation of *zakat* funds, could not be funded by *zakat* but only by *sadaqa* because it is not possible to track the recipients of the food (and determine if they are needy Muslims). In 2003, under pressure from the Egyptian Food Bank and other organizations with government influence, Mufti Nasr Farid Wasel issued a fatwa deeming it religiously acceptable to pay one's *zakat al-mal* to the food bank.[63] This fatwa opened the doors for millions of Egyptian pounds to be given to the food bank. In another act of opening up *zakat*, Muftis Nasr Farid Wasel, Ali Gomaa, and Sheikh Yusuf al-Qaradawi all issued fatwas that support the giving of *zakat* to the Egyptian Children's Cancer Hospital.[64] The 2003 fatwa by Wasel explicitly called for a *zakat* fund to support patient treatment and hospital staff salaries, a *waqf* fund to support the long-term growth of the hospital and treatment facilities, and a *sadaqa* fund to support construction, maintenance, and other hospital expenses. Subsequently, Ali Gomaa's fatwa supports the use of *zakat* toward scientific research. In 2005 *'ulama'* at the International Consultation on Islam and HIV/AIDS approved the use of funds from *zakat* for HIV-positive people in need, regardless of their religion or how they contracted the virus.[65] The same year, the president of the Fiqh Council of North America stated that "the efforts and activities of the Center for the Study of Islam and Democracy (CSID) fall under the category of 'in the cause of God' (*fi sabil Allah*) since the Center was created for, and is working toward, resisting the negative effects of oppression and dictatorship which dehumanize people and control their lives and destiny."[66] A Nigerian preacher, Oladosu Abdul Ganiyy Abdul Salam, argues that *zakat* should be used for

> job creation to solve the problem of idleness and unemployment; alleviation of hunger and starvation; eradication of ignorance by expending zakat funds on education-related ventures; provision of succour for the afflicted and bereaved; creation of social welfare programs; provision of social security monthly allowance; workshops for skill acquisition; scholarships; investment in mechanised farming and research into improving harvest; improvement of the health sector for a healthy labour force; reward of honesty and excellence; punishment of corrupt; provision of soft loans for entrepreneurs; genuine programs for the orphans, the aged, widows, almajiris, and weak members of society.[67]

These are just a handful of examples of the fatwas issued by notable *'ulama'* that offer an expanded definition of the kinds of activities that qualify for *zakat* expenditure.

One final example of the expansion of the kinds of activities that can be supported by *zakat* is an expansion in the definition of what constitutes a traveler who cannot return home. A source of contention for several years in Egypt has been the growing presence of Sudanese refugees, which resulted in several clashes between Sudanese refugees and the Egyptian police.[68] Many discussions about the refugees revolve around the perception that the Sudanese refugees are Christian. A fatwa was issued in 2006 that stated it was permissible to give *zakat* to Muslim or non-Muslim refugees, yet there was some confusion because it is still widely believed that recipients of *zakat* must be Muslim.[69] Thus while some *'ulama'* are using the flexibility of *ijtihad* to expand the definition of who qualifies as recipients of *zakat*, most individual Muslims in Egypt still prefer to err on the conservative side and pay their *zakat* to the least controversial categories. As a result of this preference, most Islamic associations in Egypt continue to focus their work on the eight categories and instead spend *sadaqa* on controversial areas. While Islamic associations still distribute alms primarily to the poor and needy, with an emphasis on orphans and widows, who have no breadwinner, how Islamic associations provide aid to the poor has changed. As a result of the fatwas supporting an expanded definition of the areas eligible for *zakat* support, a discursive shift has occurred in the interpretation of social justice—away from income equality and toward equal opportunity. Combined, these interpretations support the notion that *zakat* and *sadaqa* are best used for development work and drive Islamic charitable practices toward pious neoliberalism.

Zakat and Sadaqa for Development

Association directors argue that the publics' preference for giving to uncontroversial areas works against the best interest of the country because it discourages organizations from expanding into more controversial areas. They contend that the public's preference for *zakat* as direct distributions to the poor limits it from being deployed for development and maintain that it should be deployed to "empower the poor to help themselves." Al-Azhar sheikhs have issued fatwas supporting the notion that *zakat* may be used to encourage self-sufficiency among the poor, including entrepreneurship. We are only just beginning to see the tremendous influence of these fatwas on the charitable sector and the articulation of an Islamic paradigm for neoliberal development and the rise of pious neoliberal sensibilities in Egypt.

In a study of philanthropy in Egypt, El Daly found several scholars who justified the use of conditional giving and the transfer of *zakat* funds toward economic development. They posited that income equality is not part of social justice in Islam and that "the characters and reputation of the poor people may be taken into account in deciding whether or not they deserve help."[70] In interviews that El Daly conducted about contemporary interpretations of *zakat,* a prominent Egyptian economist, Hatem el-Karanshawy, commented:

> In principal *zakat* money could be invested in the construction of factories, as well as invested in farms and other developmental income-generating projects. . . . *[Z]akat* mainly aims at enriching the poor and not simply meeting their basic needs; investing *zakat* in projects where transparency measures are applied would allow donors to follow up on their expenditures and shareholders to review the financial statement, expand their business and increase profit. . . . [T]he main aim is to enable them (the poor) to reach their subsistence level in order to empower them to start helping themselves forward.[71]

Many of my informants echoed the sentiment that using *zakat* to meet basic needs is an inefficient use of resources. These leaders of Islamic associations saw a need to move away from giving *zakat* as direct aid to the needy and instead toward more "institutional" forms of giving that focus on conditional giving, microenterprise development, and job creation. The attention to self-sufficiency and entrepreneurship by the '*ulama*' and Islamic economists gave legitimacy to the appropriation of *zakat* funds toward development projects. After supporting orphans and widows, job creation has become the third most prominent focus of Islamic associations.

In my interview with the director of one Islamic association, he explicitly stated a desire to address poverty via job creation: "There are so many people who are actually in need. We use our friends and so on that are working and leading in each area: training centers, workshops, plumbers, carpentry etc. To create work opportunities for those who are in need in areas that need employees as well. . . . You know, because of the nationalized education system no one wants to work these kinds of jobs. But there is demand for them."[72] He identified the mismatch between available jobs and job seekers as the main reason for persistent poverty in the country. Job creation has become the task of NGOs partially because of the failures of the state. Neoliberalism draws attention away from structural explanations and toward individual improvement as the solution to poverty. Charity administrators decreased resources spent as direct aid, which they refer to as "handouts" and believe make the poor "lazy and dependent." They shifted more resources toward more "institutionalized" projects that make the poor "active and entrepreneurial." Most faith-based development organization staff spoke of a desire to see all *zakat* money be deployed "strategically" and conditionally instead of charitably, a shift that was also encouraged by the Egyptian Ministry of Social Solidarity. A shift from direct giving toward conditional giving and projects that encourage the poor to help themselves is part of the makeup of pious neoliberalism. This process of neoliberalizing *zakat* and *sadaqa* narrows the definition of the deserving poor, represents declining empathy for the poor, and asks the poor to become self-responsibilized and entrepreneurial in their quest for survival.

Thus *sadaqa* and *zakat* have undergone a transformation in Egypt in several key ways. First, *zakat* and *sadaqa* are now used as a funding stream in a much wider base of activities, including microenterprise lending, microfinance, social entrepreneurship/social ventures, and nonpoverty-related activities. Second, a desire for *thawab* (God's rewards) from *sadaqa* has inspired a revival in volunteerism, particularly in faith-based development organizations. Finally, *sadaqa* and *zakat* monies are increasingly deployed institutionally and with a definition of social justice that places responsibility on the poor for their own well-being.

A Microcosm of Islamic Economics: Rabiʿa al-ʿAdawiyya Mosque Complex

Together, the individual Islamic economic practices of *zakat, sadaqa,* and *waqf* constitute an Islamic economic system. For the most part, these practices occur in isolation from one another, thus limiting their economic functions. The Rabiʿa al-ʿAdawiyya mosque complex is an exceptional case of how *waqf, sadaqa,* and *zakat* can be deployed together synergistically (see Figure 7). It illustrates the layering of institutional forms involved in Islamic charity and the potentiality of combining *zakat, sadaqa,* and *waqf* in one complex. The mosque complex is a distinctive example of how each of these Islamic practices came together to produce what the director of the medical center called "a self-sustaining Islamic economic system." A key reason why people do not generally see Islamic charity as playing an important economic role is that there are not many examples of *waqf, sadaqa,* and *zakat* working together. In order to demonstrate the economic function of Islamic charity, I return to an ethnographic example of how these three pillars of an Islamic economy work together.

Rabiʿa al-ʿAdawiyya is one of the largest mosque complexes in Cairo and by far the largest in the bloated suburb of Nasr City. I rode past the complex nearly every day on my commute from Nasr City to other parts of Cairo. Located at one of the busiest intersections in the area, the mosque marks a critical intersection in the city and serves as a transit point for those traveling on the Autostrade between downtown and the airport. The complex consists of a large mosque, a three-story medical building, a hospital, a convention hall where Islamic book fairs are often held, an endowed water-access point, and a four-story building that houses several voluntary organizations. Historically, the Islamic *waqf* system functioned similarly, but state intervention brought this functionality to an end. The mosque is surrounded by a variety of perfectly manicured shrubbery and trees. A string of white, orange, and pink lightbulbs hangs from the edge of the mosque to the four-story building across the way, which houses an alms

Figure 7. Rabiʿa al-ʿAdawiyya Mosque. Photograph by the author.

committee on the first floor and Zidny (a youth-initiated professional skills
building NGO, discussed in chapter 6).

Rabi'a al-'Adawiyya began as simply a large mosque in a desert-bound
suburb, yet over the course of the past eighteen years it has grown to become
a premier provider of social aid. Precisely because of the mosque's role in
social service provision for residents of Nasr City and its environs, the
sidewalk in front of the mosque has become a major informal transportation node and the daylong traffic jams made it a perfect stomping ground
for tissue vendors, shoe-shiners, and mobile-phone peddlers. As Rabi'a al-
'Adawiyya grew from a modest mosque into a landmark, it demonstrated
how the space around a mosque had become a space for much more than
prayer; it had become the space of a community.

The sheer complexity of this building complex, its position as a place of
worship, health, charity, meeting, socializing, organizing, and even everyday financial transactions, epitomizes the layering of roles that Islamic institutions have come to play in modern-day Egypt. Islamic associations work
as service providers, religious organizations, development entities, and economic agents simultaneously. What appeared from the outside as a single
space was in fact several different layers of organizational entities. For
example, Rabi'a al-'Adawiyya contained at least five distinct Islamic charitable forms, each of which was administered by a different government
entity. The Rabi'a al-'Adawiyya mosque complex represents the different
institutional forms of Islamic charity. Rabi'a al-'Adawiyya is first and foremost a mosque and as such is registered with the Ministry of Endowments. Mosques are either governmental (*hukumi*) or nongovernmental
(*ahli*) and Rabi'a is considered nongovernmental because it was privately
established and does not rely on the government for finances. The Ministry of Endowments has oversight over Islamic endowments, such as the
water well at Rabi'a al-'Adawiyya, which was funded by a *waqf*. A *zakat* collection committee (*lagnat al-zakat*) is housed inside the mosque and registered with the Nasser Social Bank. Frequently a donation box sits inside
the mosque and individuals can make *zakat* or *sadaqa* contributions in
cash or by check. The mosque also has an affiliated association (*gam'iyya*,
pl. *gam'iyyat*). Because of a previous law, associations are classified as either
a peoples/popular association (*gam'iyya ahliyya*) or a charitable association (*gam'iyya khayriyya*). Organizations must specify to the Ministry of
Social Solidarity whether they work in social or economic fields. This categorization of associations also contributes to the perception that Islamic

associations are social and not economic entities. Finally, Rabiʻa housed Zidny, a younger and less-established NGO and a voluntary medical clinic funded through *zakat* and *sadaqa* but regulated by the Ministry of Health. The bureaucratic apparatus around each Islamic charitable practice (discussed further in chapter 2) also contributes to the perception that these are not economic practices.

The Rabiʻa al-ʻAdawiyya medical center was established in 1993 as an association focused on providing medical services to Nasr City. It is located in a high-rise building directly behind the mosque (Figure 8). The building is all brick and crowded with foot traffic. It is open from 10 AM to midnight and offers medical exams for a symbolic fee of 8 LE. Many medical clinics in Egypt are open late because doctors tend to work in government hospitals during the day and moonlight with private practices. The building contains a free pharmacy and a thirty-six-bed surgery division in addition to x-ray facilities, an emergency room, a kidney dialysis center, and an operating room. While the medical center charges a fee for service, no one is denied care. Instead, those who cannot pay are referred to the *zakat* committee.

The *zakat* committee, after checking on the economic status of the patient (and verifying neediness), will pay his or her way. The *zakat* committee was established in 1988, five years earlier than the hospital; the entities share five board members, which facilitates cooperation between them. While the *zakat* committee holds the funds, the medical center is involved in the actual management and implementation. The hospital allocates 70 percent of its revenue to the *zakat* committee and 30 percent remains with the association. As a longtime volunteer and leader of the committee told me: "The hospital was established separately from the *zakat* committee because no hospital can be successful (or self-sustaining) based on donations alone. We need to have some investments. . . . Those who can afford to pay more do and then it comes back into the *zakat* committee to help those who can't afford to pay. So you see there is great cooperation between the association and the *zakat* committee."[73] An important component of the compound's success, then, lies in the carefully orchestrated integration of Islamic charitable practices across various organizational entities. This system uses a mixture of charity, investments, and income sharing to provide medical care across various classes. As one of the doctors on the board indicated, "The hospital is successful because we operate like a business." The various entities within the mosque complex worked

Figure 8. Rabiʿa al-ʿAdawiyya Hospital. Photograph by the author.

to integrate the *zakat* committee and the hospital into one cohesive system that benefited from a profit-seeking model. This allowed the hospital to provide services at market price and then use those margins to provide services for those who could not afford to pay, thus serving as a model of *takaful,* or social solidarity.

Rabiʿa's organizational structure is a unique asset in that, as it has grown, it has allowed projects to take on a life of their own, rather than being threatened by them. In addition, Rabiʿa's growth-oriented structure accommodates the exponential growth of surrounding Nasr City. As a result, while many local organizations attempt to emulate it, Rabiʿa remains the premier location for social services in Nasr City. Associations all over town herald Rabiʿa al-ʿAdawiyya's success as a premier Islamic social services node and, given its status, many local associations looked to it for advice. It became a hub for coordinating association activity in the Nasr City district. The head of the association took the initiative to establish a database with personal data on individual aid recipients from twenty-five organizations operating in the district. The goal behind this initiative was to track recipients and ensure that no one was taking advantage of the plethora of *zakat* committees concentrated in Nasr City. Rabiʿa al-ʿAdawiyya is the keeper of this database and shares it with all organizations that share their recipient lists for inclusion in the database, which is testament to its special status as a trustworthy entity.

Rabiʿa also demonstrates how charity came to stand in for so much more. Volunteerism fueled the mosques' expansion. Therefore, volunteerism is also an economic act—volunteers who offer their services as a form of *sadaqa* provide in-kind services to the poor. The various arms of Rabiʿa play an important economic role in providing basic services to the community and subsidizing services to the poor, but, collectively, the mosque complex also illustrates how the practices of Islamic charity work together to form the bedrock of an Islamic economic system.

Conclusion: An Islamic Economy after Mubarak?

When describing my research to people while in the field, I frequently received puzzled looks when I described my research as examining *zakat, gamʿiyyat,* and Islamic economics: "What is the relationship? *Zakat* is one thing and Islamic economics is something else," people would retort. The perception that Islamic charity is not part of Islamic economics is a central reason why IBF is understood as the main thrust of Islamic economics. Yet as this chapter has demonstrated, Islamic charity has important economic functions that are critical features of Islamic economics. The perception of IBF as synonymous with Islamic economics is both evidence of (and a result of) the neoliberalization of Islamic economics. The IBF industry is focused solely on profit-maximization; the goal is to maximize capital gains while remaining shari'a compliant, circumventing any moral or ethical considerations. In addition, the contemporary interpretations of Islamic economists demonstrate little concern for rising inequality, while charity administrators deploy a neoliberal definition of social justice that sees job creation as a substitute for distributive justice.

The Islamic economic practices of *zakat, sadaqa,* and *waqf,* while exhibiting clear differences from neoliberal economic practices, are important parts of pious neoliberalism. Islamic economic practices are compatible with neoliberal logics, but their label as "religious" has important connotations to the actors involved. Here faith is scripted with economic rationality as individuals make ethical decisions about where to put their money while operating within a capitalist economy. Each practice entails a combination of faith-driven priorities melded with a concern for efficiency. This is not to say that there is a unified or complete transformation of Islamic economic rationality, or even that these practices are somehow less authentic than the ones that came before them. Understanding Islamic economic practices as a form of pious neoliberalism highlights the malleability and agility of both terms—"Islamic" and "neoliberalism." Labeling something as Islamic can serve a broader political agenda or add legitimacy to an otherwise capitalist endeavor. At the same time, neoliberalism is capable of merging with other political projects and processes like neoconservatism or Islamism.[74]

The Muslim Brotherhood's policies under the auspices of the Freedom and Justice Party (FJP) are a poignant example of how neoliberalism and Islamism converged. The Brotherhood's approach to Islamic economics during its one year of rule focused on IBF as the basis of an Islamic economy. While Islamic banking remains a marginal part of the Egyptian banking sector, the FJP sought to change that. As of September 2012, Egypt had only four pure Islamic banks (but several more conventional banks with Islamic windows) and one post-Mubarak–formed Islamic investment company, Ridge Islamic Capital. The four banks, all backed by Gulf financiers, include Faisal Islamic Bank, Al-Baraka, United Bank, and the National

Bank for Development. In addition, more than forty banks in Egypt have Islamic windows or branches, which offer IBF products through a conventional bank.[75] The FJP sought to increase Islamic banking's share of the Egyptian banking sector from less than 5 percent to 35 percent by creating a new regulatory framework for Islamic banks. Despite Egypt's economic decline following the 2011 uprising, the IBF market in Egypt was growing at 7 percent a year.[76]

While the Muslim Brotherhood sought to increase the role of Islamic banking in Egypt while they were in power, during the Mubarak era they were remarkably quiet on the subject. Instead of emptying their interest-bearing bank accounts, Islamists in Egypt vehemently oppose the "westernization" of social life and participated actively in charitable works, as if almost to make up for the lack of adherence to Islamic economic principles. Instead of questioning the economic motives behind this policy, the wealthy purify themselves by performing *sadaqa* (good deeds), volunteering their time, and mobilizing resources to employ the poor. The use of charity as a means of economic purification is part of the reason why Islamic charity is so vibrant in Egypt. At the same time, it is indicative of some of the contradictions of pious neoliberalism.

CHAPTER 2

Managing Poverty and Islam

T HE EGYPTIAN STATE has influenced Islamic charitable practices over the years through two major interventions: first, poverty-alleviation initiatives (including economic development policies) that institutionalized and reformed social care, and, second, intervention in Islamic entities.[1] Together these interventions produced an environment where Islamic associations played a critical role in development as well as in producing pious political subjects. Under Hosni Mubarak, the state was an amalgam of neoliberal economic policies, authoritarian technologies of rule, and antiterrorism security campaigns aimed at Islamists.[2] Here I historicize the practices of the state that led to an increase in the number and importance of Islamic associations while producing a disabling working environment for NGOs. The proliferation of NGOs is part of the "state effect" by which the state became inextricably linked to a wide network of institutions involved in governing.[3] Over the course of a century, social care for the poor moved from private endowments to a centralized state-led effort and then reverted to a local scale. While the state remained heavily involved in health care and education, the role of NGOs increased over time. As the state became the manager and regulator of NGOs, it became involved in the regulation of personal, political, and civic conduct in Egypt. I employ a genealogical analysis in order to shed light on how particular interventions became normalized, and I will trace the history or evolution of practices to construct a fuller picture of the state.

Institutionalizing Social Care

The nineteenth century marked the emergence of state-initiated forms of social care that differed from previous Islamic institutions. Although these public services began as a way for Muhammad Ali (who reigned from 1805 to 1848) to ensure the health of his military, they soon extended to the public at large. Muhammad Ali, considered the founder of modern Egypt, established a strong centralized state bureaucracy and military with a focus on modernization and integration into the international economy.[4] Secular government-sponsored and foreign schools changed the education system, once dominated by al-Azhar's religious schools.[5] Much like the nineteenth century in Europe, the first part of the twentieth century marked the beginning of secularized, centralized, and bureaucratized social care in Egypt. Yet an Islamic charitable framework remained the bedrock of social care. A new range of government-appointed officials implemented modernizing reforms like the formation of the *Dabtiyya* (central police department), which resembled the emergence of the police in Europe.[6] Mine Ener argues that the *Dabtiyya* facilitated the care of people in need, including poor children, but also acted as a disciplinary institution.[7] Government initiatives focused on managing the population, including public health and poor relief, working through schools, insane asylums, prisons, hospitals, and poorhouses. The nineteenth century marked the beginning of the exercise of moral and technical authority by philanthropists in Europe,[8] and the beginning of state and philanthropic management of the poor in Egypt, as supervision became an important technique of state rule.[9] The state became involved in defining the deserving poor, placing the state at the center of charitable giving. The deserving poor included the elderly, invalids, single women, and mothers with small children. The government provided assistance to orphans and widows of soldiers and supported religious clerics, the poor, and others deemed deserving of assistance.[10]

The charitable sector was dominated by foreign societies, private voluntary organizations (PVOs), and missionary work from the late 1800s through the turn of the century.[11] Christian missionaries infiltrated Egypt from 1815, establishing schools and charity associations. Despite political independence, Egypt's economy remained controlled by the Europeans until Nasser's reform of the 1950s. The elite expatriate community was large and influential and their PVOs provided material support for the poor. Many charitable organizations subsequently were established in reaction to colonization and the presence of foreign and missionary activities. A trait distinguishing contemporary charities (defined as late-nineteenth- and twentieth-century) from their predecessors was that a "new local bourgeoisie," rather than religious clerics or elders, established the new charities.[12] The first Egyptian PVO, Gameyat al Maaref, a publishing organization, was established in 1868, followed by the Geographical Society in 1875, the Islamic Benevolent Society in 1878, and the Coptic Benevolence Society in 1891.[13] During this period, zoos, parks, restaurants, conservatories, libraries, museums, theaters, and sporting clubs were built; the national theater opened in 1868, followed by the opera house in 1869.[14] Prior to the British occupation, there were only two Islamic associations; however, the imperial context spurred the growth of Islamic organizations.

Anticolonial sentiments spurred the establishment of a new generation of Egyptian-led philanthropic organizations from 1936 to 1952.[15] Religious organizations figured prominently, among them al-Gam'iyya al-Shar'iyya, established in 1912, the Islamic Youth Organization, founded in 1927, and the Muslim Brotherhood, established in 1928. Founded by Hassan al-Banna, the Brotherhood was an anti-imperialist group that called for an end to foreign domination and the formation of an Islamic society based on social justice. During the 1930s, the Brotherhood called for the promulgation of a new Egyptian civil code based on *shari'a*. The Egyptian government felt threatened by the Brotherhood from the beginning, and their adversarial relationship would only continue to fester in the coming decades.

The Ministry of Social Affairs (MOSA) was established in 1939 with a mandate to improve the living standards of the poor and promote social justice. The centering of the state as provider reflected the Islamic (and Ottoman) tradition of providing for the poor while serving the secular nation-building project.[16] Furthermore, the ministry could counter and monitor groups involved in serving the poor, particularly the Muslim Brotherhood. Initially, the ministry managed organizations from a distance under Articles 54 to 80 of the civic code. Law 49 of 1945 placed all charities under the ministry's supervision, while Law 66 of 1951 placed religious NGOs under the Ministry of Interior, a reflection of the regime's insecurity regarding Islamic institutions.[17] The nationalist movement grew strong between 1942 and 1952; this period was marked by numerous strikes as unions gained momentum and social strife spread to the police and army.[18] During this same period, professionals began organizing into associations: lawyers in 1912, journalists in 1940, physicians and pharmacists in 1942, engineers in 1946, and teachers in 1951.[19] These syndicates later became the backbone of the Muslim Brotherhood.

State-Led Development

After the 1952 revolution, Gamal Abdel Nasser led a critical period of state-led development with a goal of "justice and sufficiency for everyone" through economic nationalization and industrial expansion.[20] A comprehensive nationalization law in 1961 put almost every commercial and industrial enterprise under government control, including banks, insurance companies, basic heavy industry, and public works, such as energy and utilities, food distribution, textiles, transportation, film and media production, construction, department stores, and ports.[21] As a result of sequestration and nationalization, throughout the 1960s the state possessed about 33 million EGP in cash, 7,000 properties, and 293 enterprises, including the Suez Canal Company and British and French companies. The public sector controlled 91 percent of total investments and 83 percent of all production tools.[22]

Nasser concentrated state power and had a strong commitment to the welfare state. During the late 1950s and 1960s, Egypt's welfare system exploded, including universal free education, universal health care, housing, rent control, food subsidies, and job guarantees and job security for high school and college graduates.[23] The government initiated a state-led development project called "Productive Families" (al-Usar al-Muntiga) in 1964. The project's stated focus was "improving existing local products by providing technical and financial assistance; transforming local resources into industrial products with a material value; utilizing human resources of the handicapped and the elderly; exporting ethnic products to obtain hard currency," and local offices provided *qard hasan* (interest-free loans) to families.[24] Law 357 of 1952 amended Law 49 of 1945 and Nasser established a *wihda igtima'iyya* (social unit) that served to integrate the government's approach to development under a centralized state unit.[25] As part of land reforms, Nasser placed all *waqf* land under the new Ministry of Endowments.[26] From 1950 to 1970, Egypt received $884.1 million in economic assistance but no military aid from the United States.[27]

Nasser's successor, Anwar Sadat, quickly erased many of Nasser's policies, ending the sequestering of private property and instituting new laws to encourage foreign investment. Several factors created an economic debacle in Egypt, including declining productivity, depleted national savings, state overspending, Egypt's 1967 loss of the oil-rich Sinai Peninsula, and low foreign investment.[28] By the 1970s, the Egyptian economy was weak, communications and transportation systems were unreliable, infrastructure was antiquated and overloaded, industries were declining, and the welfare state had begun to disintegrate.[29]

Sadat liberalized the economy through the Law of *Infitah* (open door) in 1974 (Law 43), which opened Egypt to foreign trade and investment, established free-trade zones (with limited labor regulations), lifted currency restrictions, and encouraged the private sector to replace state control of the economy. The reforms gave foreign investors special privileges (including tax exemptions, fiscal exceptions, and exception from national labor laws, such as the minimum wage and price-setting rights), many of which Egyptian private-sector investors were not granted until Law 159 of 1981.[30] Sadat did away with guaranteed state employment for university graduates, encouraged entrepreneurship, formed private-public partnerships, and reformed the tax law. The Egyptian economy, based on oil, remittances, tourism, and the Suez Canal, flourished with impressive economic growth of 8 percent to 9 percent per year.[31] With the oil boom of the 1970s, many Egyptian workers moved to the Gulf and began sending remittances back to Egypt. Under Sadat, the country was more open to foreign interests and foreign aid, especially from the United States, while the Arab Gulf states became an important actor in the country's internal affairs.[32] USAID began sponsoring projects in Egypt in 1975; however, U.S. assistance to Egypt, only a fraction of which is development aid, became annualized after the 1979 peace treaty with Israel. Egypt is the second largest recipient of American foreign aid worldwide, the vast majority of which is military assistance in return for keeping peace with Israel.[33]

As Egypt's economy became more capitalist, a new class of bourgeoisie bankers, merchants, traders, and industrialists emerged. This new social class became avid spenders and conspicuous consumers. Demand for fashion boutiques, lavish weddings, sporting clubs, and European cars fueled a demand for larger and more spacious homes in the first ring of suburbs surrounding Cairo. State systems of education and health care were underfunded and overburdened, leading to the growth of parallel private services for those who could afford it.[34] At the same time as Cairo saw an increase in suburban living, informal housing and squatter settlements proliferated. Consequently, increased income inequality manifested spatially through the rise of suburban living and informal settlements simultaneously. Population growth exacerbated existing social problems, as the population grew from 26 million in 1960 to 40.5 million in 1976.[35] In 1977, in response to sudden increases in food prices, Egypt experienced the largest bread riots in its history. These riots made clear the significance of subsidies to the populace and, as a result, the state kept subsidies in place despite liberalization of the economy. The vestiges of the welfare state are still very much present in Egypt, despite the rapid economic changes led by Sadat.

Development under the Washington Consensus

Mubarak continued Sadat's economic liberalization program, eventually extending the private sector into insurance, trade, air transport, agriculture, banking, telecommunications, land reclamation, housing, education, and liberalization of the stock exchange and investment laws. By the mid-1980s, a dramatic fall in oil prices negatively affected the budget and the country faced another economic crisis.[36] Faced with a $40 billion national debt and rising inflation, Egypt went to the World Bank and the International Monetary Fund (IMF) for assistance.[37] In 1986 the Egyptian government accepted an IMF reform package in return for financing part of the country's $40 billion debt, and in 1991 it negotiated a structural-adjustment loan with the World Bank.[38] IMF-initiated reforms that extended into the 1990s included reducing the budget deficit, cutting subsidies, raising energy prices to international market levels, instituting a luxury sales tax, raising bank interest rates, and reducing the number of government employees.[39] As in other countries around the globe, structural-adjustment policies pulverized already stressed welfare systems, leaving the poor particularly vulnerable. Despite population growth, throughout the 1980s and 1990s spending on health care and education remained the same (See economic indicators in Table 1).

The neoliberal critique of the welfare state, framed as a need to "roll back" the state from its encroachment into the social and personal sphere, was accompanied by a "roll-out" practice of disseminating the market into the nooks and crannies of society.[40] In 1997 the government instituted a set of policies that hurt peasants and the working class by repealing the land reforms of 1952, limiting rent control, and downgrading worker protections.[41] As a result of structural adjustment, the budget deficit and inflation decreased, and by 2006 the public sector accounted for just one-third of GDP.[42] The privatization of key industries continues today. Mubarak's development agenda was driven by the pursuit of public-sector reform and deregulation, extending lines of credit to entrepreneurs and encouraging private-sector investment.[43] In addition to profits from estates and monopolies, or as agents to international companies, an elite class of millionaires benefited from corruption.[44] Between 1981 and 2001, about one thousand individuals had accumulated $50 billion within the country, more than the foreign debt of Egypt.[45]

As was typical for countries that underwent structural adjustment, throughout the last decade the Egyptian economy was marked by strong

Table 1. Egypt's economic indicators, 1965–2009

	1965	1975	1985	1990	1996	2000	2005	2009
Population (millions)	31.77	40.13	50.66	56.84	63.12	67.65	74.20	79.72
Poverty head-count ratio at national poverty line (% of population)	N/A	N/A	N/A	N/A	19.40	16.70	19.60	N/A
Income share held by lowest 20%	N/A	N/A	N/A	8.70	9.50	9.00	9.00	N/A
Income share held by lowest 10%	N/A	N/A	N/A	N/A	4.20	3.90	3.90	N/A
GDP per capita ($U.S.)	160.89	285.01	684.76	N/A	1,071.44	1,475.84	1,208.65	2,370.71
GDP ($ billion)	5.11	11.44	34.69	43.13	67.63	99.84	89.69	188.98
GDP growth (%)	9.23	8.94	6.60	5.70	4.99	5.37	4.47	7.16
GINI coefficient (%)	N/A	N/A	N/A	32.00	N/A	32.76	32.14	N/A
Foreign direct investment, net inflows (BoP, current $U.S. millions)	N/A	N/A	N/A	734.00	636.00	1,235.00	N/A	6,712.00
Net official development assistance and official aid received (current $U.S. millions)	N/A	N/A	1,756.08	5,425.06	2,189.50	1,326.96	993.63	925.11
Total Public Expenditure Spent On (%)								
Education (% of GDP)	N/A	N/A	5.60	N/A	N/A	19.7	4.80	11.90
Health (% of GDP)	N/A	N/A	N/A	N/A	4.30	7.20	5.20	4.70
Military (% of GDP)	N/A	N/A	N/A	4.70	3.90	6.10	N/A	1.70

Source: World Bank Country Data, UNDP Egypt Human Development Report.

economic growth of approximately 7 percent per year with widening income inequality.[46] Neoliberal economic policy increased consumerism, income polarization, growth of the informal economy, and a decline in public infrastructure.[47] Development funding increased, but since the poor were only becoming more vulnerable, poverty rates rose.[48] State-driven poverty-alleviation efforts continued through the Productive Families Initiative, which focused on training and production in rural areas, mostly through a vast nationwide network of NGOs that targeted the poor to engage in small and medium enterprise (SME) development. Four million families obtained training services, rotating loans, and marketing services in 2007 through 3,250 training centers.[49] While SMEs are small businesses promoted to upgrade artisan craft workers, their growth is part of the government's strategy to remove employment pressure from the state and to turn the poor into entrepreneurs.[50]

In 1990 the Social Fund for Development, a joint venture established by the World Bank, the Egyptian government, and several international donors, supplemented the Productive Families Initiative. The Social Fund again focused on SME development, this time through microenterprise lending. According to the microfinance director, the social fund for development had issued loans to almost 470,000 recipients from its inception (to December 2007) in the sum of almost 880 million EGP.[51] The fund worked with 355 NGOs to distribute these loans and calculated that, because of the multiplier effect of the loans (estimated multiplier of 1.2), the fund has created approximately 560,870 jobs. According to the Egyptian Information Service 2007 Yearbook, the social fund provided 3.9 billion LE in small and microenterprise projects, as well as social and human-development projects estimated to have provided 835,000 jobs.[52]

Many of Egypt's development initiatives were funded through USAID. Between 1979 and 2001, the United States provided approximately $25 billion in loans and grants for economic development (including debt relief, investment, and technical assistance), while military assistance was $27.6 billion.[53] USAID targeted education, economic growth, health care, water management, agriculture, environmental and natural resources, antiquities, and democracy and governance. The "secular bias" of the development industry meant that USAID funding went mostly to secular or Coptic NGOs. The areas of democracy and governance became a particular point of contention in Egypt because Mubarak saw U.S. funding for human rights organizations and democracy promotion as a threat to the regime.

The democracy-promotion efforts of USAID and the National Endowment for Democracy (NED) were supplemented with the U.S. State Department's introduction of the Middle East Partnership Initiative (MEPI) in 2002. Mubarak's authoritarian regime was very hostile to foreign funding of Egyptian NGOs and introduced strict provisions over foreign funding, provisions that continued under Mohamed Morsi, who before his ousting in July 2013 was planning even harsher legislation.[54] Most recipients of U.S. funding complained vociferously about bureaucratic hurdles between the Ministry of Social Solidarity and the Central Security apparatus.

After nearly four decades of international development funding, poverty remains one of Egypt's most pervasive problems. Yet many of the changes I observed in Cairo bear a resemblance to similar processes that have occurred around the globe for several decades. The creation of the Bretton Woods institutions in 1946 resulted in an orthodoxy about governing the economy and the emergence of an international-development industry dominated by multilateral agencies, which became known as the Washington Consensus. The Washington Consensus was predominantly a neoliberal project for the promotion of the private sector through projects that support entrepreneurship and self-sufficiency. It was also an attempt to integrate the poor into financial markets.[55] As a result, aid moved away from welfare- and charity-driven cash transfers and instead toward privatized social services and various stages of "development." While international-development ideology has gone through numerous stages over the years, from W. W. Rostow's modernization theory to a world systems theory emphasizing free trade and infrastructure building, it eventually shifted toward human development. This led to an emphasis not only on economic indicators but also on improvements in the status of women, health-care provisions, and educational reform. In the late 1990s, empowerment, microenterprise, and microfinance became the gospel of choice,[56] while U.S. human rights and democracy-promotion efforts expanded significantly after 9/11 as part of George W. Bush's foreign policy.

It is in this context that a parallel Islamic development project emerged. While the secular project of development became a huge and prosperous industry, Islamic associations remained the best connected to the poor. The decay of the welfare state created space for Islamic groups to expand their base and legitimized Islamist critiques of a westernized consumption-driven society. Islamic charities established in the 1960s and 1970s continue to believe in the efficacy of giving to the poor via direct cash transfers, while newer institutions have shifted resources away from cash transfers and toward the production of entrepreneurial and self-sufficient subjects. These newer institutions were engaged in a project to "modernize" Islam by providing efficient solutions to poverty. Meanwhile, shrinking public services led low-income Egyptians to rely increasingly on NGOs for social services that previously were provided by the government.[57] Throughout the 1980s and 1990s, the Muslim Brotherhood became a "shadow government," providing social services to the lower and middle classes while controlling numerous mosques, syndicates, unions, schools, and NGOs. While the Brotherhood was certainly not the only or even the main Islamic-oriented provider of social services, the government's fixation on the Brotherhood actually granted it greater legitimacy.

Managing Islam

The state used the discourse of Islam to maintain legitimacy; the state was symbolically represented and contested through a discourse of Islam. At the same time, Islamic associations struggled with the state for legitimacy as members of society.[58] As a result the state "found a contentious rival in the piety movement, whose authority is grounded in sources that often elude and confound the state."[59] These struggles are also struggles over public culture that played out in the everyday practices of local bureaucracies.[60] Under the guidance of three dynamic leaders, the state engaged in a tug of war over religious authority that had an impact on the practices of Islamic charity. Practically and symbolically, this war was largely framed around the question of the Muslim Brotherhood. In an effort to quell the power of the Brotherhood, the state produced a legal environment that was hostile to most Islamic institutions, regardless of whether or not they were associated with the Brotherhood.[61]

The Society of Muslim Brethren was established by Hassan al-Banna in 1928, but it was not until the 1940s that membership in the Brotherhood grew especially large; it had created an extensive network of social institutions and had between five hundred thousand and a million members.[62] The government dissolved the group and seized its assets in December 1948, after a member of the Brotherhood assassinated the Egyptian prime minister. The government arranged for the assassination of Hassan al-Banna in 1949. In 1951 the ban on the Brotherhood was lifted and members mixed with the Free Officers during the first few years of the revolution.[63] The cooperative relationship quickly changed as the Revolutionary Command Council attempted to silence reformers. After a member of the Muslim Brotherhood attempted to assassinate Nasser in 1954, Nasser's previous ambivalence toward the Brotherhood turned to animosity.

Under Nasser's leadership, tensions between the government and the Brotherhood escalated. In addition, strict regulation of NGOs became a mainstay of state-society relations, a centralized bureau took over private *waqf*, many Islamic institutions were subsidized or nationalized, and the *'ulama'* lost much of its independence. The Ministry of Social Affairs took administrative control of the Brotherhood's extensive welfare centers, arguing that they were fronts for illegal activity.[64] The ministry abolished student unions and political parties and silenced and imprisoned communists, union leaders, and members of the Muslim Brotherhood and anyone else he considered a threat to his authority.[65] Nasser initiated numerous laws governing social organizations, including associations, syndicates, unions, and endowments. He abolished *shari'a* courts in 1956 and in 1961 assigned supervision of all mosques to the Ministry of Endowments. He also stripped al-Azhar of its autonomous power, despite a marked increase in al-Azhar's budget and the dramatic increase in its student enrollment and number of foreign missions.[66] The Ministry of Endowments built several new mosques and the number of government employees in mosques nearly doubled. The ministry micromanaged imams and used the Friday *khutba* to disseminate Nasser's socioeconomic policies.[67] Hundreds of Brotherhood members were imprisoned and six leaders were executed, including the famous Islamist Sayyid Qutb.

Like Nasser, Sadat attempted to create a governmentalized official Islam; he extended governmental oversight over mosques, expanded al-Azhar even further, and engaged the Muslim Brotherhood in dialogue. Sadat frequently mobilized religious rhetoric, epitomized by his slogan "Science and Faith." The Islamization of Egyptian society grew under Sadat's rule as Islamist support increased in universities, unions, and other elements of civil society. While the number of Islamic associations exploded during his reign, he eventually chose to reinstate the government's control over religious affairs, including mosques, charities, and Islamist groups—a move that would eventually cost him his life and profoundly shape Islamic practices in Egypt.

One point of contention during the Sadat years was whether the Egyptian legal code would be secular or religious. The Ottoman Empire

promulgated an Islamic civil code in the 1870s, but, at the turn of the twentieth century, in an attempt to gain legitimacy from European powers, Egypt
codified its law as secular.[68] After the 1919 revolution of independence,
Egypt established a constitution in 1922 without any provision requiring
Islamization. Egyptian law was dominated by a secular legal code from the
establishment of the 1923 constitution until 1979, when the Committee
on Civil Law codified new laws derived from Islamic jurisprudence. Then,
in 1980, Sadat amended Article 2 of the constitution to make *shari'a* the
principal source of legislation.[69] Within the Ministry of Endowments, Sadat
established a network of district officers responsible for selecting preachers and monitoring mosque activities in each governorate.[70] Political parties were permitted to reestablish themselves on the condition that they
were not based on religion, class, or region. Muslim student associations
on college campuses across the country were encouraged and subsidized,
leading them to dominate the social and political life of students.[71] Gama'a
al-Shabab al-Islam (Youth of Islam Group) established its first branch at
Cairo University's Faculty of Engineering in 1972.[72] The greatest period
of growth for Islamic institutions was immediately after the *Infitah;* the
number of Islamic associations registered with the Ministry of Social Affairs
nearly doubled in the 1970s. MOSA supervised all NGOs until 1979,
when the ministry decided to decentralize its operations by governorate.[73]
Numerous new Azharite institutions were established, a new campus for
al-Azhar, ostensibly funded by the Saudis, was built in Nasr City, and state-
supported mosques flourished across the country.[74]

The state's co-optation of formal religious institutions undermined their
legitimacy and opened up the potential for co-optation of religion by other
groups. In the 1970s, militant Islamist groups mushroomed in Egypt, including al-Takfir wa-al-Hijra and al-Gama'a al-Islamiyya, which outgrew
its university roots to became the most powerful militant group.[75] The
mounting tension with the Brotherhood coupled with the bread riots of
1977 led Sadat to introduce a number of emergency security measures
restricting political activity and forbidding criticism of the government.
Islamists were most angered by Sadat's peace agreement with Israel, but
they also objected to Sadat's pro-Western political and economic policies.
Militant Islamists garnered support in the economically impoverished Upper
Egypt, where protests broke out in 1979. Sadat made many concessions,
but Islamist opposition grew. In response, a year later, he suspended all
Islamic associations in universities and in 1981 he accused the Brotherhood

of collaborating with militant opposition groups against the government. He began a comprehensive attack on Islamists, closing down Islamic journals, seizing Brotherhood funds, imprisoning Brotherhood members, and placing all private mosques under the Ministry of Endowments.[76] In September 1981, Sadat called for the nationalization of all private mosques. One month later, in October 1981, he was assassinated by a member of al-Jihad. Sadat's co-optation of religious institutions had the opposite of the intended effect—rather than defuse the situation, it fueled the resurgence of militant Islamists and undermined the religious establishment.[77]

Like his predecessors, Hosni Mubarak governmentalized Islam by expanding the state's religious entities, establishing the Supreme Council for Islamic Preaching, broadening the educational mission of the Ministry of Religion, and reinstituting the High Council for Islamic Affairs.[78] Immediately following Sadat's assassination, Mubarak arrested four thousand suspected members of Islamist groups and tried to strengthen al-Azhar's religious authority in an effort to undermine the legitimacy of the groups.[79] However, after more than two decades of state co-optation of religion, al-Azhar had lost its legitimacy with the public. During his first decade in office, Mubarak recognized the Brotherhood as a "moderate" Islamist group and attempted to enlist its support in a campaign to undermine the "radicals" and regain religious legitimacy for the state. Mubarak pursued limited political liberalization, including the reestablishment of political parties and the reemergence of an active press.[80] Until 1992, the Ministry of Interior attempted to counter "radical" Islam by engaging in dialogue with nonviolent Islamists.[81] Despite Mubarak's overtures to dialogue, his economic policy, political oppression, and policy toward Israel increased militant activities.

Egypt began a fervent antiterrorism campaign in the early 1990s after the militant Islamist movement reached its pinnacle with escalating violence in Upper Egypt. The government once again unsuccessfully called on al-Azhar to delegitimize the militant Islamists, but for the first time in several decades al-Azhar pushed back against the Mubarak regime and regained some of its autonomy as well as legitimacy.[82] There was a marked shift in Egypt's antiterrorism policy following the appointment of General Hassan al-Alfi as Minister of Interior.[83] General al-Alfi received two years of antiterrorist training in the United States and introduced a computerized databank for tracking terrorist threats into Egypt's security system.[84] The government pursued a policy of isolating the militant Islamists (which

Mubarak termed "terrorist extremists") through military blockades and widespread imprisonment. The state sentenced several leaders of the movement to death and infiltrated their stronghold on mosques in Upper Egypt. From 1993 onward, the regime treated all Islamists and Islamic organizations, including the Muslim Brotherhood, as a security or terrorist threat regardless of their tactics.

The antiterrorism campaign was simply an extension of the Emergency Law, which has governed the country almost continuously since 1967.[85] Thousands of Islamists, including nonviolent Brotherhood members, in addition to militant Islamists, have been subject to imprisonment under this law, and several have been subject to torture and abuse. The Brotherhood faced severe censorship and surveillance coupled with periods of mass arrest, where its members were frequently jailed and tortured. As part of the attempt to reign in Islamic opposition, the government shut down five thousand Muslim Brotherhood offices, halted the Brotherhood's partnership with the labor party, and closed the opposition newspaper al-Sha'b.[86] The government placed almost all of the sixty thousand private mosques under the supervision of the Ministry of Endowments and tightened its stronghold on Friday khutab (sermons).[87]

At the same time as militants embarked on a series of terrorist attacks on touristic venues, a younger generation of moderate Islamists was becoming politically savvy. These Islamists shifted their focus to freedom of expression and political rights through involvement in elections, calling for democracy and political reform and expressing themselves through media outlets.[88] As the Brotherhood continued to provide a wide social-service network to the poor and middle classes, it also became the most vocal and organized critic of the regime. By organizing and providing these everyday services, the Brotherhood created a permanent seat for itself at the political table; even if it was a banned political party, it was a tolerated one. The Brotherhood called for democratization and expanded its network; it permeated numerous state institutions and gained power in the judiciary, public universities, and al-Azhar.[89]

In 2006 I discussed the state's intervention in the affairs of Islamic associations with Hisham Hammami, the assistant to Abdel-Moneim Aboul-Fotouh, who at the time was a member of the guidance council of the Muslim Brotherhood. He criticized the government's stronghold on Egyptian civil society and explained why the Brotherhood had become important providers for the poor:

The government has intervened in civil society. The Muslim
Brotherhood sees poverty as a big problem and wants to
address social problems like health care. The government
thinks the Brotherhood uses social services only to get political
support and popularity. But the Brotherhood works because
they care and this sometimes leads to votes. . . . They want to
serve God and to develop our society. This is a human issue
and it is also an issue of our people and our land. . . . On July 23,
1952, *waqf* was institutionalized, and this changed state and
society relations greatly; . . . the law was utilized to make society
weaker. Organizations, media, unions, they are all the pillars that
make society stronger. But the state keeps trying to weaken and
control them. The state needs these organizations, though. . . .
The state started to feel its role weaken and it wants to hold
everything in its hands. It wants to put security, the security
apparatus, in everything—hospitals, workers, and unemployment. . . . The nationalism era is gone, but they still try to keep
it. I was raised with the Brotherhood, raised among them. And
the 'Islamic way' is the only way for people to have value, to
have meaning in their lives.[90]

Hamamy posited Islam (in this case the Brotherhood) as offering solutions to Egypt's social problems. The Brotherhood provided a large number of social services to the Egyptian public and the public recognized
their critical role in society. During the last decade of Mubarak's reign, the
Brotherhood had huge numbers of supporters in universities, courts, and
professional syndicates, including the lawyers', doctors', and engineers' syndicates, which they control to this day.[91] Operating as an informal political party running as "independents" in the 2005 parliamentary elections,
the Brotherhood gained eighty-eight seats (19.81 percent of elected seats),
up from seventeen seats (3.82 percent) in 2000.[92] The Brotherhood boy-
cotted the runoffs to the 2010 election, citing corruption, but in the first
post-Mubarak elections, in 2011, the Brotherhood collected well over 40
percent of the votes.[93] Undoubtedly the Brotherhood gained much of its
political clout by providing social services through a large network of Islamic
associations. The government's fixation on the Brotherhood as a political
threat actually enhanced the Brotherhood's legitimacy while enabling it to receive credit for the work of numerous independent local Islamic associations.

Nonetheless, the Brotherhood's influence on social institutions (including mosques, universities, syndicates, and unions) has been vital to the growth of Islamism in Egypt.

Leading up to the 2011 uprising, Egypt experienced some of its largest protests since the 1977 bread riots. Many of the protests were political in nature; protests mounted against police brutality (including the murder of Khaled Said), the Israeli treatment of Palestinians, the American invasion of Iraq, and the political cartoons in Denmark, as well as repeated election fraud. Many of the protests were also economic in nature and strikes became commonplace in reaction to worsening economic conditions for the poor. The April 6th Youth Movement, hailed as one of the sparks of the 2011 revolution, called for a general strike in 2008, which was barricaded by the police, and from 2008 to 2011 numerous casualties occurred among the poor standing in line for bread.

While the Brotherhood likely played a minor role in initiating the Egyptian uprising of 2011, it certainly benefited from it. Years of underground political organizing proved beneficial as the Brotherhood rose to power swiftly and became dominant in the post-Mubarak era. This political success was partly an outcome of the Brotherhood's provision of social services, but it was also in part because the Brotherhood had been persecuted since the revolution of 1952. The Brotherhood is politically strong because it symbolizes the *idea* of an Islamic society in the minds of Egyptians—a society without corruption, immorality, greed, and foreign interference, a society based on social justice and equality. The 2011 uprising was based on these ideals, yet none of them were ever realized in the fragile road to democracy. Of particular importance to the democratization of Egypt is the reform of an oppressive and antiquated legal environment for civil society that made operating as an Islamic charity particularly cumbersome.[94]

The State Effect: A Stringent Legal Environment for NGOs

The state's relationship with Islamic groups very much shaped the legal context for NGOs since the majority of legislation and supervision over NGOs was created in the name of protecting national security (later scripted as "antiterrorism"). Although the disabling legal environment affects all NGOs, entities seen as a threat to state power (human rights groups, Islamists) were targeted by enforcement agencies. The specific bureaucratic and legal obstacles were of critical importance because the law governing NGOs gave the government immense power to regulate group activities across space and time (what they can do, when, where, and how they do it). Creating a bureaucratic maze was a key technique of control, as they acquired information on groups and also narrowed their channels of action. The state established itself as the guardian of NGOs and enacted the first association law in 1956 under Nasser. The pronouncement annulled Articles 54 to 80 of the civic code and dissolved all associations. It also prevented NGOs from receiving foreign funds and forced them to reapply for licenses under the Ministry of Social Affairs.[95] From 1964 until 1999, Law 32 (known as the Law of Associations) gave the government extensive power over NGOs, controlling their activities and funding and shutting down associations that it saw as a threat. Through its 140 articles, the law outlined the spheres of activity that associations could work in, gave the state the right to disband and merge associations, placed organizations under the state's financial supervision, and supported activities that complemented those of government agencies. After heavy lobbying and negotiation from NGOs, Law 153 of 1999 alleviated a few of the measures in the previous law, but it did not relieve NGOs of potential interference from official bodies.[96] In fact, the law was declared unconstitutional in 2000. In practice, the current law, Law 84 of 2002, made minor changes to Law 153.[97] Law 84 requires organizations to register as either a *gam'iyya* (pl. *gam'iyyat*, association), a *mu'assasa* (pl. *mu'assasat*, foundation), or an *ittihad* (federation). Under this law, NGOs still must have permission to accept funds from outside Egypt. Organizations can have their assets seized by the ministry, if appropriate, and governing boards may be dissolved or replaced. The main features of the current NGO law include: regulations regarding the registration process and tax-exemption status; organizations must notify the ministry of any fund-raising efforts; the ministry must approve funding from abroad; and government authorities have the right to investigate the backgrounds of board members and the financial records of the organization and abolish organizations that violate restrictions. The law explicitly forbids military or political activities, acts threatening national unity, acts breaking general order or ethics, or activities that discriminate among citizens.

Law 84 had an immense impact on the NGO sector. First, it gave the General Federation of NGOs and Foundations (established in 1969) renewed importance in regulating the work of NGOs.[98] While in theory the federation was created to serve as a liaison between NGOs and the government, in essence the federation is part of the governmentalization of the state, an extended arm of the Ministry of Social Solidarity. Through 2007, only 496 national NGOs, 27 regional federations, and 11 specialized federations were members of the General Federation. Mubarak appointed ten of the thirty board members of the General Federation.

Law 84 is also significant because it created a new legal category for the creation of foundations *(mu'assasat)*. As discussed in chapter 4, this legal category allowed elite members of society to set up a Western-style foundation, a practice that replaced the co-opted practices of Islamic endowments *(waqf)*. Law 84 created the foundation as a legal category that functions much in the same way as associations but without the same stringent enforcement. For example, the NGO law requires associations to have ten founding board members, while foundations need only three and are based on a sum of money rather than a set of members. Since the 2002 law also outlined simpler rules regarding annual meetings and general procedures for foundations, Egypt witnessed an explosion in the number of organizations registering as foundations. While a foundation theoretically operates quite differently than an association, in practice many of the organizations established as foundations functioned identically to associations. They registered as foundations because of the simpler legal context. The government heavily regulated who could set up a foundation; it then used the category to mark organizations that it did not see as a threat. Thus, the category permitted the government to differentiate between suspect groups and those loyal to the regime, exercised through differentiated policing practices for associations versus that of foundations. The stringent legal environment for NGOs worked in tandem with an intrusive and brutal state security apparatus that intruded into the work of organizations.

The effects of this stringent legal environment on NGO activity cannot be overstated. It includes a lack of cooperation and communication among NGOs, a culture of secrecy and lack of transparency in the sector, and rapid growth in the number of new NGOs without a concomitant increase in their effectiveness (i.e., thousands of redundant NGOs without functionality). Among the organizations I visited, the directors cited a lack of cooperation among NGOs and a culture of secrecy—where NGOs were afraid to divulge their activities to one another—as their greatest problems. This is partially a result of the Emergency Law, which creates a climate of fear around any form of organizing. In addition, strict ministerial rules prohibited collaboration, which was seen as a security threat. Whenever I questioned anyone about the lack of coordination and collaboration in the sector, they reiterated the security concern. An entrepreneur involved in development work told me: "The problem with large scale is that you become influential and a threat. As long as you are small, no one bothers you. When you show you can influence people, have direction, make a difference, change—then they get threatened."[99]

The *they* in question are the security authorities. In my interview with an architect who provided in-kind services to charities and mosques, he also mentioned that large-scale associations threaten the government. A major reason, then, for the huge number of associations was the unspoken understanding that organizations that grew too large, or had too much influence, would be seen as a threat to the government and run into problems. This was particularly true of organizations with an Islamic association due to the state's tumultuous history with them.

The NGO Landscape

Important political issues are at stake in the categorization and classification of NGOs.[100] Most scholars of Egyptian civil society have gone to painstaking lengths to decipher the categories developed by the Ministry of Social Solidarity. Law 32 of 1964, which was not amended until 1999, categorized associations as either charitable associations (*gam'iyyat khayriyya*) or community development associations (CDAs, or *gam'iyyat tanmawiyya*). This dichotomy of charity versus development profoundly shaped the ministry's policies.[101] Charitable associations were usually religious in nature and were often attached to a mosque or church. In contrast, CDAs were usually secular development organizations that frequently received foreign funding. In contrast to religious charities, CDAs had very few limits on the type of work they were permitted to do. They were commonly administered by current or former government employees in consultation with international agencies such as the Ford Foundation, AMIDEAST, CIDA (Canadian International Development Agency), and USAID.[102]

In October 2006, there were 21,639 associations, 299 foundations, and 23 federations registered with the Egyptian Ministry of Social Solidarity (Table 2).[103] Of these, approximately a quarter of all associations, half of all foundations, and 10 percent of all federations were located in Cairo. Growth estimates are about one thousand new associations, one hundred new foundations, and ten new federations per year, leaving 2012 estimates at twenty-eight thousand NGOs, eight hundred foundations, and about

Table 2. Associations, Federations, and Foundations by Region, (2006)

Region	Associations	Foundations	Federations
Cairo	5245	136	5
Giza	2076	20	7
Alexandria	1595	40	3
Suez	347	3	0
Port Said	214	1	0
Urban Governorates	9477	200	15
Upper Egypt	4722	24	26
Lower Egypt	6472	43	10
Desert/Frontier Governorates	819	6	1
Central Associations	149	26	11
Total	21639	299	63

Source: Ministry of Social Solidarity, 2006. Upper Egypt Governorates include Aswan, Qena, Suhag, Asyut, Luxor, Minya, Beni Suef, and Al-Fayoum. Lower Egypt Governorates include Kafr el Sheikh, Dumyat, Dekahlia, Behera, Gharbia, Ismailia, Minufia, Kalyubia, and Sharkia. Frontier Governorates include Red Sea, New Valley, North Sinai, South Sinai, and Matrouh.

one hundred federations.[104] Using the 2006 figures for associations, 44.8 percent (9,687) fell under the unitary category "cultural, scientific, and religious services." This categorization obscures the number of Islamic associations by grouping them in with cultural, education, and Coptic associations.[105] Understating the number of Islamic organizations was part of the government's strategy to underplay the influence of Islamic associations.[106] The government further classified associations based on eighteen categories of activity.[107]

Given the limitations of working with the category "cultural, scientific, and religious," scholars created other classification systems. Saad Eddin Ibrahim emphasized the difference between "welfare PVOs," categorized as associations working in health care, housing, or environmental protection, and "developmental PVOs," which are involved in upgrading standards of living.[108] Within the category of PVOs, community development associations (CDAs) represent the single largest category of organizations engaged in income-generating activities for the poor. Ibrahim used the term "social Islam" to describe an extensive network of "advocacy-service" PVOs—organizations involved in both social service provision and advocacy work of some kind. Amani Kandil classified nonprofit organizations into six categories: associations and private foundations, professional groups, business groups, foreign foundations, advocacy organizations, Islamic *waqf,* and Christian charities.[109] This categorization, however, is somewhat problematic now because the lines between public and private are blurred; many associations and private foundations are funded through Islamic charity, and, furthermore, welfare and advocacy activities often go hand in hand. Kandil recognized the slipperiness of these categories and created a catchall category of "borderline institutions," which includes cooperatives, Sufi groups, religious and private hospitals, research centers, and the quasi-governmental Nasser Social Bank. Abdelrahman categorized NGOs into five groups: Islamic NGOs, Coptic NGOs, community development associations, advocacy groups, and businessmen's associations.[110] Yet once again the boundaries between businessmen's associations, advocacy organizations, and development organizations are becoming blurred. Another important part of this blurring of organizational categories is the encouragement by the Ministry of Social Solidarity for associations working from a welfare/charity framework based on cash transfers to transform their work to a development framework focused on job creation and conditional giving.

Birth of a Dichotomy: Charity or Development?

In March 2006, I found a directory of development NGOs in Egypt. Rummaging through the uncatalogued library at the Ahram Center for Political and Strategic Studies, a government-funded research center that focuses on civil society in the Arab world, I was surprised to come across the directory, since numerous scholars of the sector had told me no such thing existed.[111] In fact, the Ministry of Social Solidarity is the only entity capable of producing such a document. Initially I inquired at the ministry, but employees directed me to the National Federation of Egyptian NGOs, which I was told was in the process of creating a directory of NGOs. The NGO federation was supposed to act as a mediator between NGOs and the Ministry of Social Solidarity but essentially was an extension of the ministry. In my subsequent visits to both the federation and the ministry that year, I was told that a directory was "in the works" and would be completed within the following year. When I returned to Cairo in December 2007, the directory still had not been completed and rumor was that even if it existed it would never become accessible. Nearly five years later, I gave up on the directory, having come to understand that the state's monopoly on information and bureaucratic incompetence prevented informational transparency in the nonprofit sector.[112]

Delighted to find some sort of directory after months of frustration, I arranged a meeting with the author, Dr. Ayman Abdel-Wahab, a researcher at the Ahram Center. In our interview, we discussed the numerous difficulties he faced in compiling the directory. For one, the classification of NGOs as developmental (as opposed to charitable) was a major problem because the definition of what actually constituted "development" was set by the NGOs themselves and not by the central authorities.[113] Many organizations were classified as developmental but were far from it; for example, many organizations that assist in funeral and burial arrangements were classified as developmental. In addition, the documents the ministry provided often did not match the activities of the organizations he consulted. Given the difficulty associations faced when trying to amend their founding documents, they tended to register in numerous areas from the beginning even if they had no immediate plans to operate in those areas.

Abdel-Wahab discussed religious charities, primarily based on the practice of *zakat*, as obstacles to development. Despite pressure from the government to become development organizations, the fact that so many organizations began as charities meant that they continued to focus on cash transfer to categories established for *zakat* recipients in the Quran.[114] Under Law 32 of 1964, 75 percent of organizations had been classified as charity and aid and 25 percent had been classified as developmental.[115] Abdel-Wahab estimated that only 10 percent to 15 percent of organizations were actually involved in development work, defined mostly by income-generating projects. He also noted that Islamic associations were increasingly involved in *tanmiya khayriyya* (charitable development) as part of their *takamul* (social integration) ideology.[116] In my visits with ministry officials, they reported that almost all organizations were engaged in some sort of development work and that charity was a thing of the past. However, as Abdel-Wahab noted, development work requires far more resources (financial, human, planning, etc.) than charity work and therefore organizations that had been operating as charities for decades had a difficult time making the transition.[117] I questioned the need for a transition.

Abdel-Wahab confirmed my sense that a great ideological transition was under way as charities strove to become developmental, but that this transition was far from complete. Most organizations continue to work in the areas of food, clothing, and medicinal provision as well as direct aid for the poor and disadvantaged groups such as female heads of households and orphans. As part of the shift toward development, many organizations had begun to transition their work into income-generating projects such as skill upgrading or microfinance. In the process, associations had to negotiate a whole new set of meanings and become skilled in the language of development. They had to reconcile varying perspectives on social care, including Islamic notions strongly rooted in traditional interpretations of *zakat* with so-called human development.[118]

Since so many of my interlocutors spoke of the NGO sector using this same charity-development dichotomy, I repeatedly inquired about this distinction. The Egyptian Ministry of Social Solidarity played a critical role in encouraging NGOs to move away from operating as "charities" and instead to become developmental "engines of empowerment." Since 1995, when it was called the Ministry of Social Affairs, the ministry developed a solidarity program whose stated objective was to "alleviate poverty and integrate the poor into the development process of financial aid and the establishment of income generating projects."[119] In my meeting with Aziza Youssef, the director of the Central Administration of Associations at the ministry, she emphasized the ministry's new role:

> We play a role in directing organizations. We are encouraging them to transition from charity to development. . . . Our own name change better reflects our role now. This name change, and the shift from charity to development, are really based on the largest problem that our country and society faces, that the solutions must address poverty. . . . We have seen growth in the sector fueled by a number of organizations working in development . . . small and medium enterprises, loans, computer training centers, etc. Some have been working in this area for a long time, but we also see increases in the emerging fields of environmental organizations, consumer-rights advocates, youth programs, administrative development, IT and communications. . . . So this a transitional phase.[120]

When the ministry changed its name from the Ministry of Social Affairs to the Ministry of Social Solidarity, it moved from a direct provider of social services to the central manager of NGOs.[121] The demise of the welfare state led associations and NGOs to become increasingly important; they provided the services the state no longer could or wanted to accommodate. As a result, the NGO sector in Egypt became incredibly crowded, with more than 22,000 organizations, 7,321 of which operated in Greater Cairo alone.[122] This huge number of organizations is evidence of the important role of the NGO sector as an actor in governance. As the state's role in service provision declined, NGOs and, more recently, the private sector became important partners in social-care provision. Despite the huge number of new players, the swelling in the number of NGOs has not necessarily led to improvements in quality or outputs. Egypt continues to face tremendous poverty as average citizens struggle to meet their basic needs. Youssef had indicated to me that, despite the growth in the number of organizations, many were not functional. For Abdel-Wahab, this period of transition for NGOs also included unprecedented exponential growth in the number of associations:

> During the past ten years, there have been many changes. First, there is a huge increase in number, although quality vs. quantity is questionable. . . . There were one thousand new organizations each year over the past four years; before it was about five hundred new organizations a year. So that's a huge jump. And the agenda has changed; it increasingly features building civil society, rights, and defense of environment, etc. . . . And there are monetary changes—more businessmen involved and the wave of privatization has meant a move toward consumer-rights organizations as well.[123]

The Ministry of Social Solidarity, then, played a critical role in shaping the agenda of NGOs, but it was not the only government entity involved in the management of NGOs. In addition to the central security apparatus, the Nasser Social Bank also governed local *zakat* committees (*ligan zakat*), entities that are not registered as associations but often serve the same function. The Nasser Social Bank was charged with managing the *zakat* accounts and monitoring the activities of *zakat* committees across the country.[124] The bank had a particular stronghold over committees that receive government funding, controlling virtually everything it could. The bank has 89 branches and 4,690 *zakat*-raising committees, raising approximately 594 million EGP.[125] Local *zakat* committees also played a critical role since NGOs "have been encouraged by the government to shift from being charities to providers of microfinance, the Nasser Social Bank is seen as playing a role, through both co-funding and by setting an example through its own financing methods."[126] The ministry thus used the Nasser Social Bank to disseminate its development-oriented approach to Islamic charities.

Islamic charities entered the world of development by drawing on a long history of *zakat, sadaqa,* and *qard hasan* as well as the history of poverty-alleviation approaches from the Nasser era onward. While many Islamic charities simply went along with the ministerial pressure and changed to development associations in name only, others quickly jumped on board the development agenda. Having watched "secular" development organizations receive funding by international aid agencies for over three decades, many Islamic associations were eager to tap into the same lucrative networks. The organizations did not blindly import a development paradigm; instead, they wove Islamic charitable practices into the existing orthodoxy on development championed by the state and multilateral institutions.

Conclusion

Practices of governmentality initiated in the nineteenth century as part of the formation of modern Egypt institutionalized poverty alleviation. Prior to the nineteenth century, social care was dominated by the Islamic practice of *waqf.* The state's intervention in *waqf* has produced new forms of philanthropy into the twenty-first century, a phenomenon discussed in detail in chapter four. The state and private voluntary associations became increasingly involved in poverty alleviation during the nineteenth and early twentieth centuries. As more institutions and organizations became involved, the practices became bureaucratized and depersonalized, shifting the focus from the poor to poverty and later from social justice to economic growth.[127] A tension emerged between the state and associations over who was responsible and capable of caring for the poor. After the 1952 revolution, under the leadership of Nasser, the Egyptian state became a welfare state, providing extensive government guarantees, including education, employment, housing, and health care. Until the 1980s, when Egypt implemented a series of structural-adjustment policies, Egypt was a comprehensive welfare state. During the 1990s, Egypt's welfare programs, governed largely by what was then the Ministry of Social Affairs, were drastically reduced. Although many programs continued to exist, they were drastically underfunded and unable to keep up with the expedient population growth.[128]

Egypt witnessed a spike in Quangoization or GONGOs (government-organized NGOs) as the binaries of state and nonstate blurred.[129] Quangoization occurred directly in line with the state's withdrawal from the welfare state, a phenomenon that is emblematic of the dissemination of neoliberal governance. The gaps in wealth created by neoliberal development policies led not only to increased poverty but also to an increased role for Islamic associations in society. As the government's provision of social care declined, Islamic associations provided social services for the poor.[130] As NGOs became more involved in the direct provision of social services, Islamic organizations in particular became key providers of social care.[131]

The government also engaged in an intense battle with Islamists over religion and the policing of conduct. State-governed Islamic entities lost a great deal of their legitimacy as a result of this intervention, which in turn opened up a space for multiple religious authorities. The government targeted Islamic groups, particularly those with an overtly political agenda. This served to strengthen the involvement of Islamic associations in social care, which in turn only strengthened their position in society. At the same time, the care work done by Islamic associations enabled the survival of the poor in the wake of neoliberal economic policies. The social work of Islamic associations also benefited the Muslim Brotherhood. The state's interference with Islamic associations seems to have produced the opposite of the intended effect. The current state of Islam in Egypt is largely a product of the state's intervention in and attempt to co-opt Islam under its own agenda. An attempt by the state to control "popular" religion laid the groundwork for a subsequent religious revival.[132]

CHAPTER 3

A Space and Time for Giving

The mosque floor is covered with dark green carpet. An empty
well sits in the center of the room; rusty pipe remnants protrude
from the well. Scattered columns with historical engraving support
the foundation of this side of the mosque. Several long tall shelves
in the corner are filled with women's shoes, left by the women
praying, or in the case of the widows coming to collect their aid,
plastic flip-flops. Women volunteers, organized by committee, sit
on the perimeter of the room; all veiled, mostly elderly, they guard
the few chairs in the building. As a visitor, I am allowed to sit on
one of the chairs. Every first Tuesday or Thursday of the month,
upward of two hundred women swarm into the mosque to receive
their aid. They must first attend a brief sermon [*khutba*] given
by one of the Quranic reading-group leaders [*da'iya*] and then
perform the noon prayer. The look of dread is apparent on many
of their frowning faces, sweat dribbling down their black abayas
[loose traditional cloaks], as they kneel on the ground, waiting
impatiently. After the prayer, the women's names are called out
one by one, and each woman must present an ID card to the
Hagga, sign on the line indicating her monthly aid amount, and
verify her address and number of children. Many of the women
are illiterate and so the Hagga reads the information to the women
and then requests their *khitm,* a small stamp that they carry around
with them and use in lieu of a signature. After receiving their
envelopes, the women symbolically kiss it and softly utter
"al-humdulillah" [Thanks Be to God]. On their way out of the
mosque, many stop by another Hagga and ask if there is bread
today. The Hagga hands them a small voucher, and the women
scurry off to collect their shoes or slippers and proceed to the
warehouse for leftover bread collected from local bakeries.
(author's field notes, March 15, 2006)

This scene from the Salah al-Din Mosque in the middle-class neighborhood of al-Manyal describes a procedure that occurs at literally thousands of mosques in and around Cairo. I visited more than a dozen such *zakat* committees scattered around town and found very little variance between them. The women come from near and far, collecting between 25 and 200 LE from the charity committee at a local mosque to supplement the meager social security benefits available from the starved welfare state budget. Many of the women, with no formal education and little or no family support, work as well, peddling Kleenex to drivers at busy intersections, housekeeping for the wealthy, or sewing garments for two LE apiece (about 20 American cents).

Support from *zakat* committees often came with the requirement to attend moral and religious instruction *(irshad dini)* on topics such as cleanliness, organization, honesty, consistency between words and actions, neighborly relations, relationships with relatives, marital relations, and other disciplinary and behavioral issues. *Zakat* committees in mosques across the country coupled direct aid with religious lessons. The Hagga, a soft-spoken austere yet energetic woman now in her late seventies, was a founding member of the Salah al-Din Mosque's *zakat* committee in 1971; the committee officially became the country's first women-run *zakat* committee in 1973 (Figure 9). The Hagga explained to me why religious lessons are given along with aid: "We want to raise the level of the women, teach them manners and cleanliness. Yes we want to help them, and we give them monetary assistance. But they also need education. God gives rewards *(thawab)* for knowledge sharing. . . . So we combine charity with religious lessons, which has an effect on human development" (interview, Cairo, March 22, 2006). The Hagga articulated a postcolonial civilizing narrative; helping the women meant giving them money and educating them in how to lead a proper life. The organization linked receipt of monetary aid with disciplinary practices, including religious and moral lessons, thereby grafting "morality onto economics" and using assistance as a "sacrament of moralization, control, and dissuasion."[1] The veiled recipients attended prayers, listened to sermons, and followed the orders of the Hagga because they knew that the *zakat* committee members had discretion over how strict or lax they were with respect to contingencies for aid. The women thus performed such "technologies" of the self and complied with invasive social-research practices that investigated the details of their situation, home life, and neediness. The women did so because aid was contingent on their willingness to submit and they needed this aid to survive.[2]

Figure 9. Entrance to the zakat *committee at Salah al-Din Mosque in al-Manyal.*
Photograph by the author.

In this mosque, there was a strong literacy and a high-school equiva-
lency program. Many graduates of the literacy programs were also bene-
factors. In addition to the aid given to widows, *zakat* committees also
focused on providing aid to Egypt's estimated 2.5 million orphans.[3] Once
a year, on Orphans' Day, thousands of mosques around the country hold
a large party where hundreds of orphans come and enjoy a large meal and
receive small plastic totes filled with school supplies and sweets. Egyptians
from all walks of life participate in Orphans' Day in order to recognize the
plight of orphans. Most *zakat* committees also provided a variety of other
community services, including day care (subsidized by the ministry), tutoring for school-age children, burial services, emergency aid, and either support for or direct provision of health services.

One day I asked the Hagga about the bread vouchers, or the tiny slips
of paper I heard some women ask about as they exited with their monthly
stipend. The Hagga asked an aid recipient to show me the way to the office,
where women pick up day-old bread and used clothing. The woman, in
her mid-forties, wore a black ʿabaya and beige flip-flops. On the way there
she was silent, walking briskly and paying little attention as I struggled to
dash across the congested roadway. We walked several blocks through a
maze of alleys to the ground floor of an old apartment building where the
zakat committee kept its supplies. Two younger women managed the
stashes of day-old bread and allowed the women to pick through the piles
of donated clothing. The woman I followed saw an acquaintance there
and stopped to chat with her. On the walk back to the main road, the
acquaintance said to the woman, "It is worth it to come here just for the
bread. I can't bear to wait in line for the (subsidized) bread. My 200 LE
barely covers food for my children." The other woman replied, "God is the
provider of all. May He help us and guide us on the righteous path." Bread,
a staple of the Egyptian diet, is subsidized and offered to the poor through
a vast network of state-run bakeries. Since demand is greater than supply,
women often wait in line for hours to receive their allotment. Fights frequently break out as people wait in line for the subsidized bread; thus, the
women would rather pick up day-old bread from the charity. Despite their
financial hardship, most Egyptians thank God for what they have, holding
on to the belief that God provides everyone according to their need. Even
women as needy as these two were likely to give charity since giving is
such an important part of Egyptian culture.

There are more than twelve hundred *zakat* committees like this one scattered around Cairo. Mosques and their associations constituted a crucial space for the poor and the lower middle class to receive social services that formerly were provided by *awqaf* and the state. Given the decimated public health-care and public school system, medical clinics, hospitals, and tutoring services became part of the list of regular services provided by mosques. Since so many children are enrolled in quasi-private schools (and even those who go to public schools have to pay high fees for tutoring), mosques also frequently supply back-to-school boxes with books and supplies for students. Women like those described above continued to receive aid from *zakat* committees because of their status as female heads of households. Particular categories, like the poor and needy, have special status in mosques because of the common interpretation of a Quranic passage that protects the eight categories of *zakat* recipients, including widows and orphans.[4] Thus mosques created social service divisions where they support female heads of households with monthly stipends. Because orphans are also a clearly identifiable group of the "deserving poor,"[5] based on *Surat al-Tawba,* every charitable organization I visited served them as well.

In the wake of privatization, mosques and their associations became key providers of social services. Many mosques helped couples with the costs of marriage since the costs have been escalating for years. And of course marriage, as an institution, serves to preserve the religious requirement for abstaining from sexual relations outside marriage.[6] Given the expansion in services that mosques provided, different forms of giving were kept separate through a system of accounts that ensure that all *zakat* was spent in the requisite time period. Most mosques also held an account for each of the following areas: *zakat al-fitr, zakat al-mal,* orphans, widows, medical cases, and *sadaqa gariya* (which is used for mosque maintenance). Some mosques placed labeled boxes in the mosque for each area so people could donate as they wished, while others simply had virtual boxes kept through an accounting system.[7] Despite the large number of *zakat* committees and associations, across a vast array of charitable associations (regardless of their size or resource base), a sentiment of scarcity prevailed. *Zakat* committees resorted to limiting their operation to a specific locale. In order to receive aid from a particular mosque, the recipients needed to live within a specified district. At the same time that giving became more localized, it also expanded geographically. The spatial expansion of giving was triggered by a transformation in the space for religious discourse. Islamic charity played a role in this transformation, which resulted in changed spatial relations throughout Cairo.

Islamic Charity as a Form of *Da'wa*

Da'wa literally means "call or invitation" and refers to the practice of urging others (Muslims or non-Muslims alike) toward Islam, an "Islamic lifestyle," or public piety. A *da'i/ da'iya* is one who implements *da'wa*. Traditionally this was a Quranic recitation leader or teacher in a mosque, but today the number of self-proclaimed religious authorities has multiplied and *da'wa* frequently takes place outside the mosque setting. Individuals engaged in *da'wa* gained prominence because they spoke to the daily concerns of people in everyday spaces, discussing "transportation, bureaucracy, corruption, unemployment, and social and gender inequalities."[8] The rise of the *da'iya*, or female preacher, in particular brought religious discourse directly to women as they coupled religious lessons with morality.[9] *Da'wa* involves much more than preaching and can encompass any activity performed with the intention of integrating Islam more fully into society or bringing the practices into people's everyday lives.

Volunteerism is a form of *da'wa* and an important expression of religiosity. Islamic charity is literally "putting *da'wa* into practice."[10] It is also a form of *da'wa* because in performing *khayr* (a good deed, including charity) one has the ability to open the hearts of others to Islam. Islamic charity as a form of *da'wa* plays a critical role in the formation of Islamic subjectivities; religion is the driving force behind the majority of Egyptians' engagement with poverty alleviation. As one philanthropist told me, he was motivated to help the poor in order to encourage people to "think about what it means to be religious. I do it for God first, my country second, not for the poor people themselves. . . . I want to improve the image of Islam and I do that by starting with good deeds [*a'mal khayriyya*]. . . . Community service leads to religiosity. And religious motives are behind 90 percent of good deeds in Egypt."[11] The sentiment of doing good deeds for God is encapsulated in the phrase *khayr wa-khalas,* as givers were most concerned with how their good deeds would be received by God.

Over the past ten years, Islam has moved into everyday life and thus everyday spaces discursively, symbolically, and materially.[12] Hosts of self-proclaimed *da'i/ da'iya* were concerned with public morality and sociability;[13] therefore they shifted preaching away from "Islamist polity to personal piety and ethics."[14] A shift from Islamist polity to personal piety required greater focus on individual subjectivity and the expression of religiosity in everyday life rather than a focus on formal politics or state building. *Daʿwa* illustrates the forms of ethical and political subjecthood produced by Islamic charitable institutions in Egypt as acts of piety become acts of polity. With a new emphasis on piety and ethics, volunteerism and participation in local mosques or associations became as important a marker of religiosity as daily prayers, modesty in dress, and abstinence from alcoholic beverages. While the new *daʿi* led to a growth in Islamic volunteerism, Islamic associations also fueled the growth of *daʿwa*. These associations were an important means of articulating religiosity in daily life; at the same time, the vast majority of Islamic charities were engaged in *daʿwa* work in addition to assisting the poor.

The growth of *daʿwa* in Egypt is to some extent an unintended consequence of the state's co-optation of Islam. As the state cracked down on Islamist organizing, people felt disillusioned and afraid of being associated with formal Islamic institutions. *Daʿwa* was a safe way to implement Islam informally into all aspects of society and daily life, or what many scholars refer to as Islamization.[15] The Islamization of society is the insertion of Islamic discourse and practices into everyday life, making piety a much more visible act. Islamization "involves the process whereby various domains of social life are invested with signs and symbols associated with Islamic cultural traditions."[16] Islam also became a larger part of public life because more people dedicated themselves to *daʿwa* work. *Daʿwa* then contributes to the Islamization of society because it allows people to articulate Islamic practices and norms publicly. *Daʿwa* can traverse space and time because "*daʿwa* is constituted whenever and wherever individuals enter into that form of discourse geared toward upholding or improving the moral condition of the collective."[17] However, one may participate in *daʿwa* without being part of an Islamist agenda.[18] While the Islamization of everyday life is certainly an important component of the Islamist agenda, many individuals who participate in *daʿwa*/Islamization are not Islamists.[19] *Daʿwa* blurs the distinction between Islamization and Islamist politics.

The blurring of Islamization and Islamist politics has led Janine Clark to assert that "working or volunteering for or donating to an Islamic social institution as a form of activist *daʿwa* (ideology through activism) is an important component of Islamist identity."[20] While *daʿwa* can be a form of activism, it is also frequently simply a form of volunteerism. All practicing

Muslims—not just Islamists—perform Islamic charity. Most of the volunteers in Islamic charities that I spoke with identified themselves as volunteers, not as activists. In contrast, members of the Muslim Brotherhood frequently saw themselves as activists. The prevalence of the activist label for *anyone* engaged in Islamization stems from a Eurocentric tendency to view Islam as a threat to secular values.[21] I therefore refer to Islamic charity not as a form of activism but rather as an act of volunteerism. Islamic charity is both a form of *da'wa* and also operates side by side with preaching and religious lessons given by volunteers in a wide range of Islamic associations.

A prime example of a *da'wa* organization is al-Gam'iyya al-Shar'iyya. Established in 1912, it is the oldest and largest *da'wa*-oriented organization in Egypt, with a network of 3,800 committees and offices spread throughout the country.[22] The leader of the organization, Mohammad Mokhtar al-Mahdy, stated that the goal of al-Gam'iyya al-Shar'iyya is "to apply Islam to daily life, to teach it in our lives and put it in its place. *Da'wa* is tied to understanding Islam."[23] Their *da'wa* work is based on a link between Islamic charitable practices and disciplinary practices. For example, they support more than half a million orphans and accompanying this support is health care, hygiene, and religious lessons. The organization sends al-Azhar scholars to different areas of Cairo to give talks outside the Friday prayer lectures (*khutba*) and has more than 950 offices around the country for the memorization of the Quran alone.[24] Their branches also send international relief abroad covering a vast area, from Niger in the West to Indonesia in the East. Under the broad category of *a'mal saliha* (good deeds) comes social work and medical care, including orphan care, productive power, scholarships, catastrophe relief, Ramadan food bags, Eid celebrations, and medical services. Their fund-raisers are so efficient at collecting donations that they told me they raised 35 million EGP (about $6 million) for the cancer hospital. The central office distributes more than 50 million EGP (about $10 million) for the organizations' own projects. The project manager emphasized that the "number-one activity of the organization is *da'wa*" and includes preaching, knowledge production, publications, seminars, panels, a daily magazine, and memorization of Quran. These projects were all linked to their *a'mal saliha,* thus inextricably linking Islamic charity to *da'wa*.

The organization houses ten of its twenty-six centers in Cairo. The project manager explained its size by the fact that "we emphasize action over words, and do so by thinking about the everyday issues that people face, rather than focusing on, say, changing the political atmosphere or the government."[25] In fact, the organization went to great lengths to avoid political engagement and therefore appeared to have a good relationship with the Mubarak regime. The organization also had a good relationship with wealthy businessmen, who fund its projects. Once a project was identified, the organization would approach these businessmen, who gladly offered their resources anonymously to fund the project and in return received rewards from God *(thawab)* for *a'mal saliha*. Al-Gam'iyya al-Shar'iyya employees are driven by the same desire to gain rewards from God for their good deeds. As the project manager told me, "I began working with the organization out of a desire to go to heaven, to build my house in heaven. I believe that the organization is the best in the nation for showing people religion through action rather than through words."[26] Al-Gam'iyya al-Shar'iyya is certainly one of the largest Islamic associations in Egypt, geographically as well as financially, yet a culture of secrecy means that the everyday functions of the organization remain a mystery.[27] Despite this mystery, the organization clearly demonstrates the coupling of charity and *da'wa*. While mosques and their charitable associations are key sites for *da'wa* in Muslim societies, Islamic associations expanded *da'wa* outside the mosque.

Spaces of *Da'wa*: Producing Pious Neoliberalism

The growth of the *da'wa* movement came with a new spatial dimension. While the mosque remains a critical site for the formation of religious subjectivity, the new generation of *da'i* shifted *da'wa* outside the mosque and into everyday spaces and online forums.[28] Preachers used new media formats, including satellite television shows and the Internet to expand the circulation of religious discourse into everyday life.[29] These religious leaders gave advice in everyday spaces across neighborhoods of various classes, from a car on the metro line to a dinner party or a shopping mall. *Da'wa* expanded to street corners, cafés, stores, parties, and even gyms. The presence of these preachers in public space led to "an orientation that stresses rituals, appearances, prayers, fasting, pilgrimage, veiling and other outward signs of religiosity."[30]

The production of pious neoliberal subjects was fueled by both the enlargment of religion in the public sphere and the expansion of the market mechanism in Cairenes' everyday lives. This visible religiosity came with observable contradictions, described by El-Tawil as "Muslims wear-ing colorful veils and tight trousers, relying on commercial banks that pay interest, or engaging in many other 'un-Islamic' modes of behavior."[31] The concomitant rise of Islamism and neoliberalism created contradic-tory images throughout Cairo. For example, patrons at the City Stars mall were greeted with holiday lights, Santa Claus, and Christmas trees during the holiday season, while signs invited patrons to pray in the ground-floor mosque. Outside the American-style food court with all the fast-food brand names sat a Resala Charitable Association table soliciting volunteers and donations. The presence of Islamic associations in everyday spaces, from sporting clubs to shopping malls, is part of the message that Islam is com-patible with a Western-influenced, consumption-driven lifestyle.[32] The public nature of Islamic practice manifested visibly in Cairo's symbolic landscape via Islamic dress (including the number of women donning the veil), a proliferation of prayer rooms, the public presence of preachers in the street, the public's commitment to Friday prayer, and the growth of an "Islamic sector." The Islamic sector (discussed in the next chapter) is a multimillion-dollar goods and services industry that markets itself as Islamic and includes publications, educational institutions, businesses that sell "Islamic commodities,"[33] from *halal* meat to modest clothing; entertain-ment, art and religious gatherings; and Islamic banking and finance.

The changing nature of *da'wa* also had a resounding effect on the spa-tial distribution of Islamic charities. Historically, Islamic charities were based in upper-middle-class neighborhoods that funded them, such as Mohan-diseen, Heliopolis, or Nasr City. Despite the concentration of poverty in specific neighborhoods in Cairo, associations rarely chose their location based on communities of need. Instead, many of the newer associations I visited were physically located in buildings adjacent to these historically important mosques, which allowed them to save costs and take advantage of existing networks and sometimes even evade the security apparatus. The neighborhood of Nasr City, for example, has several large mosque com-plexes, including Rabi'a al-'Adawiyya, al-Azhar, al-Rahman, al-Nour, and Dar al-Arqam, as well as hundreds of small NGOs. These large mosques are based in middle- and upper-middle-class neighborhoods and are sup-ported by the people who live there. In contrast, smaller mosques and prayer rooms are pervasive throughout working-class neighborhoods. Nasr City had a particularly strong concentration of these newer associations located near large mosque complexes. As one charity administrator told me, "The new style of *da'wa* [popular *da'wa*] encourages civic engagement and volunteerism and has had a big influence on the way people think about charitable work. There are lots of different factors here. We have al-Azhar here, Rabi'a al-'Adawiyya is here, lots of sporting clubs, and this has led to lots of associations being here as well."[34] While charities were still stationed in wealthier neighborhoods, they became more mobile, using vans to bring services to informal settlements. These younger associations have changed the spatial distribution of services, bringing them to working-class neighborhoods instead of having the poor come to them.[35] Islamic charities formed clusters or nodes around large mosque complexes while spreading spatially across the parameters of the city in order to reach those most in need. While Islamic charities changed spatial relations, the month of Ramadan designated a special time for giving.

The Spirit of Ramadan

The holy month of Ramadan is a time of deep internal reflection. Individuals suppress their human urges and exercise a great deal of restraint as they refrain from eating, drinking, smoking, sexual activity, cursing, fighting, and impure thoughts from dawn to sunset for nearly thirty days. After dusk, people connect over elaborate meals, breaking their fast and either socializing or spending the evening in prayer. Ramadan is also a time in which individuals are asked to think about all they have to be thankful for and help those who are less fortunate.[36] Almost everyone gives charity during Ramadan, be it to a neighbor, through a local mosque, a local *zakat* committee, or a *ma'idat al-rahman* (table of the merciful).[37] "Table of the merciful" is the name given for free *iftar* (the meal at which one breaks fast) distribution during Ramadan. Large tables and chairs are set up on street corners, in tents, and in vacant lots and are open to all at sundown. At the end of Ramadan, before the Eid prayers, there is a compulsory *zakat al-fitr* (almsgiving on the feast) in which every Muslim who can afford to must feed a person in need for one day. In Egypt, the *zakat al-fitr* is between 5 and 8 LE (slightly more than $1) per person and must be paid before the Eid prayer at the end of the month of Ramadan. It is believed that a person's fasting will not be accepted if this *zakat* is not paid.[38]

Ramadan is a heightened space and time for giving in Egypt. A combination of an increased sensitivity among Egyptians to the feeling of hunger and a religious invocation to give in Ramadan makes this a time of immense generosity. When asked why they are fasting, hundreds of people expressed to me, "So that I can feel what it is like to be hungry, to have thirst, to understand the sentiment of those less fortunate than me." The poor receive food in the form of Ramadan food bags, "tables of the merciful," and zakat al-fitr. Ramadan food bags are distributed to families by Islamic charities throughout the month and usually with no questions asked. These bags almost always contain the staples of an Egyptian diet: rice, cooking oil, flour, sugar, macaroni, lentils, beans, salt, tomato paste, and tea. Nearly every Islamic association in Egypt, including mosques, zakat committees, and social service units, distribute Ramadan bags. Families can pick up the bags, but they are also delivered, particularly in well-known informal settlements and lower-class neighborhoods. As the poor become the source of everyone's attention, they eat well for one month of the year.

The table of the merciful at Iman Mosque served hundreds of men, women, and children each evening (Figure 10). Six male employees ran the kitchen, cooking enormous pots of rice, meat, stewed vegetables, and beans from the previous evening, and continued to cook all day for those who came to break their fast (Figure 11). At 3:30 in the afternoon, a few hours before sunset, about two hundred men and women lined up at the garage door with their own dishes to be filled, which they would take home to feed their families. A staff of volunteers dished out the food with metal mallets; one distributor served rice, another, vegetables, and another, meat. At sunset, another three hundred people broke their fast with the same food in the mosque complex. Many similar mercy tables are organized as large tents on street corners and run entirely by volunteers.

The proliferation of tables of the merciful was a product of the Mubarak era. Previously, Ramadan tables were not as plentiful and were located outside mosques and organized by local communities. As structural-adjustment policies put food subsidies on the line, it heightened the need and demand for charity. Those who benefited from privatization felt a particular compulsion to help the poor during Ramadan and therefore the practice of businessmen establishing tables of mercy became commonplace over the course of the past twenty years. Ramadan tables of mercy were an easy way to "build a house in heaven" without having to commit to year-round giving. Many believe that the acceptance of one's fast by God is contingent upon doing good deeds throughout the month. In the minds of many people, mercy tables amount to additional godly rewards (thawab). Neighbors

Figure 10. "Table of the Merciful," Iman Mosque, Nasr City, at sunset during Ramadan, 2006. Photograph by the author.

Figure 11. Volunteers at Iman Mosque prepare food for the poor to break their fast during Ramadan. Photograph by the author.

and friends used to initiate mercy tables collectively, which led to a far less concentrated pattern of tables. Today, since most businesspeople like to have their own table, the practice has led to a huge concentration of tables across the city. In the polarized neighborhoods of Nasr City, tables of the merciful were few and far between in the wealthy residential areas and shopping-mall districts, but they were present on virtually every street corner in the more poverty-stricken or industrial districts (Figure 12). In contrast to much religious giving, tables of mercy were very public, and people spoke openly about their involvement with them. Seif, an entrepreneur and philanthropist, had volunteered at a number of organizations before deciding to set up his own table of the merciful in a poor neighborhood in the 10th district of Nasr City, "I decided to do a Ramadan table there in front of a store, office, and a garden. . . . We ended up having four hundred people each night. I hope to get to eight hundred next year, *inshallah.*" He said that he was driven to create his own table of the merciful out of faith. While religious motivations continue to drive charitable work, the rise of a bourgeois class seeking to purify their wealth intensified the scale of giving.

Figure 12. During Ramadan, people break their fast for free at a "Table of the Merciful" in a working-class neighborhood of Nasr City. Photograph by the author.

Cultures of Giving

An estimated 40 percent of Egyptians live at or near the poverty line, and yet even those struggling to get by give to others even less fortunate. Over 60 percent of Egyptians give charity of some kind, and conservative giving estimates for Egypt are 5.5 billion EGP (approximately $1 billion) annually.[39] Although GDP per capita for 2006 was $1,801 (at constant 2000 prices), giving was approximately $14 per capita, or .78 percent of income.[40] Monetary donations are the most prevalent form of giving followed by in-kind donations and volunteerism.

Religion remains the driving force behind Egyptian giving; 46 percent of Muslims indicated that their motivation for giving was "a personal religious act," 45.6 percent said that it was "for the sake of God," and 37.9 percent were primarily motivated by "poverty eradication."[41] A different survey found that 45.8 percent said they gave out of religious duties, 37.2 percent gave in order to get closer to God, 13.3 percent gave out of custom and tradition, 2.4 percent gave to reduce the number of poor people in society, 1 percent gave to cooperate with government efforts to reduce poverty, and 0.5 percent gave for general economic and social benefits.[42] Combined, this means that at least 90 percent of giving in Egypt is motivated by religion. Most Egyptians "give because of a religious motive, and their aim is to gain credit from God *(thawab)*, not because of a sense of responsibility toward their society."[43]

Faith-based giving has several distinguishing characteristics. First, most people prefer to give secretly and through individuals rather than institutions. These giving preferences are driven by beliefs (supported by *hadith*) that giving in secrecy and to people one knows increases the merits in the eyes of God. Second, a huge amount of Islamic charity is given during Ramadan through *zakat al-fitr*, Ramadan food bags, and tables of the merciful. Together, these practices constitute a culture of giving that is reinforced annually. Third, giving motivated by faith once meant to be driven to do *khayr wa-khalas*, or good deeds, seeking only credit from God with little concern with impact. Today, faith-based givers are as concerned with changing the conditions of poverty on the ground as "building their house in heaven." As a result, Islamic charities are engaging in a plethora of practices that run the gamut from traditional patterns of religious benevolence to systematized, measurable, and calculated giving.

Most Islamic association directors described Egyptian giving as "scattered, charity-oriented and mostly person-to-person based."[44] They described giving in Egypt as "haphazard," "unstrategic," and "inefficient," and held practices of giving during Ramadan responsible: "Yeah, there are so many players, like 5,000 Ramadan bags from Bank al-Ta'am, 8,000 at al-baraka, 8,000 at Sam'a. All around that's like 200,000 or 300,000 Ramadan bags. But we are all distributing in the same locations—and there are all the same problems . . . communication, commitment, continuity."[45] Despite a large number of Islamic associations engaged in charitable giving, associational directors felt there was a repetition of efforts and an inefficient distribution of resources. Many Islamic association directors told me this problem stemmed from a lack of communication among organizations. They also wished to see a cultural shift away from "traditional" patterns of giving (*khayr wa-khalas*) and toward "human development" (*tanmiya bashariyya*) initiatives. Egyptian giving patterns indicate that a change is under way, as 74.2 percent of donors would prefer to "direct philanthropic resources to development rather than unorganized charity."[46] The Egyptian Food Bank has combined an emphasis on food and Ramadan with private-sector specialization, accountability, and professionalization. The story of the food bank illustrates how a religiously driven culture of giving combines with a business-driven approach to produce new forms of giving and subjectivity simultaneously.

"We can cover the entire nation": The Egyptian Food Bank (Bank al-Ta'am al Musri)

The Egyptian Food Bank, established in 2006 in Cairo, brought innovation and business expertise to the giving practices of Ramadan. The organization was associated with Niazy Sallam, the CEO of the Olympic Group, who played a pivotal role in the organizations' founding. I met Mr. Sallam at the Olympic Group headquarters and began by asking him how he became involved in charitable work. He paused and said:

> I reached a point in my life where, thanks be to God, my business is successful and growing prosperously. And at that point, a person often tries to do something, something for society in return, for Allah, especially since the best thing a person can do for the day of judgment, to better his position in the eyes of God, is charitable work.[47]

He went on to tell me about a paradoxical experience that he took as a sign that this work really needed to be done:

The day before our third meeting, I was invited to attend a
wedding in Moqattam and during the same time, an employee, a
security guard, his father had died, so I went to mourn in the
Azhar neighborhood before the wedding. On the way to go
express my condolences to the employee, there were so many
poor people everywhere, but one sight that day gripped me
and did not leave me. There was a woman passing by with her
eight-month-old child who began to cry. So she just stopped,
looked around her, and picked up any old thing off the street.
She didn't wash it off or anything and gave it to the crying child. . . .
And then afterward as I went to the wedding, it was so extravagant,
so much money and so much waste. A seafood buffet, dessert
buffet, famous singers and other extravagances—you name it, it
was the last thing.[48]

This dichotomy of excess and need that Sallam saw that evening became
one of the foundations of the association, which aimed to create a more
equitable distribution of food in Egypt. Sallam and a group of business
partners founded the Egyptian Food Bank as an association aiming to
minimize food waste from the hotel industry and instead assemble a system for delivering leftover food to those in need. Given the essential role
of Sallam, the food bank was often associated with the company. In fact,
until Betech donated a building to the food bank in 2006, it operated at
the Olympic Group Headquarters in Nasr City. Based on a fatwa from the
Mufti Ali Gomma (Fatwa 168/622), believers can distribute their annual
zakat al-mal to the food bank.

The most popular program was the "oath of khayr," which allowed
donors to sponsor a family with a "Zad Pack," a bundle of food staples, for
a period of six to eighteen months. The food pack contained rice, flour,
sugar, pasta, white beans, black-eyed peas, lentils, black lentils, fava beans,
salt, tea, tomato paste, cooking oil, and a packet of meat and vegetables
(Figure 13). The food bank also had several thousand volunteers who regularly participated in packing food during the month of Ramadan. Food
Bank CEO Moez El-Shohdi wanted to create a distribution network that
could cover the entire nation. He coordinated work with hundreds of
implementing partners across the nation. In Cairo, private schools such as
Cairo International College and the American International School, integrated service learning into their curriculum, sending their students to pack

Figure 13. The Egyptian Food Bank's "Zad Pack" of staples offered to families during Ramadan. Photograph by the author.

food for the bank, while in 2011 Procter & Gamble held its employee volunteer day at the organization.

During the month of Ramadan, the food bank held its own Ramadan gift program called *"Iftar Sa'im"* (breakfast for a fasting person). The bank distributed a similar, but smaller, food bundle as the "oath of *khayr"* package, which included the traditional fast-breaking dried dates and apricot nectar. It also collected *zakat al-fitr* (almsgiving of the feast) during the heightened Ramadan campaign. The money was collected and converted into dry food and distributed to the poor. In 2009 El-Shohdi's goal was to deliver ten thousand cartons of food (each carton feeds five people for a month at a cost of 150 LE). Growth and cooperation were two of the main goals of the organization, as El-Shohdi explained:

> We grew our food bank program from 21,000 meals the first year to over 3 million meals served now. We will continue to grow. We have put in place policies and procedures for handling the food, job descriptions, an internal control system—approved by Ernst and Young, the criteria for NGOs in our network—social research department, and a database that we are sharing with all organizations as long as they are willing to work under our system.[49]

The organization's principal goal was to develop charity on a national scale. To this end the bank established the "Hunger-Free Village Program." The idea was to match businesspeople with a poor village and meet the food needs of everyone in the village who qualifies for aid. A company would commit to feed the village for a set time period and according to the qualification scheme set up by the food bank. This direction built on the program's intent "to apply business principles and our morality to charity. We are successful here because of the link to Islam and *zakat* as a tenet. If those give that which is not in use today and it is distributed properly, we can cover the entire nation."[50]

In addition to Ramadan, Eid al-Adha (feast of the sacrifice) is another concentrated period of giving in Egypt. During this annual holiday, which coincides with the hajj pilgrimage to Mecca, Muslims symbolically slaughter an animal to symbolize the biblical/quranic story of Abraham's sacrifice. During the celebration of the sacrifice, families pool resources and slaughter an animal and distribute the meat to the poor (Figure 14). A huge amount of meat distribution over the course of three days results in a great deal of waste because the meat spoils before it can be distributed across the country. The food bank hoped to create a more even distribution of food year-round by freezing and canning. In 2008 the Egyptian Food Bank partnered with United Bank on a coupon campaign for the

Figure 14. Preparing to slaughter a lamb in celebration of Eid al-Adha. Photograph by the author.

annual Eid lamb sacrifice. The *Sakk al-'Udhiya* (sacrificial bond) program asked individuals to purchase a coupon in advance for either 999 LE or 777 LE. The coupons gave the bank the authority to perform the act of sacrifice on the donors' behalf, while the advance purchase allowed the bank to plan distribution. The fee of 999 LE covered the traditional slaughter during the official holiday, while the cheaper fee allowed for the slaughter to occur at a special halal meat facility in Australia, where the meat was packed, shipped, and distributed year-round. In the inaugural year, one thousand animals were slaughtered in the rural town of Ismailiya and numerous organizational partners were employed to create a broad distribution network. The project uniquely attempted to can and flash-freeze different parts of the animal in order to prolong the availability of meat to the poor.

Many pious individuals engage in sacrifices to commemorate other occasions, like the birth of a son, weddings, or simply as a way of seeking God's blessings—be it for a large purchase or a recovery from illness. The food bank's "Redemption, Vows, and Atonements Program" performed a sacrifice and distributed the meat to the poor on behalf of the faithful and in the name of their desired goal. The donation would fund the slaughter of a cow (9,000 LE) or a sheep (1,500 LE) and the meat would then be distributed in packs or frozen. The bank thus brought greater efficiency to the act of charity. The food bank demonstrates how a business ethic merged with the culture of charity to produce new charitable ventures and new forms of subjectivity. Most of the volunteers at the food bank valued the enterprising approach of the organization and yet wanted to feed poor people, whom they saw as deserving of their charity. In my interview with one volunteer, I asked her why she became involved in charity work. Her response was, "Have you seen the film *Pay It Forward*"? Confused, I shook my head and she continued:

> Personally, this was my inspiration for getting into this work.
> I think the film came out in 2000, but the idea is when you benefit
> from something, you can give back by using it as credit. You know
> it isn't just about calculating your *zakat* as 2.5 percent. Pay it forward.
> If God gave you a lot in this life, then you can and should. . . .
> I think a lot of wealthy, they don't realize, they don't see the state
> of poverty here. Some streets, you can't even enter them because
> the stench there, the sewage in the street. So I think by working in
> *khayr* it is a way to pay it forward.[51]

Faith is the driving force behind this volunteer's involvement with Islamic charity. She chose the food bank as a way to pay it forward because in professionalizing food distribution, she could help others who were in greater need while also "building her house in heaven."

Conclusion

Islamic charity is a mainstay of Egyptians' interaction with the poor. *Zakat* committees remain committed to providing direct aid to orphans, female-headed households, and others who fall under the eight categories of *zakat* recipients in the Quran. Direct aid comes with an obligation to attend religious and disciplinary lessons, inextricably linking Islamic charity to *da'wa*. Despite, and perhaps even because of, the state's regulation of social care and its intrusion into Islamic institutions, *zakat, sadaqa, da'wa,* and the ethos of *khayr wa-khalas* remain the bedrock of Islamic charitable practices. Islamic charity is first and foremost about pleasing God, since faith remains at the heart of the practice. *Da'wa* increases the presence of religion in everyday life, leading to even more Islamic charity. Thus *da'wa* and Islamic charity reinforce each other and are mutually constituted.

Although the mosque remains the most important space for Islamic charity, a new generation of actors moved charity and *da'wa* into everyday spaces. Islamic practices became even more embedded into daily life partially because these practices expanded outside the mosque. The holy month of Ramadan provides an annual time of concentrated giving that is evident through Ramadan bags, tables of the merciful, and *zakat al-fitr*. Together, Ramadan and the new spatiality of *da'wa* capture the essence of giving in Egypt. And yet, while there are thousands of *zakat* committees and associations, the predominant sentiment among leaders, givers, and recipients alike is that of scarcity.

Because association leaders framed the problem of poverty as a problem of scarcity, they also framed the solution as an issue of efficiency, thereby producing a new approach to Islamic charity. Half a century of international development initiatives, the state's promotion of private-sector social ventures, expanding national and regionwide interest in social responsibility, and a conviction that charity needs to be supplanted by development initiatives have led to more business-driven Islamic charities. These associations believe that the charitable sector in Egypt would benefit from more "systematization," "professionalization," and "accountability." This discourse has been imported from the private sector, as particular forms of knowledge and means of calculation remake the nonprofit sector. Thus while Egypt has a strong culture of giving based on *da'wa,* the holy month of Ramadan, and an ethos of *khayr wa-khalas,* Islamic associations are also engaging in human development marked by the rise of conditional giving, a focus on job creation, and the promotion of pious neoliberal subjectivity through an emphasis on self-sufficiency for the poor. This paradigm of Islamic human development is fraught with contradictions as centuries-old practices of Islamic charity are merged with market-based solutions. Before looking in greater detail at the new cultural production of business-driven Islamic charities, I discuss the broader context within which this particular iteration emerged. New institutional forms accompanied pious neoliberalism, including private mosques, foundations, and an Islamic private sector. I refer to the melding of the private sector and Islamism as "privatized Islam."

CHAPTER 4

Privatizing Islam

PRIVATIZING ISLAM is the production of a market-oriented Islam that generates new institutional forms. It is a manifestation of pious neoliberalism and in the case of Egypt is a response to a nationalized or statist Islam. Using security as a pretext, the Egyptian state gradually escalated its intervention in Islamic institutions throughout the twentieth century. The state intruded in Islamic institutions of all kinds, but its interference in mosques and the co-optation of *waqf* most poignantly illustrate the consequences of such an intervention. Mosques and *awqaf* formed the bedrock of Ottoman Egypt through Mohammad Ali's modernization of Egypt in the early twentieth century. After the 1952 revolution, decades of state intervention by the Ministry of Endowments undermined the independence of these religious institutions and eventually led to their privatization. Wealthy individuals historically funded *waqf,* and these endowments provided social services to the public. Recognizing the great capacity of *waqf,* Gamal Abdel Nasser nationalized and bureaucratized the institution, leading to its eventual demise as an institutional form.[1] In its place emerged Western-style foundations established from 2002 onward by a new bourgeois class that had made its money during the rapid privatization of state-owned industries in Egypt from the 1970s until about 2010. In the past, most mosques were built with *awqaf* funds, and communities frequently collected donations to transform their small prayer rooms into mosques. There are two kinds of mosques in Egypt, private (*ahli*) and governmental (*hukumi*). Today, most are governmental mosques and even privately funded mosques (*masagid ahliyya*) eventually become governmentalized.

The state recognized mosques as a critical space of community and Islamist organizing and therefore through a process of annexation put community mosques and their imams under state control in the name of national security. While Hosni Mubarak wanted the ministry to annex all mosques, he allowed elites to establish privately funded mosques. Foundations and privately funded mosques are a key part of a privatized Islam in Egypt, but globally an Islamic sector is the most visible marker of privatized Islam. The Islamic sector is a multi-million dollar market for religious goods and services provided by Islamic businesses that market their products as such. It includes publications and multimedia, educational institutions and products, businesses for Islamic goods from halal meat to fashion, entertainment, art, and religious gatherings. In Egypt, the development of this industry complemented the growth of *da'wa* and enabled Islamism to flourish despite an authoritarian regime that was hostile to Islamic entities. These new private religious spaces and institutions played a critical role in the promotion of pious neoliberal subjectivity.

Managing Mosques

During the January 25 uprising of 2011, the congregation of millions of people in mosques at Friday noon prayers constituted a major organizing opportunity that led to mass protests across the nation. After the sermon (*khutba*, pl. *khutab*), people left the mosque and went straight to Tahrir Square. Sermons held after the Friday midday prayers are a key space for disseminating ideas because they give the preacher a weekly captive audience. Most preachers gained popularity and clout by speaking to the everyday issues that matter to people.[2] The mosque thus was a critical space for organizing the fall of the regime in 2011. During the eighteen days of the January uprising, then Minister of Endowments, Mahmoud Hamdi Zaqzouq, specifically warned Egyptians against using mosques to launch protests against Mubarak.[3] Mosques served as a communal gathering point and thus authoritarian leaders felt particularly threatened by this space.

During the 1990s, Mubarak attempted to gain authority over the piety movement by nationalizing nongovernmental (private) mosques and requiring all *da'iya* to attend a state-run two-year training program.[4] Toward the end of the Mubarak regime, the mosque came to signify tensions over social identity and ethical consciousness, while the Friday sermon became the heart of public discourses over religion. The state consequently tried to extend regulation over both.[5] In my interview with a manager at the Ministry of Endowments, I asked about the ministry's management of mosques. His response:

> In order to ensure that there isn't any type of political motives or
> other undesirable motives and to ensure that mosques are led

down the clear, right path, we centralized the administration over them. That way we appoint the imam, and test them to ensure they are capable of the task and that they have good aims. . . . There is a system in place in each district and each manager is responsible for monitoring a certain set of mosques. They monitor the mosques by rounds, sending a manager to various mosques to hear the Friday *khutba* and observe the activities of the mosque. That person then reports to the undersecretary.[6]

The ministry understood the organizational potential of the mosque. The state intervened in the affairs of mosques by appointing and micromanaging the imams, controlling and monitoring the *khutab,* and putting the mosques under the authority of a centralized bureaucracy. Community donations or wealthy individuals fund private mosques. Government mosques are supported by a combination of government funding and private donations. All mosques have imams who must be approved and paid by the Ministry of Endowments, but the ministry also appoints imams in government mosques. An architect who designs mosques at cost (as opposed to for profit) described government intervention in mosque affairs:

All the mosques are government supervised, even the private ones. The government provides the imam and his salary, but the mosques that *can* try and provide extra salary and support. But the government is sure to control the preachers and what they say. The board of directors runs the mosque, but in coordination with the Ministry of Endowments. . . . There is no cooperation between mosques—each one is operating in a desert island. They can't transfer funds between wealthier and poorer mosques because of the rules around the monitoring of accounts and the fear of national security.[7]

The government believed that mosques in lower- and middle-class communities could serve as organizing nodes for Islamists and so state interventions were aimed there. Nonetheless, anyone perceived as having too much clout became a target of state security. The state monitored all mosques; the difference was merely a matter of degree.

Mosque subsidization and nationalization began in 1961 under Nasser;[8] Anwar Sadat briefly decentralized mosque control, fueling the growth in private mosques, but then recentralized it in the late 1970s.[9] Mubarak tightened the control that the Ministry of Endowments had over mosques according to his perception of an Islamist threat, starting in 1982 with Ministerial Decree 16.[10] This law defined the ministry's authority over donations designated for mosque building. In 1992 Mubarak began a long process of state annexation of mosques.[11] In December 1996, Law 238 annexed all unlicensed mosques and placed mosque preachers under the authority of the Ministry of Endowments. It required the appointment of state-approved al-Azhar graduates as preachers and required permits for any other sermons delivered in mosques.[12] In 2001 the ministry issued a set of ten conditions for mosque building that governed landownership, architecture, location, the size of the mosque, and the distance between mosques. It required the inclusion of space for social and health services and mandated a 50,000 EGP deposit in a bank account before the ministry would grant permission for construction.[13] While technically anyone could apply to build a mosque, the financial requirement coupled with government discretion created an obstacle to legal mosque building that favored elites who were unlikely to threaten the regime. Between 1996 and 2002, the government annexed thirty-five thousand private mosques as part of Mubarak's plan to place all mosques under government control.[14] Yet the process of nationalization faced numerous hurdles. Islamists and local governors contested the right of the central authorities to control mosques, while the state had trouble justifying the escalating costs and found it difficult to implement the changes.

There is no clear figure for how many mosques there are in Egypt; even official statistics from the ministry itself vary significantly and several estimates contradict one another. Nonetheless, Table 3 is my attempt to aggregate a variety of estimates that demonstrate the rise in the number of government mosques. Nationalization of mosques occurred during the past decade at a rate of approximately six thousand mosques a year.[15] In Cairo alone, there are an estimated thirty-five hundred mosques and twenty-five hundred *zawaya* (small prayer rooms, often on the ground floor of apartment buildings).[16]

The ministry decided to pursue mosque nationalization because monitoring mosques was an obstacle to Islamist organizing and led to a culture of fear and self-regulation inside mosques. The Global War on Terror (GWOT) also provided further legitimacy for state intervention in Islamic institutions.[17] The United States insisted that many Muslim-majority

Table 3. The estimated number of mosques in Egypt

Year	Total Mosques	Governmental	Private	Source
1961	17,000	17,000	0	(Gaffney 1994)
1979	34,000	n/a	n/a	(Gaffney 1994)
1986	50,000	n/a	n/a	(Gaffney 1994)
1993	70,000	30,000	40,000	(Gaffney 1994)
1998	n/a	65,000	n/a	(Encyclopædia Britannica 1998)
2003	83,000	63,000	20,000	(Wattad and Rizzuto 2003)
2006	150,000	74,500	18,000	(U.S. Department of State 2006)
2008	n/a	91,457	n/a	(Department of Islamic Affairs and Charitable Activities 2008)
2011	105,000	93,000	12,000	(Addeh and Fuad 2011)

countries create a system to deter the use of mosques and Islamic charity to support acts of terror. For example, as part of antiterrorism compliance, the United States demanded the removal of donation boxes from mosques and required that all donations be traceable.

In 2006 the ministry announced that it was synchronizing the *azan* (call to prayer), another sign of the government's attempt to control the mosque.[18] Minister Zaqzouq was careful to note:

We are unifying the call to prayer, not the Friday sermons. . . . It is not possible that an imam in Zamalek deliver the same sermon as an imam in Upper Egypt. They tailor their message to the needs of their communities. But we are giving them guidelines. We tell them not to spend too much time speaking about the Afterlife and Judgment Day. *We are in need of more practical sermons.* Work ethic, time management, and education are all very relevant topics that need to be addressed in our mosques. I want the imams to give people a message of hope so that they may ultimately lead a better life and become more productive [emphasis added].[19]

The minister defensively addressed the issue of sermon unification in response to opposition groups who had rallied around the issue. The state's intervention in mosques was ironically couched in neoliberal language; while neoliberalism espouses a rollback of the state's involvement in social affairs, here the state increased its role in mosques. The minister justified the intrusion as a way to make sermons more "practical" and "efficient," yet the intervention demonstrates how the state participated in the production of pious neoliberalism by encouraging neoliberal values (including a work ethic, time management, and the dissemination of particular kinds of knowledge) through Friday sermons. Labor unions and Islamists opposed mosque synchronization because they were worried about the numerous *muezzin* (prayer callers) who might be laid off in the process. Synchronization of the call to prayer was also symbolic of the state's extension into the nooks and crannies of everyday Islamic practices in the name of security. Mubarak's mosque-management strategy was a unique product of neoliberalism and authoritarianism.

The state marked the beginning of Ramadan 2010 with the rollout of the first phase of *azan* unification in the Cairene districts of Nasr City and Heliopolis. Out of the estimated 107 mosques in Nasr City, only 40 had unified the call to prayer.[20] Only the largest mosques, such as Rabiʿa al-ʿAdawiyya and al-Khulafaaʿ al-Rashideen had installed the device, which costs 170 LE and broadcasts a live transmission of the call for prayer.[21] In response to sharp criticism, the driving force behind the project at the ministry, Sheikh Salem Abdel-Gelil, said, "Any new technology is always controversial here because people like sticking to the old ways. But change and progress are required if we are to stay up-to-date as the world moves forward."[22] The ministry used a narrative of progress and modernity to justify the synchronization, but many Islamists saw the move as another act of state power, since the state used the same justification for annexing unauthorized (*ʿashwaʾi*) mosques. The ministry also warned that the use of mosques for political activities was forbidden and declared that it would create a database of licensed mosques as part of a wider plan aimed at "improving management" of state resources.[23] Mosque management was thus a key apparatus of security for the Mubarak regime.

Dar al-Arqam is an example of a communal mosque that experienced annexation. It is a large mosque complex in an upper-middle-class neighborhood of Nasr City. The mosque complex, which includes a hospital under construction, wide-open green space, and an event center, was established by a group of neighborhood sheikhs who raised all the funds to build it. The property was distributed by al-Azhar in the late 1980s. The neighborhood had lots of *zawayas* but no mosque until the sheikhs built one in 1991. I met with one of the oldest employees and discussed the mosque and their association. He told me that they used Rabiʿa al-ʿAdawiyya as a model and that in order to gain approval, the government required the mosque to include social space, greenery, and an association registered with the Ministry of Social Affairs (now the Ministry of Social Solidarity). The mosque complex provided all the usual services: support for widows and orphans, Quranic memorization, sewing and crochet training for women, marriage expenses, medical services provided for a "symbolic fee," a sports center, library, and day care. A physical-therapy clinic and large hospital were under construction. Although the board, consisting of mostly sheikhs, fund-raised for the association, "nothing was planned on a large scale. It just turned out that way because individuals from al-Azhar built and supervise it." The employee told me, "Like all others, the mosque was taken to be supervised by the Ministry of Endowments." The ministry appoints and pays the imam, but the association takes care of the staff of forty employees. Hesitantly he objected to the government's intrusion: "We are a bit set back by the ministry. They refused to allow our center for Quranic recitation and learning to be developed as an actual certificate program with al-Azhar. It's hard to systematize the quality with al-Azhar. . . . We have no problems though. We have good relations with the government." While the creation of this mosque was predicated upon privatization (through the selling of al-Azhar–owned property), the private mosque could not escape government control, illustrating some of the contradictions of a privatized Islam.

Mosques served as a crucial space for organizing the fall of the Mubarak regime, yet the fight for authority over religious houses of worship remains strong in the post-Mubarak era. After a wave of sectarian violence broke out in March 2011, the Ministry of Endowments called on all imams to address "national unity" in their Friday sermon.[24] On June 1, 2011, the Egyptian parliament passed a unification law that governs the building, demolition, replacement, restoration, and modification of both mosques and churches.[25] Building-permit applications for houses of worship must "go through the public engineering office in the governorate where the church or mosque would be built. It sets a maximum period of two months for approval or rejection of an application, and stipulates that no house of worship can be built closer than a kilometer to another church or mosque."[26] Christians viewed this law as an attempt to curtail church building, since Christians tend to be concentrated in particular neighborhoods and therefore build churches closer together. Islamists also condemned the law as creating hurdles to mosque building.

The state's annexation of private mosques into government mosques under Mubarak transpired alongside growth in the total number of mosques in Egypt. These new mosques were not grassroots mosques funded by community donations. Instead, they were private mosques created by wealthy businessmen who were less likely to threaten the regime and therefore were not subject to the same level of scrutiny as community mosques. The decline of community mosques in Egypt occurred at the same time as the growth of private mosque complexes built by businessmen in the sprawling suburbs of Cairo.[27] While the Ministry of Endowments wanted to nationalize all mosques, it could not afford to do so. Instead, mosques are either nationalized (under the Ministry of Endowments) or privatized (operating independently with funding from large businessmen). The growth of private mosques in the wake of mosque nationalization illustrates the contradictory tendencies of pious neoliberalism. The state could not stop the growth of private mosques, which was fueled by the merging of wealth and piety. Annexation of mosques was a failed attempt by the state to regain legitimacy over religious affairs. The state's co-optation of religion only served to deepen the public's suspicion of the government and fueled support for Islamists. Together, the state's lack of legitimacy over religious affairs, its intervention in Islamic institutions, and a legacy of state failure and corruption fueled privatized Islam. Privatized Islam occurred in response to, yet is outside of, the state's influence and refers to the application of market principles to create new institutional forms like the private mosque or the foundation. No institution illustrates this process of institutional destruction and rebuilding more poignantly than the history of *waqf* and its subsequent "revival" as a private foundation.

The Demise of *Waqf*

Waqf as an institution changed drastically over time. During the mid-thirteenth-century Mamluk period, more than half of Egypt's agricultural land and the majority of buildings in Cairo were *awqaf*.[28] Under the Ottoman Empire, mixed *waqf* was the dominant form, where "massively endowed soup kitchens, hostels, and schools made far greater contributions to poverty alleviation than any *zakat*-based transfer scheme."[29] Approximately six thousand *awqaf* were founded during the eighteenth century; these *awqaf* were important public institutions and often took the form of large mosque complexes that provided basic social services to the public.[30]

Ottoman *waqf* provided shelter, health care, education, water supply, and soup kitchens for the poor, in addition to financing the building of roads and bridges. At the start of the nineteenth century, between one-half and two-thirds of the Ottoman Empire were *awqaf*. The centralization of states, however, threatened the independence of *waqf*.[31]

Muhammad Ali created the Egyptian *waqf* ministry in 1835 and nationalized six hundred thousand feddans of *waqf* land formerly used to finance mosques and religious schools.[32] In 1851 the government confiscated a huge amount of *waqf* land and created a central administration. The period of constitutional monarchy (1923–52) marked an intense struggle between the king and the parliament over the administration of charitable *awqaf* and reform of al-Azhar. Despite many attempts to reduce the power of 'ulama' during Mohammed Ali's reign, King Farouq (1936–52) supported the 'ulama' and even opened his private treasury to nearly triple the religious budget during his reign.[33] By the start of the twentieth century, government and philanthropic associations asserted their responsibility and capacity to care for the poor and began to compete with *waqf* as the predominant institutions of social care. As more institutions and organizations became involved, there was a shift in focus from the poor to poverty.[34] The act of caring for the poor became bureaucratized and depersonalized. From 1952 onward Nasser extended the bureaucratization of *waqf* that began under Muhammad Ali so far that the practice nearly disappeared from Egyptian society.

The changes to *waqf* that Nasser initiated eventually led to the annihilation of *waqf* as a form of charity in Egypt because, as the government became more involved in *waqf*, people's trust in the government declined. Nasser abolished private inheritance *waqf*, eroded the sovereignty of the endower over his endowment *(shart al-waqif)*, appointed governmental endowment supervisors, imposed taxes and fees on *waqf*, and created a massive bureaucratic structure governing *waqf*.[35] He changed the rules for the establishment, distribution, supervision, preservation, and dissolution of *waqf* through a long series of legal changes.

Nasser's complete overhaul of *waqf* was an important part of his state-led development plan and his attempt to curtail Islamism in Egypt. Collectively these changes and the legacy of Nasserite policies led endowers to look elsewhere for ways of institutionalizing their giving. Family *waqf* is still prohibited by law and the governmentalization of *waqf* is one of the most poignant memories in Egypt's public memory. Wealthy families who had their endowments confiscated by the government continue to recount their stories. The restrictions on endowments and confiscation of private property in Egypt changed *waqf* so profoundly that the custom of establishing *waqf* for public purposes eventually fell out favor in Egypt and today the practice is minuscule in comparison to other institutions.

In my interactions with philanthropists, they mentioned that creating a *waqf* under the Ministry of Endowments was "like throwing money down a trash chute." Philanthropists always linked Nasser-era reforms to their negative perception of *waqf*. In 2006 I interviewed the general manager of the Ministry of Endowments to find out why they had done nothing to stop the decline of this important historic institutional form. He told me that existing *waqf* support mosques (about 60 percent), coffin/burial ceremonies (about 30 percent), and Quranic schools (about 10 percent). I asked him why there were not more *awqaf* being established in areas like health care or education, since this has become increasingly popular in Turkey and the Arabian Gulf. He became despondent, "You want me to tell you that the ministry is going to steal the money or get involved and people don't want the ministry involved in their affairs, that's why they don't set up *waqf*?" He was understandably defensive because the ministry had a reputation of being one of the most corrupt in the nation. I quickly replied that was not my intention at all but that I was interested to hear his perspective on why endowments were declining and what the ministry might do to encourage more *awqaf*. He calmed down a bit and said, "If the ministry does a good job, then people will create *waqf* to support it. If not, then people will not have faith in the system and therefore will doubt the ministry and not contribute. Before the [1952] revolution, *waqf* was much stronger and there was much more money. Now we have maybe ten new *awqaf* per year. . . . Instead people put their money in private projects."[36] Evidently, the ministry was not doing a "good job" because no one established new *awqaf* and existing *waqf* revenues were in decline. Instead of reforming *waqf*, a 2002 change to the NGO law allowed the establishment of private foundations. Foundations replaced endowments as an institutional form of giving; philanthropists finally had an alternative form of institutionalized giving subject to far less government intrusion.

Egypt's New Foundations

Since 2000 development experts from the World Bank, the Brookings Institution, the Ford Foundation, and Islamist groups alike have called for a *waqf* revival.[37] These experts tout a *waqf* revival—modeled after its successful revitalization in Iran,[38] Turkey,[39] and the Arab Gulf states of Kuwait, Saudi Arabia, Qatar, and the UAE—as a means of creating sustainable enterprises. Daniela Pioppi described the call for the revival of the institution of *waqf* as "part of a new understanding of Islamic principles, this time in line with the international neoliberal trend."[40] While some read the emergence of foundations (*mu'assasat*) and social entrepreneurs as a new "class of institutions that collect and channel *zakat* (religious charitable contributions)" and "a new form of indigenous "mass" or "community self-help" charity,"[41] these institutions fall short of a *waqf* revival. I found that these new foundations were mostly a local form of Western-style Ford or Rockefeller foundations. While there was a tremendous amount of excitement about the emergence of new Arab philanthropy and the potential for a home-grown source of funding for NGOs, only a few foundations were actually "revamping old ways and adopting new modalities to structure and target private giving beyond the provision of basic consumables to effect sustainable societal change."[42] I read this new form of institutionalized philanthropy as an attempt to revive *waqf* while actually replacing the fifteen-hundred-year-old practice. From 2002 to 2006, wealthy families, corporations, and others who wanted to establish associations without the hassle attached to the label and who could afford the 10,000 EGP fee established nearly three hundred foundations. From 2006 to 2009, the number of foundations nearly doubled again (Table 4).

The trend of establishing foundations (based on a sum of money dedicated to a particular cause) arose out of a more lenient legal environment and in response to the rise of the private sector as a player in the development process. While the number of foundations more than doubled from 2006 to 2009, in practice I found that many associations had registered as foundations with the Ministry of Social Solidarity because it was easier than registering as an association. As international aid to NGOs came under more scrutiny, many Egyptians who could afford to strove to create foundations that could provide domestic grants to Egyptian NGOs. The rise of foundations was thus also depen-dent upon the new prosperity of a bourgeois class that had benefited from Mubarak-era privatization schemes.

The Al Alfi Foundation is an example of one of Egypt's new foundations that presumably would have been set up as a *waqf* if there were not a history of state intervention. Moataz Al Alfi, the CEO of Americana, a successful packaged-food company in Egypt, lays claim to a long "history

Table 4. The number of foundations by governorate

Governorate	2006	2009
Cairo	136	260
Giza	20	109
Kalyubia	4	12
Suez	3	2
Port Said	1	3
Ismailia	4	9
Behera	1	2
Alexandria	40	58
Dumyat	5	7
Sharkia	7	18
Dekahlia	2	5
Kafr el Sheikh	3	7
Minufia	8	15
Gharbia	9	11
North Sinai	2	4
Matrouh	1	1
Al-Fayoum	3	8
Beni Suef	3	9
Minya	1	29
Asyut	4	7
Suhag	2	10
New Valley	1	1
Luxor	1	5
Red Sea	1	1
Qena	2	3
Aswan	8	13
South Sinai	1	2
National/centralized	26	34
Total	299	645

Source: Ministry of Social Solidarity, 2009.

of philanthropic giving . . . since 1892." Al Alfi told me about the various schools his family had established through *waqf* in the governorate of Shar-kaya. One *waqf* established in 1905 was terminated in the 1950s, when, after Nasser-era reforms, the family gave the school to the Ministry of Education. The family established several health centers and schools, inspiring Al Alfi's current focus on education. Although in our interview, he described the family's building of health centers, schools, and mosques as "*waqf*," the website steers away from the term, doubtlessly to avoid the government's watchful eye.

On his website, Al Alfi's "Message from the Founder" opens with verse 261 from *Surat al-Baqara*: "The likeness of those who spend their wealth in the way of Allah, is as the likeness of a grain; it grows seven ears, and each ear has a hundred grains. Allah gives manifold increase to whom He wills. And Allah is All-Sufficient for His creatures needs, All-Knower." Although clearly inspired by faith, the Al Alfi foundation makes no other mention of religion and instead focuses on human resource development, education, leadership, and entrepreneurship. A melding of divine inspiration with management science is typical of pious neoliberalism. Al Alfi described the organization's aim as "developing people with high capability to improve their surrounding social and economic environment" and as a "high-impact foundation seeking the highest social return." The organization targets "talented youth," "future leaders and entrepreneurs," and promotes a "culture of participation." I asked Al Alfi if he thought giving needed to happen in secrecy in order to be recognized by God. He eagerly responded, "People don't like to talk about it [giving], because they think how can I say that I am supporting one of my family members or something. But we have to create a role model, and show people that they are giving and that they have to be giving and that when you give you are rewarded and so giving transparency is a good thing not a bad thing."[43] He asserted that a culture of giving in secrecy and excessive government had stunted Arab philanthropy. Al Alfi avowed that the private sector was essential to the development of society, but he emphasized that this was supplemented by something else, "I'll tell you something, in general in Egypt there is what you call *takaful,* people take care of each other, their brothers and sisters. If I have a good income, I can take care of my family. . . . There is probably an equal amount of money in the GDP of Egypt being spent on families, this is what you can call a hidden figure."[44] Other philanthropists also emphasized the importance of *takaful* alongside religion when describing their motivation, yet they also distinguished their work as development and not charity, "Charity is when I feed someone in Ramadan, but if I built a school or send someone to get a post-grad degree, that's philanthropy. . . . Philanthropy is not deeply understood in the Arab world, because philanthropy involves building schools and training people. But here the government builds the schools and education is free. Then why would you pay to build a school? . . . The mindset of the community is not ready yet for education, they are more interested in giving money to mosques or churches, more charity work."[45] Many other philanthropists and NGO administrators drew a distinction between charity and development, calling for a replacement of the former with the later, while highlighting the importance of *takaful*. Marwa El Daly asserted that *takaful* was central to Egyptian giving but that there was a lot of misunderstanding about philanthropy in Egypt. The lead researcher in the CDS study on Egyptian Philanthropy, she initiated Waqfeyat al-Maadi in May 2007. Although labeled a *"waqf,"* the entity is legally registered as a foundation and operates as both a grant-making and operational foundation. El Daly set up the foundation to revive the concept of *waqf* in Egypt and to connect the wealthy suburb of Maadi to its poorer environs.[46] Waqfeyat al-Maadi encourages companies to extend their Corporate Social Responsibility (CSR) programs and support the foundation. As part of their "reviving and modernizing the social endowment program," they held a variety of workshops and training courses for other organizations. In the courses, they emphasized the mobilization of local resources and "the role of religion and culture in boosting sustainable development."[47] The foundation plans to expand and create health, education, employment, community service, and environmental protection endowments in order to serve as a model of how *waqf* could be revived.

In response to the call for a *waqf* revival, in 2007 the Grand Mufti Ali Gomaa initiated the Misr el Khayr Foundation with several prominent businessmen. Gomaa is the chairman of the board of the foundation and refers to it as a development institution. It focuses on human development in the poorest governorates of Upper Egypt and has projects under the categories of relief (for debtors), education, health care, scientific research, and *takaful* (social solidarity). Its goal is to serve as an internationally renowned foundation working to eliminate unemployment, illiteracy, poverty, and disease. The foundation funds projects through donations collected as *zakat, sadaqa,* and relief funds, and it holds separate bank accounts for each type of fund to ensure that *zakat* spending is *shari'a* compliant. The *sadaqa* funds are invested, primarily through a separate but affiliated community development fund, the Misr el Khayr Investment Fund, and the income is used to support their other activities. The foundation is also affiliated with Ard el Khayr, a joint stock company focused on SME development.

While the foundation does work through a network of more than twelve hundred NGOs throughout the country, its model is a hybrid operational and grant-making foundation. Under the category of *takaful,* the foundation balances direct-aid with income-generating projects. Its internal documents emphasize strict guidelines for determining the deserving poor, stringent follow-up procedures, and a contractual obligation between the aid recipient and the foundation that gives the foundation the right to withdraw the project if the recipient exhibits a "lack of seriousness." The foundation represents the ethos of pious neoliberalism. In his chairman's speech, Grand Mufti Ali Gomaa begins by highlighting the importance of Islamic charity to society and then seamlessly shifts his language to development. He states his appreciation for the foundation's supporters by invoking religion, "May Allah reward them, the prosperity is from Allah," while the website describes the foundation's values as "transparency, respect, excellence, responsibility, accountability and equity." Pious neoliberalism is characterized by this precise melding of neoliberal language—transparency, responsibility, and accountability, with a clearly articulated dedication to faith.

Most of the new foundations established by a new bourgeois class were inspired by dedication to God, yet the founders and staff tended to minimize religious language and instead described their activities as human development. Since Misr el Khayr was established by the Mufti, it has a clear religious connotation to most Egyptians, but the language of the website is that of development. One organization that stood out as an exception to this emphasis on development was a foundation so mysterious that I felt like an investigative reporter in my quest to find it.

Rumor had it that one of Egypt's business tycoons was very charitable. In 2001 he had started a fast-food restaurant and put all its proceeds toward charity, in essence creating a de facto *waqf*. He also established a foundation and, in contrast to all the other foundation staff I met with, the director spoke to me on the condition of anonymity. The foundation director, a retired army general, indicated that the founder insisted his name not be attached to his work because of a deeply held belief that giving in secrecy maximized rewards from God and led to better results: "When you believe in something and you do it entirely with the aim of God knowing and for his sake only, then you will succeed."[48] The businessman who established the foundation refused to have his name on anything, even the mosques he built. The director boasted that they were the first (foundation): "You see many projects sprouting up now, but keep in mind that we were the first." In contrast to the Western development-oriented foundations, this foundation focused on typical Islamic charity projects, providing medical care and direct social services as well as donations to a well-known *da'wa* organization. The foundation accepts no donations from individuals or state funds. All of the money came from their *zakat* and *sadaqa* from the founder's businesses, amounting to more than 100 million EGP. Despite giving in secrecy, the organization was actually one of the most transparent in terms of sharing its financial data with me. I noticed that organizations run by former military were far more transparent than the others. Their overall lack of suspicion might be related to their military backgrounds, which made them less susceptible to state intervention, and therefore gave them much less to fear.

The foundation spent the majority of its funds on supporting widows and orphans, but it supplemented cash support with access to discounted services. It issued ID cards to the recipients and then gave them a list of associated businesses—"friends" of the foundation that had agreed to provide discounted or in-kind services to those with a proper ID card. The general elaborated, "Let me give you an example. There is a family that has three children; it gets 20 LE per child, that's 100 LE for five people. Of course that's not enough to cover their needs. But when they get free meat, free health care, and free shoes, that helps."[49] He also talked about a large orphanage that the foundation funded and boasted that the orphans wore designer clothes: "The lowest thing they wear is Daly Dress." Again, in contrast to the other foundations, which were fixated on quantifying the neediness of recipients and on demonstrating a focus on efficient use of resources, the general was proud of the fact that the foundation spent munificently.

The foundation also engaged in income-generating projects for the needy, although it did not use the language of development like the other foundations. The general described a program where they teach women how to sew. They started a sewing school with fifty machines and cloth donated from stores and then expanded into eleven governorates. They pay the women 1 LE per *gallabiyya* (a long, loose traditional Egyptian garment) and then they distribute the products for free as *zakat* to the needy. The general was particularly proud of this system: "That way we are making these women productive, helping them and at the same time helping others in need." Through these sewing schools, they have employed 170,000 "working mothers." Finally, the general took out a picture that had vans of goods being sent to Palestinians. The vans had banners that read "From the Egyptian people to the Palestinians." He told me, "I'm personally responsible for making sure these vans made it there." Then he said that the *da'wa* organization they support financially had changed the banners to their name for publicity. The manager proudly laughed, "I don't care if they put their name on everything. God knows everything."

The foundation sponsored several public (government-run) hospitals and provided free medical care, including radiology services. I asked the general why the foundation decided to support the government instead of opening private hospitals and he said, "The state lacks funding, but some hospitals have good managers but without the means to do good work. We know some of these managers are very capable but do not have the money they need to make their hospital a success. So we handpick them, and we fund them." Doctors I spoke with echoed the success of these privately funded public hospital units, describing them as some of the best in Egypt. Given their partnership with the government, I inquired about their relationship: "We take nothing from them, and they leave us alone. We follow all of the rules, like providing them annual financial reports. But they would never dare intrude into our books. They get the basic information and that's it. Because, like I said, we don't need them, they need us. We don't collect funds from anyone; other organizations run into problems because they don't follow the government's rules about gathering money and they implement projects in areas they aren't authorized to fund."[50] While foundation staff in general were far less critical of the government than association staff, most still complained about bureaucratic procedures getting in the way of their work. But certain institutions, particularly those run by retired military, seemed to have an easier time than others.

This foundation went against the trend of establishing Western-style foundations. While it did engage in some income-generating work, this clearly was not the priority. In addition, the director emphasized the good deeds (*khayr*) of the organization over efficiency, sustainability, or professionalization, even though the foundation work easily could have been described by these three characteristics. He spoke openly about the religious motivations of the founder and tended to focus on categories of recipients in line with *zakat* requirements, rather than market the foundation as doing development. Finally, the foundation had not established a clear link between the company and the foundation. In fact, the general went out of his way to ensure the anonymity of the donor. Unlike community foundations, which gather a group of funds and are few and far between, private foundations are primarily based on private wealth. The growth of private foundations epitomizes pious neoliberalism, as wealthy individuals merged their faith-driven giving with "business development" or "venture philanthropy."[51] In the case of foundations, businesspeople are driven by faith to give but are not content with a *khayr wa-khalas* approach. Instead, they build institutions that bring their professional expertise to giving.

Pious neoliberalism of course is not just Islamic. Coptic construction mogul Naguib Sawiris was one of the first businessmen to establish a foundation from his family's fortune in 2001. Inspired by the work of the first director, Ibrahim Shihata, with the World Bank, the Sawiris Foundation for Social Development focused on employment, entrepreneurship, and microcredit. While his wife was renowned for her work with the Coptic Church as well as the predominantly Christian garbage collectors, other philanthropists speculated that he was permitted to set up an endowment outside the Ministry of Endowments precisely because, as a Christian, the *waqf* laws would not apply to his endowment. The Sawiris Foundation leadership was very proud of being one of the first, as Hoda Sawiris told me, "Today creating a foundation is easier than it was five or six years ago. There are many more businessmen involved, and more people in the field, and so the fact that these businessmen are there has added value because it has improved the image and pointed to their role in the community."[52] The Sawiris Foundation was not just a pioneer, but it is also one of the most professional foundations in Egypt and has won various international awards. It seemed as though it had inspired several other foundations or, as Mrs. Sawiris called them, the "copycats."

Numerous other businessmen established both private and corporate foundations because they saw it as a win-win situation. The businessmen involved in foundations received minimal financial benefits from their philanthropy because Egyptian law permits only limited income deductions and tax benefits for philanthropy,[53] but the businessmen surely improved their public image as a result of their philanthropy. In postrevolutionary Egypt, wealthy businessmen who had engaged in philanthropy were spared the wrath of activists calling for the prosecution of former NDP affiliates on corruption charges. In interviews I conducted with philanthropists, they continually referred to their religious obligations as the driving factor in establishing foundations.

Privatized Islam and the Rise of an Islamic Sector

In addition to private mosques and foundations, the third aspect of a privatized Islam is the emergence of an Islamic private sector, otherwise referred to as a Muslim or Halal "lifestyle market."[54] In a special issue of the

Journal of Middle East Women's Studies dedicated to "Muslim Women, consumer capitalism and the Islamic cultural industry," Banu Gökariksel and Ellen McLarney posit that "Islamic knowledge, performances, and selves are more and more mediated through increasingly commodified cultural forms and spaces."[55] The merging of "ethical consumerism and Islamic beliefs"[56] has produced a global multibillion-dollar sector that includes halal food, Islamic financial products, a veiling fashion industry, children's products, matrimonial and networking services/websites, Islamic educational institutions and reference resources, and Islamic media and entertainment, including satellite TV channels, music, entertainment venues, restaurants, and leisure resorts.[57] While any ordinary business that voluntarily pays *zakat* might qualify as an Islamic business, the focus within the lifestyle market is on consumption. From ethical colas to Islamic beach resorts, Islamic businesses responded to the increasing demand for products that mesh with a "modern" Islamic lifestyle. Lara Deeb and Mona Harb analyze Hezbollah's development of an "Islamic milieu" in southern Lebanon through a focus on leisure sites and spaces.[58] Another particularly visible manifestation of Islamic commodities is the rise of veiling fashion. As more and more women donned the headscarf over the course of the past fifteen years, a vast array of veiling fashions emerged, as did stores that catered to the newly differentiated forms of veiling.[59] Segregated or women-only beach resorts that do not serve alcoholic beverages also appeared across Egypt's North Coast, as did magazines of global reach marketing to Muslim women's lifestyles.[60] The proliferation in the number of *da'iya* and the popularity of Quranic recitation classes fueled the growth of Islamic bookstores that sell Islamic commodities like Qurans, framed Islamic calligraphy, books, and sermons on cassette tapes, CDs, and DVDs.[61] Pious neoliberals shaped both the consumption and production of commodities and their circulation through Islamic businesses.

The 2012 World Halal Forum in Kuala Lumpur aimed to bridge "the halal supply chain" with Islamic finance in order to address the "emerging halal economy." The emphasis on shifting from a halal sector to a halal economy is indicative of the widespread global growth of pious neoliberalism, while the merger of Islamic finance and the halal market is emblematic of privatized Islam. The largest and most developed aspect of this privatized Islam is IBF, which is now a $1 trillion industry that includes *riba*-free bank accounts, Islamic investment vehicles, derivatives, credit cards, mortgages, insurance, and microfinance.[62] Islamic financial products, including

Islamic equity funds, bonds (*sukuk*), and hedge funds represent the biggest growth areas within IBF.[63] From the 1986 to 2006, IBF global capital, assets and deposits grew at 15 percent to 20 percent annually.[64] IBF doubled in size between 1998 and 2001 alone.[65] After the 2008 global economic crisis, IBF remained one of the fastest-growing sectors of the global financial industry. In the recent financial crisis, IBF was hit much less hard than conventional finance, shielded precisely by the fact that the very traits that lie at the core of Islamic banking made credit swaps and derivative trading difficult. However, the rapid growth of the sector largely results from the dilution of the core principles of Islamic economics (such as the avoidance of *gharar* and *maysir*) in order to compete with Western finance. Islamic economists Hassan and Lewis argue that this trend threatens the legitimacy of Islamic banking practices, so that "Islamic banking looks like an issue of branding, like Mecca Cola instead of Coca Cola."[66]

IBF is a clear example of pious neoliberalism as it "reflects a desire to give an Islamic legitimacy to the financial system."[67] It also reflects a desire to give a neoliberal capitalist legitimacy to Islamic practices as part of a broader modernity narrative. Pious neoliberalism is reflected in both the producers of IBF and the consumers, offering new financial instruments that blend capitalist logic with religious ethics. A similar logic resulted in the creation of Socially Responsible Investment Funds (SRIs) in the 1990s. SRIs operate by dictating a set of moral guidelines that limit the set of investment opportunities that are included in a given portfolio. Many SRIs eliminate alcohol, tobacco, weapons, gambling, and pornography from their investment portfolios, while green funds measure the sustainability and environmental practices of companies. Religious investment funds develop investment portfolios that they see as complying with a set of moral codes. For example, Islamic investment funds eliminate investments in pork products, conventional financial services, weapons/defense, and entertainment products (including hotels, casinos, cinema, pornography, and music, which are perceived as being wholly un-Islamic). Many Christian funds use similar screens and avoid investments in companies involved in abortion, pornography, gambling, alcohol, firearms sales, tobacco and nontraditional/homosexual lifestyles, or those that offer nonmarital partner benefits. These religious investment funds are part and parcel of pious neoliberalism; piety and profitability are equally weighted in investment decisions.

In addition to Islamic mutual funds and financial instruments, privatized Islam manifests in the reinvention of Islamic microfinance. I say reinvention because Islamic microfinance is the pious neoliberal version of a centuries-old Islamic practice called *qard hasan* (benevolent loan). The development of Islamic microfinance is celebrated because it has the potential to produce significant financial returns. Practitioners who support an Islamic microfinance use Quranic passages in support of *qard hasan* to justify the practice. However, Islamic microfinance produces profits at the expense of the poor. *Qard hasan* is intended to help the poor without taking advantage of their misfortune. By focusing on generating a bottom line, the ethos of *qard hasan* is compromised. Islamic microfinance becomes another means of privatizing Islam since it adapts a historically significant Islamic economic practice to capitalist norms.

Loans for the Poor: *Qard hasan* and Islamic Microfinance

For decades the poor have had their own coping mechanisms for dealing with their lack of access to credit. In response to financial exclusion, they formed their own small lending circles based solely on trust in order to meet their needs.[68] Lending circles usually consist of anywhere between four and twelve individuals who commit to pay a lump sum each month (for example, 100 LE). A schedule is set based on need and consensus, and thereafter each month one individual in the circle receives a lump sum equal to the monthly contributions of all members combined (for example, 1,200 LE). Lending circles serve as a way to help those with no access to credit and limited financial means to meet their needs—be it wedding preparations, housing repairs, debt to the landlord on past due rent, or capital to start a peddling business. This practice is extremely prevalent among the working class. Despite the existence of these indigenous and less exploitative forms of capital sharing, microfinance, with its exorbitant interest rates, proliferates in Egypt because it represents formal market access to capital.

International development experts do not take the self-help lending circles of the poor seriously because they are not formalized contracts. In my interview with an employee at the International Financial Corporation (IFC), the arm of the IMF that promotes the private sector in emerging markets, he explained that the stated goal of IFC was "to build and improve the financial infrastructure of emerging markets, and we do so by encouraging microfinance, by facilitating the creation of private credit bureaus." When I asked his opinion of the informal money-lending circles in Egypt, he belittled their importance as a form of credit:

I suppose they are a form of credit, but they have limited use—
they are short term and they don't replace the need for proper
financial services and access to long-term money. In Egypt, there is
a serious problem with credit in the long term. Here the maximum
even big businessmen can get is credit for five to seven years. This
stems from the perception of risk, from ignorance, from the financial industry's perspective on the ability/willingness of individuals
to pay back loans. And this stems from a serious lack of financial
intermediaries, who can ensure that savings don't just sit there.[69]

Before credit can be extended to the poor, they must prove themselves
risk-worthy, and because they do not have traditional forms of collateral,
microfinance institutions usually use the notion of group responsibility to
minimize risk and ensure a repayment. The use of *qard hasan* programs in
conjunction with interest-based microfinance serves as one final example
of a privatized Islam. While practitioners try and limit moral hazard and
maximize payback on loans, they also recognize an Islamic injunction toward debt forgiveness.

A *qard hasan* is an interest-free loan with a set payback period.[70] Called
a benevolent/gratuitous loan, it is believed that God rewards the lender in
multiples.[71] Once a prevalent practice of Islamic associations, today the
cash-based interest-free loan has been replaced by Islamic microfinance
and an in-kind goods form of microenterprise lending. For example, Dar
al-Orman's *qard hasan* program gives an entrepreneur 7,500 LE to start
his own project. The receiver pays back the loan interest-free over eighteen months. If their project succeeds, the entrepreneur receives another
loan and then is only required to pay half of it back. If they successfully pay
half of the second loan back, they receive a third round as a grant, a reward
for their success.

Many committed to the idea that the poor need access to capital to exit
poverty found the concept of an Islamic microfinance attractive. As the
director of al-Azhar's Salah Kamel Institute for Islamic Economics told
me, "*qard hasan* is a thing of the past. . . . Very few organizations are issuing interest-free loans . . . microfinance is the current trend, the wave of the
future." While the prohibition of *riba* made many Islamic organizations
weary of microfinance programs, over the past ten years Islamic economists have suggested that *sadaqa* and returns from *awqaf* could be used to
finance microfinance institutions (MFIs).[72] The fund manager of Faisal

Zakat Fund (of the Faisal Islamic Bank) told me that he is regularly approached by individuals who "want to use their *zakat* to donate to microfinance and vocational training centers."[73] While microfinance exploded in Egypt over the past fifteen years, most of the market is conventional microfinance, which most Islamic associations find objectionable. A few did transition their *qard hasan* programs to interest-bearing microfinance following Sheikh Mohammad Sayyid Tantawi's 2002 fatwa proclaiming that fixed interest was not *haram*.[74] With the global celebration of the success and promise of microfinance, Islamic banks have expressed momentous interest in expanding into microfinance and becoming "agents for development" alongside NGOs.[75] Microfinance, then, represents a form of privatized Islam as the nexus between "the world of business and profit and the world of social solidarity and altruism."[76]

World Bank economist Habib Ahmed, a champion of Islamic microfinance, argues for the use of a *takaful* (mutual/social insurance) reserve to reduce the risk of financing the poor. A *takaful* reserve could be "created by small weekly/monthly contributions from the beneficiaries. This *takaful* reserve would be used to support beneficiaries who are unable to pay their dues on time due to some unexpected problems like natural calamity or death in the family."[77] Ahmed's use of *takaful* demonstrates a shift in the meaning of the word, away from social solidarity or insurance based on a principle of joint-risk sharing and toward a form of capitalist insurance. Furthermore, some Islamic scholars have started to argue that banks are permitted to charge a small service fee to cover the cost of administering these microloans.[78] In support of this, Azuzul Huq, executive vice president of the Islamic Bank of Bangladesh, states, "The *Shari'ah* does not permit and Islamic banks do not receive any income from interest-free investment loans. The lending banks can, however, recover the administrative costs directly related to the investment as a service charge."[79] As with many IBF practices, many institutions take the ability to charge a mark-up fee as an opportunity to translate fixed-interest-like charges into profit, enabling old neoliberal practices to take on new faces.[80]

The replacement of *qard hasan* with Islamic financial tools such as *murabaha* and *ijara* reduces the risk or "moral hazard" of a loan because an asset/good exchange occurs rather than a cash exchange. This decreases the likelihood of a diversion of funds and reduces the default risk and therefore increases profitability.[81] Many Islamic associations gave *qard hasan* as a microloan paired with a particular employment opportunity and the necessary tools to work in that craft. For example, the public relations representative of Dar Al-Orman explained their use of *qard hasan,* "We provide *qard hasan* to women in rural areas, we give them 180 LE a month for six months so they can try and sell the goods they are producing. We have also distributed over 9,500 cows in Upper Egypt. We give loans of 100 LE to help farmers buy supplies. They then pay it back interest-free at 20 LE a month."[82] The Nasser Social Bank also engaged in a microenterprise-based *qard hasan* program. In my interview with the head of the *zakat* arm of the bank, he told me: "Many people have the ability to work but don't have any means. We provide them with tools like air-compressor machines. We'll give someone a compressor for 1,000 LE, leave him three months to profit, and then take half of his daily profits as payment toward the 1,000 LE. The goal is to increase employment."[83] Once the recipient's business was up and running, they would return the tools to the organization that gave it to them or pass it along to another person in their neighborhood. Islamic association directors prefer microenterprise rather than cash *qard hasan* because they see microenterprise as less risky. While the number of organizations involved in microfinance grew by the day, only a handful of organizations gave out interest-free loans in Egypt.[84] One of the only organizations I found that still issued monetary *qard hasan* is called *Taharrur Iqtisadi,* which literally means "economic liberation." *Taharrur Iqtisadi* is a small, local service-oriented organization mostly engaged in the provision of direct social services. As part of its approach to becoming "self-sufficient," this organization has taken on the economic development strategies of microfinance, computer training, and microenterprise development. It combines Islamic debt forgiveness in the form of *qard hasan* with an interest-based microfinance program. Located in downtown Cairo, the association occupies a floor of one high-rise building on a crowded narrow street in the neighborhood of Saad Zaghloul (Figure 15). The neighborhood is nestled between Sayyida Zaynab, a very old and *sha'bi* (popular) neighborhood, and the lavish and manicured mansions and embassies of Garden City on the other side.[85]

The organization's sign was barely visible and the building was mostly residential. When I arrived, the sidewalk was difficult to navigate because of the overflow from the noon prayer at the mosque nearby. I made my way up the stairs and walked into their tiny office. They were very welcoming and eager to share their experiences. Although the organization was involved in a variety of activities, including running a day care, support for

Figure 15. Taharrur Iqtisadi is an association that provides microfinance to individuals and created a qard hasan or interest-free loan program for those who qualify. Photograph by the author.

working mothers, educational panels, job creation, and interest-bearing loans, I was most interested to hear about their work with *qard hasan*. In my interview with one of the directors, she said:

> We give out loans, like any bank. Our loan program began in 1999 and our return rate on our loans is unheard of—100 percent. But our *qard al-hasan* program started only in 2005. We started a department for aid one year ago and made twenty loans as *qard al-hasan*. . . . Lots of people ask for loans but are not qualified. Loanees must be a government employee—that is a form of guarantee. We also ask for a phone bill or some other ID. . . . We also get small electronic goods for small businesses—this is ongoing. They get the loan and then pay it back. We sometimes have communal loans. . . . We have granted 174 regular loans this year but only a few *qard al-hasan*. . . . The interest rate on our regular loans is 14 percent.[86]

Working with the Bank "Iskan wa-l Ta'mir," they provide individual loans up to 6,000 EGP and communal loans for groups of up to six people totaling 30,000 EGP. Interestingly, their return rate on these loans is stated at an extraordinary rate of 100 percent. The rate, however, includes the transfer of a potential defaulter's loan into a *qard hasan*.

I inquired about the roots of the *qard hasan* program, since this organization seemed to go against a general trend. In 2005 a young man asked for a loan to prevent his home from being repossessed. The organization was known around town for providing free legal aid. Departing from the interest-bearing loan program established in 1999, the organization provided him with an interest-free loan. Only months later, a youth came to them with another problem. As part of his attempt to get on his feet, he had signed on to a debt for goods that he intended to sell at a profit, but he did not succeed and was unable to service his debt. He was on the verge of being imprisoned in one of the new industrial towns, the 10th district of Ramadan City, for not paying his debt. The organization offered him free legal aid but then also provided him with an interest-free loan. This gave them the idea of creating a formal *qard hasan* program. The organization is able to sustain its *qard hasan* program as a result of its interest-bearing sister. In this way, the reemergence of *qard hasan* has a great deal to do with the explosion of microfinance. Numerous borrowers, unable to pay back the exorbitant interest rates that are common to microfinance schemes, are turning to Islamic principles of debt relief to bail them out.[87] Associations use zakat to help overburdened debtors since they constitute a category of rightful receivers designated in the Quran. Islamic microfinance epitomizes how experts narrate an Islamic neoliberalism, one that relies on principles of neoliberalism and simultaneously draws upon an Islamic narrative to make it attractive to a Muslim clientele. Islamic microfinance extends credit to the poor, while the architects of the halal marketplace offer modern, middle-class Muslims a niche consumer market.

Conclusion

The Egyptian state has a long history of meddling in Islamic institutions that it has attempted to co-opt as a form of state building since the twentieth century. As the state tried to limit the power of Islamic institutions, piety was expressed through other means. The co-optation of Islamic institutions, particularly mosques and *waqf*, eventually brought into being new institutional forms predicated on individual wealth, or a privatized Islam. These new institutional forms include private mosques, private foundations, and an Islamic lifestyle market, of which Islamic finance is an important component. These institutions established a new space for the expression of Islamic piety in relation to neoliberal ideology. Private mosques proliferated in the new gated communities of Cairo; private foundations attempted to transform the charitable sector by providing an alternative domestic yet development-oriented source of funding for associations. An Islamic sector provided new outlets for expressing one's religious identity as a consumer. It is part of a privatized Islam that caters to a bourgeois class of Muslims who choose to express their identity through the purchase of Islamic commodities. The rise of a new bourgeois class that directly benefited from privatization, Gulf remittances, and (often) government corruption, are part and parcel of neoliberalism, as is the expression of culture and identity through commodities. The new middle-class Muslim consumers express their religiosity not just through consumption but also in how they save, invest, and give charity. Collectively, these individual practices craft a new form of subjectivity—that of the pious neoliberal subject.

CHAPTER 5

Business with Allah

THE LADIES OF THE HELIOPOLIS SPORTING CLUB raved about the food they purchased from Zahrawan.[1] Zahrawan sells prepared foods that women could heat and serve for their families. Out of a small shop on Omar ibn el Khattab Street, they sold labor-intensive goods like stuffed grape leaves, moussaka, savory pies, and French cookies. The backroom shelves were filled with these foods while the side room displayed hand-made jewelry; downstairs, home goods like pillowcases and tablecloths as well as *gallabiyyat* and veils were on display. Although my first encounter with Zahrawan was as a consumer, every mention of the place was accompanied by praise for the wonderful *khayr* these women had done. Zahrawan was engaged in business with Allah and yet it was not a business at all; it is a charitable and developmental foundation affiliated with Hagga Sherine, a beloved female *da'wa* star who gave religious sermons and lessons to women in this upper-middle-class neighborhood. Once considered a suburb of Cairo, Heliopolis houses the Baron Palace (*Qasr al-Baron*); al-Korba, a busy commercial street with nineteenth-century belle-époque architecture and loads of trendy cafés, and the presidential palace. The foundation occupied three stories of a high-rise building, where they sold their goods and engaged in a variety of charitable activities (Figure 16).

Zahrawan Foundation, established in June 2011, focuses on *da'wa*, charity, and development. The foundation is run by a voluntary administrative team of six women and a salaried cleaning staff. A majority of the fifteen hundred volunteers are upper-middle-class women who participate in a variety of activities that include: *zakat, takaful,* productive families, prepared foods, Ramadan and Eid distributions, youth camps and after-school activities, street beautification, and social services for the illiterate, elderly, orphans, and others with special needs. Some women teach Quran memorization for youth from nine years through college age and the foundation is licensed to provide Quranic certification for *da'iya* in the mosques. They also hold seminars on volunteerism and give moral lessons coupled

Figure 16. The Zahrawan Foundation's promotional materials for prepared foods cooked by women who receive assistance in addition to wages.

with assistance to women in informal settlements. Zahrawan is an operating foundation rather than a grant-making one, but it is run like an association. Like many other foundations I had visited, it could establish itself as a foundation because it had the necessary capital (10,000 EGP) to do so. Foundations are subject to less government intervention and are able to sell goods without violating the stringent NGO law. Many charities had complained about their inability to sell anything during the Mubarak years. Since Zahrawan was established after the uprising, it was not subject to government interference. I arranged to meet the chairwoman, Hagga Shahira, to find out more about this institution of privatized Islam.

When Zahrawan was established, it marketed itself as a women's charitable foundation, a voluntary association, and a foundation for sustainable development at the same time. The foundation preached that faith and work are two sides of the same coin and its goal was to "translate faith into positive work." The prepared-foods market and artisan crafts shop, initiatives that provide income opportunities to poor women, were the most well known of their projects. This model is a market-based solution to poverty and the women used a "systematic" approach to ensure quality control over the food. They had opened a factory that produces sheets and towels to employ women who also receive aid. In addition, the founders would soon open a for-profit school. Thus Zahrawan is an example of how some Islamic charities were engaging in business with Allah. As more businesspeople became involved in charitable work, I noticed they brought with them a different approach to charity work, one that sought out market-based solutions to poverty, relied upon a systematic approach, and created strict accountability parameters for aid recipients. Although only one association director described his work as "business with Allah," I observed numerous other associations built on the idea of applying business expertise to the charitable sector.

Don't Give a Man a Fish

Islamic charity administrators with private-sector backgrounds described the poor in a common manner. All of the associations I visited collected and distributed *zakat,* but the administrators of some organizations voiced concern that aid recipients were taking advantage of the system. For example, one charity administrator said, "People are not honest about their income, assets, etc. . . . which makes it difficult to really identify the neediest families. But with experience, our research team learned who is telling the truth and who is not." Several charity administrators believed the poor were in pursuit of infinite aid, that they preferred to receive "handouts" rather than earn their own income. A young entrepreneur involved in charitable work, echoed this skepticism toward aid recipients, "These women go from committee to committee getting aid rather than working. Some of them make upwards of 1,000 LE a month, taking advantage of the system. It's like those beggars on the street. You know some people even amputate their limbs so people will feel sorry for them? They know they can make more money as beggars than working!"[2] He saw the aid recipients as working the system and as endless seekers of aid.

Other charity administrators voiced a concern with efficiency, "Poverty is so widespread, we have a hard time figuring out whom to give to, who are the most needy. . . . People who donate are sometimes not convinced of the needs of the poor. You know the Chinese proverb, 'Don't give a man a fish. Teach him how to fish'? . . . Sometimes people are hesitant to give."[3] Charity administrators sought to ensure that charity only went to those who deserved help. Their notion of deserving stemmed from the categories of *zakat* recipients outlined in the Quran, but they preferred to give direct aid to those who could not work—orphans, the disabled—and to help the unemployed or underemployed improve their lot through income-generating projects. Individual donors often asked charity administrators, "How do I know your recipients are *really* needy?" and therefore charity administrators pursued "measures of neediness" and conditional giving in order to ease donor anxieties.

One administrator described a "social research system" he set up to determine who is "really needy and who is able to work. . . . We sponsor families until they are ready and able to generate income for themselves."[4] Other charities implemented similar systems that sought to quantify and verify neediness while tracking charity-recipient behaviors. Charity administrators in this sense are "travelling technocrats" who applied their private-sector expertise to charitable work.[5] While the experts involved saw this change as a natural and logical transition, it was one that drew upon neoliberal development ideology and was reproduced by private-sector experts who are part of a particular social network.[6] These social research systems are an act of governing; they define parameters of neediness, delimit the deserving poor, and manage the poor in their everyday lives.[7] Social research systems empowered charity administrators to feel confident that recipients were truly deserving of aid.

Many charity administrators yearned for a centralized distribution database that would allow organizations to check individuals' need-worthiness, most importantly to ensure that aid recipients were not double-dipping and receiving aid from numerous organizations at once. The executive director of the Egyptian Food Bank was a key advocate for such a network. He told me, "We want to study the state of organizations, develop criteria for organizations working in a particular area, and then create a framework in which they can cooperate. This includes having common storage, databases, and a computer network to ensure that aid recipients are not taking from multiple organizations."[8]

As an experiment, twenty-five mosques in Nasr City collaborated to establish a database of aid recipients that they share among themselves. The purpose of the database was to establish a system that verified how much aid a recipient was receiving and prevent resourceful individuals from working the system. Numerous other informants indicated that they hoped a citywide system could be established to ensure that aid reached the most deserving recipients. Charity administrators voiced a commitment to helping able-bodied individuals increase their income, while hoping those aided would eventually become givers of charity rather than recipients. Many organizations counted their ability to turn recipients into givers as a measure of success. As one association director told me, "We turn recipients into givers; we have sixty children who were once recipients now giving. An example of a recipient who now gives is a doctor, once he got his degree and his sister got married, they sent the money back as a thank-you to another family."[9] The associations directed by former businesspeople were the most likely to create systems of verification and apply a systematic approach to their work. The next few case studies illustrate how different associations drew upon their private-sector expertise to systematize their work while crafting market-oriented solutions to poverty.

The Egyptian Food Bank Revisited

The Egyptian Food Bank is so successful that in 2010 the United Nations Private-Sector Initiative facilitated the exportation of its model to other countries in the Middle East. The founders of the Egyptian Food Bank used their business savvy to develop a "bank" model and drew on their powerful social network for help. Given his busy work schedule as CEO of Olympic Group, a household appliance and consumer electronics company, cofounder Niazy Sallam decided to draw on his social capital: "As a businessman, I have strong ties with important people, ministers, other businessmen. I felt that I could use some of those connections and try and apply my own expertise from my work, to this other area [charity] but as a businessman."[10] Sallam and his associates entered the charitable sector as businessmen, with the intention of applying their private-sector expertise. Their goal was to create a more efficient distribution of food by minimizing food waste and assembling a system for distributing leftover food to the needy. The founders told me that a responsibility to engage in *takaful* and a desire to "build a house in heaven" led them to establish the organization.[11] These businessmen sought to organize charity on a scale never seen in Egypt, "We wanted to do something on a larger scale, on a national (*qawmi*) scale. So I sat down and began to write the names of businessmen I knew on a piece of paper. I asked them to help in some capacity in this project. This work is really then, *'amal 'amm'* (public service) seriously, not like other charitable projects that operate on a small scale. It isn't just *khayr wa-khalas*. . . . God wants me to be in the middle of these powerful men for a reason."[12] Sallam had a clear strategic vision for alleviating poverty when he began the Egyptian Food Bank. His business colleagues liked the bank model and began assembling resources to apply the model to other areas like vocational training, housing, clothing and medical care. When I returned to Egypt in 2010, the food bank had converted its registration from an association to a foundation. As a foundation, it could use their existing social network to expand their bank model thereby facilitating a "coordinated charity network" that could address "broader social issues in a systematic way." When I returned in 2012, the foundation had succeeded in creating a coordinated charity network, including a sister entity, The Egyptian Cure Bank, that provides medical treatment for those who cannot afford it. I asked Food Bank CEO Moez el-Shohdi, a transnational hotel manager who quit his job to run the food bank, if they had any other banks in the pipeline. He smiled widely, danced around the question a bit, and then described the Egyptian Clothing Bank and the Egyptian Hope Bank for Training and Employment. The Egyptian Clothing Bank will provide clothing to the poor by collecting donations from factories and distributing them seasonally for a nominal fee to students, factory employees, and others who cannot afford market-priced clothing. Yaser Abdel Fattah will head the Egyptian Hope Bank; through a 2012 cooperation agreement with the food bank, the Hope Bank will oversee rehabilitation, training, and employment for fifty thousand food bank beneficiaries.

The Food Bank's unprecedented growth and successful creation of a charity network was a clear indicator that the foundation had achieved a goal that an employee described to me back in 2006: "to shift concepts of charity work in Egypt." The banks apply to other social problems the same business savvy, checklists, investigation procedures, and databases that the food bank created. The banks will collectively move into an office in New Cairo where each foundation will share resources, including five departments: information technology, human resources, NGO assessment, case and research divisions, and monitoring and evaluation programs. By sharing a central database with all information on partner organizations, shared equipment, staff and other infrastructure, the banks benefited from economies of scale. The bank model was central to their success from the very beginning: "Ali Gomaa, the mufti, was at our launch and he mentioned the idea of banks—of setting up different banks for each cause. Many businessmen were there and got excited about it. Several board members are well-known businesspeople involved in the American Chamber of Commerce and transnational companies like the JW Marriott Hotel."[13]

The food bank was a clear example of doing business with Allah. The staff did not consist of volunteers but salaried professionals. Salaries, administration, and marketing expenses were covered through the sponsorship from local businesspeople. El-Shohdi was not an executive director, but rather a CEO who ran a multimillion LE enterprise:

> The reason I quit my job in hotel management is that I'd like to treat the problem of the ʿashwaʾi approach (haphazard development approach) in the next fifteen years. I want to increase the number of families that will receive benefit from our different "banks." I want to reach 4 million families. In ten years, if the average family has five members, that's 20 million people whose lives have been improved. That's what—12 to 15 percent of the 75 million in Egypt? . . . If those who give that which is not in use today and it is distributed properly, we can cover the entire nation.[14]

El-Shohdi also differentiated the foundation's professionalism from the rest of the sector:

> Lots of people are working in khayr, but it is ʿashwaʾi (haphazard).[15] Of the twenty-two thousand organizations registered with MOSA, maybe ten thousand are working and each organization is operating individually. There isn't really the idea of specialization of organizations, although this is increasing. Most organizations are operating at a local level, resulting in duplication. In our vision, there is more specialization and we will try to make sure organizations are not duplicating one another.[16]

El-Shohdi emphasized strategic planning and spoke disapprovingly about charities that were less strategic in their giving. He described other charitable work as *'ashwa'i*—unplanned, unorganized, uncoordinated, unprofessional. In contrast, the CEO set up measurable benchmarks for the association and expanded quickly through a vast network of partner NGOs. He focused on infrastructure and the institutionalization of the management processes so they could grow quickly, building an elaborate database of partners and protocols disseminated across governorates. He created stringent accountability parameters for all partner organizations involved in distribution. Any organization that became part of their network went through rigorous evaluation and training, including building their social marketing skills, fund-raising capacity, and ensuring quality control across the network.

The underlying vision of this bank model was "to address poverty on all fronts, especially via job creation." The Hope Bank will create a job bank, to match employers with employees, because while there is demand for low-end, manual labor jobs there are not enough potential employees. El-Shohdi believed this mismatch was a result of "the nationalized education system, no one wants to work these kinds of jobs." The unemployment rate also exacerbates the enormous problem of marriage.[17] "There are lots of bachelors who don't have the means to get married. In today's world, many can't afford the necessary items for marriage, and the biggest issue is often housing, since the cost of housing is so high."[18] Since access to housing for young men in Egyptian society is inextricably linked to their ability to get married, the escalating cost of housing is a major obstacle to marriage. El-Shohdi saw the business sector as a potential partner in combating the affordable-housing crisis. He explained that if large construction companies involved in the growth of Cairo's new exclusionary suburbs could "set aside a few units nearby for the service industry that will be needed to support these houses," it could serve the dual purpose of bringing much-needed labor to the gated communities, at the same time as involving the businesses in *khayr*.[19] According to El-Shohdi, this created a win-win situation: "There are lots of possible incentives for companies, such as tax-deductions, advertising, sponsorships—the benefits they get by participating in these projects. . . . You know that today media costs are very high, so corporations are far more willing to do stuff in return for having their name reach people."[20] Businesspeople involved in charitable work were also much less concerned with secrecy than those who worked in *khayr wa-khlas*–type organizations. They saw the culture of secrecy around giving as a limitation on the growth of organized giving. El-Shohdi's emphasis on transparency also shaped his interactions with me; he was more than happy to share the details of the organizations' operations, plans and reports, and welcomed me back in his office time and time again.[21]

Another factor shaping the food bank's success, and a benefit of having executives from the private sector as board members, was access to capital. As the marketing manager explained:

> Our launch cost one million LE. We had one campaign on TV that cost one million, but we only paid half price. [The satellite TV channels] Dream, Mahwar, they give us spots on TV for free and from our campaigns we get about 3 million LE back to pay for projects, so they are very strategic and successful. We also have an arrangement with Diner's Club so that people can transfer their points to the food bank instead of redeeming them at restaurants. We get 50,000 LE monthly from this arrangement. These arrangements allow us to focus on sustainability.[22]

The executives of the food bank, given their access to capital and personal connections, were in a good position to embark on their large-scale charitable project, but they also could not have reached such acclaimed status without government support. In addition to having connections to several prominent businesspeople, they had connections with the then Minister of Social Solidarity, Ali Musalhi. El-Shohdi was on a first-name basis with the minister: "I met with Ali—he is absolutely willing to help, he is open to taking on new ideas." In fact, the food bank advisory board also had cozy relations with Ali Gomaa, then the Grand Mufti of Egypt, second in religious authority only to the sheikh of al-Azhar University. Ali Gomaa was the overseer of Dar al-Ifta, the highest body residing over religious law in Egypt. Gomaa also had a business background; he had studied commerce before completing his graduate studies in Islamic jurisprudence and eventually became a full professor at al-Ahzar University. In 2004 he was appointed Grand Mutfi by President Mubarak and issued several controversial fatwas. Notorious for his so-called liberal interpretation of religion, his conservative lifestyle protected him from widespread criticism. Examples of his controversial fatwas include a fatwa forbidding female genital mutilation, a staunch stance against terrorism, a fatwa in favor of women becoming judges or heads of state, and an additional one permitting fixed interest rates. He took a strong stance against "radical" clerics and their "fanatical" followers and became famous through his newspaper column, television appearances, and Friday sermons at Masgid Sultan Hasan.[23] In addition to attending the food bank's launch, Ali Gomaa issued a fatwa on *zakat* for the bank. The fatwa stated that *zakat* could be used to serve all those in need, regardless of their religion, thereby validating donations made to the food bank.

While the Egyptian Food Bank does not describe itself as an Islamic charity, faith was an inspiration for its leaders. *Zakat* and *sadaqa* were important funding sources and the bank's association with the Mufti provided the foundation with another layer of legitimacy. Even organizations that did not identify themselves as Islamic had close ties to religion. It is this merging of private-sector expertise and faith that constitutes pious neoliberalism. The food bank is one of the clearest examples of how pious neoliberal subjects change the charitable landscape; it is one of Egypt's most distinguished charities precisely because of the way it was able to bridge a commitment to faith with private-sector leadership. These businessmen used strategic planning, access to capital, and a vast and powerful social network to turn the food bank into a household name. The food bank took the existing culture of charity, applied a private-sector perspective, and produced an organization that transformed food politics across the nation. This trend of bringing business and charity together was transforming numerous other charities as well.

"Not just from the heart, but from the mind": Mustafa Mahmud Mosque Complex

The mosque complex of Mustafa Mahmud has received unmatched scholarly attention as an exemplary Islamic association.[24] Armando Salvatore, a German social scientist, describes it as the "most significant case of public Islam in post-Nasserist Egypt."[25] Founder Mustafa Mahmud was renowned for demonstrating the compatibility of science and faith and then linking them with services. Denis Sullivan, one of the first to write about Egyptian associations, saw Mahmud as an "Islamic entrepreneur," while Salvatore referred to him as "a normative entrepreneur able to invest the moral view of individual responsibility, social obligations, and imperatives of progress."[26]

Mustafa Mahmud was born to a modest family in the Nile Delta town of Tanta in 1921. He was trained as a medical doctor and practiced medicine from 1952 to 1966. A proficient writer, he spent many years questioning religion, which led to a radical change of faith in the late 1960s, when he became known as a deeply religious man and a pivotal public figure in the reconciliation of science and religion. In the 1970s, he invested a great deal of money in causes he supported; as he gained popularity, people began to donate money to these causes. He built a mosque and the association in 1975, which included the first free medical clinic in Egypt at a time when there were no international organizations working in this area. After the medical clinic was established, the square where it was built became a key space for social services as schools and other service providers mushroomed in and around the square.[27]

The mosque sits on a crowded boulevard, Avenue of the Arab League (*Gami'at al-Duwal al-'Arabiyya Street*), in the upmarket Giza neighborhood of Mohandiseen, named after the middle-class engineers who inhabited the district in the 1960s. In front of the mosque is Mustafa Mahmud Square, a large patch of green space in an otherwise concrete jungle (Figure 17). The fame of the mosque complex stems mostly from the medical clinic; patients from the entire governorate trek through horrendous traffic to receive services here. Having heard a great deal about the mosque, I was eager to interview the association's administrators. I arranged for an interview with Refat, the director of social services at the Mustafa Mahmud Association.

Figure 17. The Mustafa Mahmud Mosque complex sits on a crowded boulevard in the upscale neighborhood of Mohandiseen. It serves as a node for social services in Giza. Photograph by the author

Upon my arrival at the complex, Refat welcomed me with great enthu-siasm. He told me, "I become inspired when I see young people like you become interested in *khayr* (good deeds)." He was very proud of the asso-ciation, which he described as a social foundation (*mu'assasa igtima'iyya*), because of its involvement with numerous smaller organizations. He began by telling me, "I take my job seriously. I want to help the poor, not waste time," and described the organization as a charity organization (*gam'iyya khayriyya*) engaged in development (*tanmiya*). Refat explained that the organization relied heavily on charity to sustain itself: "Much of the work we do is through people's *zakat*. In 1976, I began working in the medical cen-ter. In 1986, just three years after I finished college, I came here. . . . At that time, we had really limited evaluative facilities, but today we have every-thing we need. . . . We get one million LE or more in donations a month. These donations really enable the work we do."[28] Mustafa Mahmud was a charity, but what distinguished it was a systematized and professional approach to charity (Figure 18). Refat emphasized their professionalism:

Most charitable organizations work based on a handouts model. We entered the charitable scene as professionals—our board is all highly educated. [The founders] used to discuss handouts but were interested in the issue of human development. So the project started with caravans, medical caravans. They would arrange for professors to go to rural areas and deliver health services in cycles, because these areas lack health resources. But what they discovered was that they don't have the human resources either; they were very weak and so they thought about a way to develop them.[29]

By entering the charitable scene as professionals, the founders brought their work experience to bear on the association and explicitly labeled their work as development. As part of their development program, Mustafa Mahmud ran a *qard hasan* program based on animal production rather than cash lending. The program began as a spinoff of the health caravans: "We decided to provide a rural farmer with a pregnant cow, and then he needs to pay back the cost of the cow by giving the baby to his neighbor. Then we started to train them to begin making milk, cheese, etc. That way they can produce for themselves."[30]

Refat saw poverty as a problem of production: if the poor were given the proper tools and skills, they would be able to help themselves instead

Figure 18. Advertisement for Mustafa Mahmud on a truck used to transport goods to those in need. Photograph by the author.

of relying on charity. He repeated the "fish and the fishnet" analogy and explained that the organization focused on giving the poor tools and culti-vating an ethic of self-reliance. An ethic of self-reliance assumes that people are capable of and willing to monitor and regulate their own conduct. At the same time as the poor were being taught to have self-discipline, they were also subject to intense systems of monitoring and evaluating that implicated the poor "in the order into which they are integrated."[31] The organization provided the Egyptian farmer with tools and training that en-abled him to be productive rather than rely on charity.

Refat described the association's unique structure. It collected funds and used that money to fund its activities as well as the medical clinic. The medical clinic operated on a sliding scale, based on need. Evaluative serv-ices at the clinic were offered for a symbolic fee between 2 to 8 LE and treatment was offered at different discount rates based on income. The doctors received one-third of the fees collected. Most doctors worked in state-run hospitals in the daytime and ran private practices in the evenings. They volunteered one or two days a week at the clinic and were more interested in receiving godly rewards (*thawab*) than additional income, so most donated their fees back to the clinic. All workers other than doctors and the board were employees. Refat saw this as an advantage: "If I had volunteers instead of employees, we'd be slowed down. So we are employees except for the board. . . . I think having volunteers is sometimes problematic. When you give someone a salary, the person works harder, they are more dedicated. With a volunteer, you can't really rely on them."[32] While many associations, such as Zahrawan and Resala (discussed in the next chapter), saw volunteerism as an asset and a key pillar of their work, Refat considered a reliance on volunteers a liability. Volunteers are usually middle or upper-middle class, while those employed in charitable associations seemed to come from a variety of class backgrounds. Having salaried employees further professionalized charity since these employees could then be held accountable to the organization, not just to God.

In the medical center, there were various classes of rooms, based on payment. Those patients who could afford to pay full price did. Such individuals might request their own room, although most patients who paid for regular treatment usually share a room with one or two others. Patients who received free care were placed in a room with a number of other patients. Refat explained that the money of the well-off subsidized the others. The clinic supplemented the nationalized system, where individuals might have waited years for service. Despite the huge number of medical clinics, these voluntary associations could not accommodate everyone. Several medical centers I visited used the same model of sliding scales and echoed the importance of full-paying patients whose payment subsidizes services for the poor. Sullivan described this as a "capitalist enterprise founded in the name of Islam" and asserted that it is a "model of achievement with financial benefits accruing to the staff and low-cost health care for thousands of patients."[33] Given the terrible state of health care in Egypt, most mosques were affiliated with a *zakat* committee that in turn was associated with a health clinic. Collectively, faith-based health clinics were a low-cost alternative to poor state care, and the lower and middle classes preferred the care these clinics provided to that of the state.

Like the health-care system, a parallel, privatized education market arose to supplement the faltering and underfunded public education system. Over the past fifteen years, approximately twenty new private universities opened and private secondary schools proliferated by the day. Traditionally reserved for the wealthy, private education spread to the middle class with mid-tier private schools, an indicator of the neoliberalization of education. Since public educators are poorly paid, many give private lessons on the side. These lessons are not really optional, many students fail without private lessons from their instructors. Many mosques provided private tutoring to schoolchildren, or helped families with tutoring fees, especially those preparing for their final year of high school exams.[34] The educational system had become a labyrinth of institutional arrangements. Private universities frequently issued a handful of scholarships to students at the top of their class, while numerous Islamic charities provided full-scholarships for international Muslim students from low-income countries to study in Egypt. Like the Al Alfi Foundation, discussed in chapter 4, Mustafa Mahmud provided scholarships for university students to attend *private* universities. While Al Alfi provides scholarships for expensive schools like the American University in Cairo or the British University in Egypt, Mustafa Mahmud provided scholarships to mid-tier universities. Refat explained: "Today there is a huge problem in education. Students with scores less than 93 percent can't even go to the universities they want to go to; some can't afford the expensive private universities. So we are providing funding for students to go to the less-expensive private schools, the ones that cost 2,300 LE tuition. That way, those who want an education but can't afford the outrageous fees will get an opportunity."[35]

Refat recognized that there was a systemic problem with the education system in Egypt, but he did not suggest a systematic solution. The organization's response was to help students enroll in the second-tier private-sector schools rather than attempt to address the failing public school system, thereby perpetuating class hierarchy over generations. The organization paid directly for students' educational needs while subsidizing privatized care. Refat acknowledged that the association was "filling in the gaps" in social care left by a decimated welfare state, but he was also careful not to describe the state as incompetent. Instead, he emphasized how they helped the state:

> We were the first ones to do a food bank. . . . There are the artisan workshops. . . . We also built training centers, we have a computer center in Agouza, literacy programs and sewing classes. We train women how to weave carpets. . . . In addition to our *qard hasan*

program for youth in rural areas, we also support microenterprise projects for youth in Cairo. We provide them with training as well. . . . Have you seen any organizations of this size in your work? All of Mohandiseen relies on us, the Governorate of Giza relies on us for our services, especially medical. . . . What the government can't do, we do.[36]

His statement reinforces the notion of state failure; the voluntary sector stepped in where the state was incapable. The Mustafa Mahmud Mosque complex provided social services, medical care, and employment opportunities that the government no longer could provide. By "filling the gaps" in social care, Mustafa Mahmud was "supplementing" rather than providing an *alternative* to state care: "We are supporting the government social service work, by supplementing it. They can't do it alone anymore; society can't continue to rely on the government only for social development. Look at America, 90 percent of social care there is private."[37]

Refat argued that the supplementation of state care with privatized care was a positive change, but privatized care legitimates budget reductions for social services. Starving the state is a key technique of neoliberalism, as budget reductions make state services less effective, thereby leading more people to pursue private services. Thus the introduction of private care was a self-perpetuating cycle that extended neoliberalism into social service provision. Charities needed larger donations to keep up with the demand for privatized care, so more donations came from businessmen, who in turn had made their money in the previous wave of privatization. The organization received large donations from businessmen and relied on Islamic charity to support its programs. Yet financial pressures compelled charities also to pursue income-generating projects. Refat explained, however, that strict government rules regarding revenue generation created an obstacle to the sector's efficiency: "One problem we have is we can't produce things. If any organization could work in productive areas—factories for example, then we could get increased efficiency. . . . We could use the revenue from those factories to support our social programs."[38] Although the ministry had pressured organizations to become development-oriented, it continued to enforce restrictions on their activities. Under increasing financial pressure, charities fund-raised aggressively, sometimes competitively, in the private sector. An associations' ability to fund-raise relied on a combination of private-sector allies and religious legitimacy that is emblematic of pious neoliberalism. At the same time, as charities pursued private-sector donations, CEOs, frequently exposed to the CSR mantra, judged that it was in their interest to engage in charitable work. They saw their participation as a win-win; they could support projects, improve their public image, and gain free publicity. Refat did not mention any specific businessmen who supported his organization, but casually indicated that the association consistently exceeded its fund-raising goals. However, he was critical of businessmen who used charity for publicity purposes: "Everyone wants credit for himself. . . . They don't want to work together. So many people are using charity as a public relations tool because advertising and marketing pages in newspapers are up to 2,000 LE now. When you hear [names specific organizations], then [names specific companies] come to mind."[39] Refat criticized corporate social-responsibility campaigns that spend equal amounts on projects and the advertisements showing what they have done. He believed that corporations should stick to their business expertise and seemed to resent their entrance into the charitable sphere; he preferred to see private-sector expertise applied by individuals.

Refat also described the importance of job creation in helping to decrease poverty in Egypt. Many businessmen had told me that unemployment was not due to a lack of job opportunities but rather a mismatch between the jobs people expected to hold and the type of jobs that were actually available. The problem was compounded by the legacy of guaranteed employment during the Nasser years, which led young men away from manual labor. Refat echoed the sentiment that people are too selective about their employment: "Not everyone has to have an office job. But that's what they want. I have a nephew who works in tourism, that's his degree. He got a good job in a hotel and got upset about serving alcohol. But to me, that's a waste of time. That's his job—tourism. He shouldn't have gone into it if he was so concerned about alcohol! That's the thing these days—people are so misguided."[40] Refat reiterated that religious and cultural perceptions of acceptable work contribute to the unemployment predicament. His stance was unusual; I had never heard a pious man employed by a mosque voice acceptance of alcoholic beverages being served. It seemed that Refat's pragmatism trumped any kind of moral judgment on the issue. This led me to ask Refat more questions about his view of religion. Bringing Islam into the conversation struck a chord with Refat as he proclaimed:

In my opinion . . . in many ways, Islam is more strongly
implemented in Europe than here! Because there is so much
development, so much thought, so much ethics in the way people
do their work—much more so than here. There is no comparison;
it is not an issue of income, but of thought, of culture. . . . The
thing is, organizations don't understand that things have to
come not just from the heart, but also from the mind. Most
organizations don't know how to deal with human development. . . .
There is a big issue of not knowing how to implement things.[41]

Refat saw Europe as more Muslim because he perceived Europeans as
more organized and in possession of a strong work ethic. His understanding of what it meant to be Islamic included strategic thinking, honesty,
education, competitiveness, and competence—business with Allah. He was
adamant to demonstrate that the "backwardness" of many charities marked
them as un-Islamic and characterized his association's work as development. His reference to Europe led me to ask if he had traveled or lived
abroad. He responded:

I went to school in Beirut for some time. . . . I was an avid reader of
German culture and philosophy. I read a lot of psychology and philosophy. And [one founder], he lived abroad extensively; half of his
year is practically in Europe. But for me, reading is half of traveling.
Dr. Mustafa Mahmud, when he was alive, he used to have discussions with youth of the *hara* [small neighborhood]. The problem
now is that there is so much ignorance and misunderstanding.[42]

Refat's admiration of German culture and philosophy seemed to influence
his interpretation of what was Islamic. Linking piety with professionalism
is a core tenet of pious neoliberalism. Many of the professional charity
administrators I met received Western education and spoke admirably of
the West's educational and industrial advancements.[43] But they also spoke
proudly about Islam's golden past and told me that Muslims had taught
the West algebra. This narrative of progress and regression worked to
legitimate the merging of piety and neoliberalism. Refat emphasized the
Islamic tenets of social solidarity, trusteeship, and concepts of justice that
informed his charitable work. At the same time, he believed in the Western

project of development and sought to professionalize Islamic charity. Combining Western efficiencies with an Islamic framework of social care is the task of a neoliberal Islam.

"Your Door to Good Deeds": Dar al-Orman Association

Dar al-Orman Association is one of the largest and most well known Islamic charities in Egypt. It was awarded the first "Most Successful NGO" prize by the Ministry of Social Solidarity in 2011–12. The director of operations proclaimed, "We are successful because people have faith in us. We have built trust over time and we have transparency."[44] Headquartered in the lower-middle-class neighborhood of al-Haram, bordering the Pyramids, the association has 32 chapters, 740 employees, 6,500 volunteers, and more than 33,500 projects, across 17 governorates, mostly in Upper Egypt. Ahmed al-Qabbany, his business partner, Dr. Khaled al-Noury's wife, Zeinab, and a professor named Magdy Batran, founded the organization in 1985. Qabnoury is the name of their successful metal and aluminum company; although the company had no direct affiliation to Dar al-Orman, it certainly provided a stream of private-sector donations. From its inception, the association was concerned with supporting orphans and cancer patients. The organization provided transportation, meals, and accommodation for cancer patients from rural areas to enable them to receive care at the government-run Kasr al-Ainy Hospital in Cairo. Since its formal registration with the Ministry of Social Solidarity in 1993, the association extended its work into income-generating projects for the poor.

Dar al-Orman is headquartered in a modest multistory apartment building in a remote alley (Figure 19). In my interview with the public relations manager, Moustafa, he talked about the organization's income-generating work:

> Around 1993, we started to limit handouts and to focus on getting small projects off the ground, giving out cows, getting kiosks started, training women to sew or do tricot [a type of knitting]. Lots of activities. . . . You know the Chinese proverb, "Don't give a man a fish. Teach him how to fish?" The idea then is to get some kind of income going for them. . . . That's the only way to deal with social problems from the root. Income generation is the major goal of these initiatives.[45]

Figure 19. Dar al-Orman Association headquarters in al-Haram. Photograph by the author.

Despite Moustafa's focus on making individuals productive, the association balanced charitable projects with development initiatives. Dar al-Orman's slogan, "Your door to good deeds" (*bawwabtak li-l khayr*) invokes the Arabic word for charity (*'amal khayri*) directly. Dar al-Orman provided support for twenty-five thousand female heads of households a year, medical treatment for nearly five thousand disabled individuals at a cost of 35 million EGP, and funded cancer treatment for twenty-six thousand patients a year. The association ran an orphanage with more than sixteen hundred orphans and was a primary sponsor of Orphans' Day. Orphans' Day occurs on the first Friday of every April; between 2004 and 2009, more than seven hundred and fifty thousand children participated. The organization was an important advocate for orphans; it had lobbied the government to change laws regarding orphan care; opened hundreds of community halls for orphan day care; arranged for waivers for all school fees for orphans, including access to higher education; and created a database to facilitate Orphans' Day across associations, leading to two hundred and fifty thousand annual participants.[46] The association entered the 2010 *Guinness Book of World Records* for having the largest numbers of orphans participate in Orphans' Day and the holiday was taken up by the Arab League to become a regional phenomenon.

While Dar al-Orman was engaged in a vast array of activities, Ahmed al-Qabbany emphasized the projects that made villages more "productive," such as a microenterprise program called "the small farmer," a *qard hasan* program, and vocational training for men and women (Figure 20). He described "the small farmer" program as a microenterprise building initiative that helped individuals in rural areas start income-generating projects, be it a *kushk* (street kiosk), a phone and copy shop, or a café. The association helped construction-trade workers (electricians, plumbers, and carpenters) open their own businesses (Figure 21). The association gave 31,500 farmers livestock that produced an average income of 550 LE, for a total of EGP million LE. They helped establish more than seventy-six hundred kiosks that produce an average income of 500 LE per month. Individual kiosks cost 7,500 LE to create, coming to a cost of 120 million LE. The association emphasized "development and production." Microfinance and microenterprise development gave the poor the tools, training, and access to capital to become self-sufficient. Ahmed described some indicators of income-generating success; the typical cow project generates income for the farmer of 550 LE a month, while kiosks create revenue between 450 and 600 LE

Figure 20. Dar al-Orman's "small farmer" program provides farm animals to the poor to help them improve their livelihoods. Photograph by the author.

a month. Like other associations, Ahmed was proud of turning recipients into donors and shared these stories as indicators of their success—"a young man in Minya that we helped turn a *kushk* into a supermarket, enabling him to become a donor of *zakat* rather than a recipient."[47]

The *qard hasan* program provided loans of 180 LE a month to poor rural women over a six-month period that they used to produce arts and crafts. The wireless company Mobinil had recently created a partnership with Dar al-Orman to fund *qard hasan* for artisan craft workers, particularly carpenters. The *qard hasan* program also provides farmers with money to buy supplies. The loanees were expected to pay back the loans interest-free at 20 LE a month. Despite a focus on income-generation, the association had not converted its *qard hasan* program into microfinance but still gave out interest-free loans, reflecting the association's religious roots. In 2006 the association went back to its roots in another way. Its growth moving forward would rely on private-sector partnerships. The managing director told me that 25 percent of donations came from businesses, 50 percent from prominent businessmen, and the remaining 25 percent came from individual donors and student groups. Businesses such as TE Data, the private university called the 6th of October University, Bank al-Ahli, and Swiss General were among their donors. In a 2012 follow-up visit, I asked how the business had been affected by the poor economic climate. He indicated that donations from small business donors had increased, individual donors had decreased, and yet overall donations had doubled since the year before to 145 million LE, "Now more than ever, donors appreciate that we do our work with precision and dedication to God. . . . We follow up on our villages and donations for years and years. That is why our donations keep increasing."[48]

Dar al-Orman became even more reliant on private-sector funding expertise with the 2006 establishment of a philanthropic initiative called "A Foundation for Every Village." Forty businesspeople donated nearly 3 million LE to develop eight villages on the list of Egypt's one thousand poorest villages.[49] The businesspeople were financially responsible for a

Figure 21. Dar al-Orman's qard hasan program helped this electrician to open his own shop. Photograph by the author.

village, from beginning to end, including food procurement, health care, literacy, medical treatment, and infrastructure building. Dar al-Orman drew upon its founders' social network to mobilize private-sector expertise and provide private-sector funding, planning, and supervision to help the villages improve their standard of living. The businesspeople provide the ideas and donations but were not involved in the administration. Dar al-Orman maintained close relations between the businesspeople and the villages, including holding a monthly strategy meeting. They worked in the areas of skill-building/upgrading, including training for carpet-weavers, potters, and other artisans. By 2009 the association had covered nearly twenty-six villages at a total cost of 150 million EGP.

By 2012 they had developed sixty-seven villages, taking on approximately twelve new villages per year. I accompanied the board of directors on a visit to one of the "completed villages" in 2012. The association rented an air-conditioned bus and several board members brought their children along. A videographer and photographer accompanied us to document the work, which could serve as publicity for the success of the association

Figure 22. Girls walk home with jugs of clean water in Fayoum. Dar al-Orman created a water-treatment facility for this village. Photograph by the author.

when recruiting other business donations. The director of the board, a generous and boisterous man, led the tour. He recited passages from the Quran while describing all of the association's achievements. The association had paid to connect homes to the public electricity grid and ensured clean water through a water-treatment facility nearby (Figure 22). They set up literacy programs, provided transportation to the nearest medical facilities, provided cash assistance for those unable to work, and sponsored income-generating projects for those able to work. They had renovated homes with roofs, flooring, bathrooms, and tiling (Figure 23). I inquired why some homes were renovated and others were not, as I had previously thought the entire village was covered by the "Foundation for Every Village" concept. The director told me that only those households that qualified were renovated. In order to qualify, the family had to undergo an extensive social research process that entailed an assessment of their property, bank accounts, income statements, household size, and other assets such as livestock. The director reminded me that everyone benefited from the electricity and water. Dar al-Orman's goal was to find private-sector

Figure 23. Dar al-Orman renovated this man's house as part of its foundation for the "Every Village" program. Photograph by the author.

partners to cover one hundred villages over the next eight to ten years. As the public-relations representative explained to me, "The private sector is the third actor in the development triangle with civil society and the government. . . . The future of civil-society organizations in Egypt lies with businessmen. They are taking the lead."[50]

Dar al-Orman is an example of how associations evolved over time and in relation to broader processes in the economy. Unlike many of the organizations I studied, they saw charity and development not as polar opposites but as two sides of the same coin: "The charity projects help people meet their needs; development projects improve living conditions. We believe you have to work on both fronts. Charity is a part of development."[51] The association promoted private-sector engagement in the development process and fostered entrepreneurship and an ethic of self-reliance among beneficiaries. Yet religion was an important way in which they propelled their growth; their advertisements to solicit donations drew on Islamic invocations to give and their reputation as servants of God drew in donations by the millions. They relied on Islamic charity as a major source of donations, regardless of whether the giver was an individual or a business. Their reputation as an honest Islamic charity provider gave them the legitimacy to further their developmental projects. Despite their identity as a charity, the association is well regarded by pious neoliberals. In 2009 the association joined an informal network of "the main charity associations in Egypt" to coordinate the distribution of Ramadan food bags. Ahmed was proud that Dar al-Orman could sit at the table with the other prominent associations, including Misr el Khayr, the Egyptian Food Bank, al-Gam'iyya al-Shar'iyya, and the Cancer Hospital. While a broader alliance was unsuccessful, it at least put some of the biggest charity players at the same table (Figure 24). The biggest charitable associations in Egypt were also able to begin collaborating because they were all in the good graces of the Mubarak administration. The collaborating associations shared faith and a business ethic, both of which are essential to pious neoliberalism.

Conclusion

The entry of private-sector players and values into the social sphere is a core tenet of neoliberalism; it resulted from the rising supremacy of corporate power, concerns over competitiveness, the incorporation of businesses into the management of welfare states, and the outsourcing of social

Figure 24. Although associations often work in isolation, the biggest associations collaborate on Ramadan food-bag distributions. Photograph by the author.

care.[52] Surprisingly few people were critical of the increasing role of business in social enterprises. In fact, charity administrators, the staff at the Ministry of Social Solidarity, and international development experts all praised the growing role of the private sector in development. In my interview with a corporate social responsibility (CSR) consultant, he told me that "market-based solutions are benefiting the poor" by providing employment opportunities, SME (small and medium enterprise) development programs, CSR, "pro-poor investments," and "sustainability through supply-chain integration."[53] The poor also voiced a preference for income-generating projects. One aid recipient said, "Loans are better because I became able to work, open a house, and feed myself," while another said, "A kiosk is preferable because the one who would give me today, will not give me tomorrow."[54] The poor were not seekers of infinite aid, as the entrepreneurs had feared; rather, they sought to meet their basic needs, which their stagnant wages no longer covered.

The inclusion of private-sector players into the charitable landscape profoundly shaped the priorities of associations and their attitudes toward the poor. Associations used intensive social research systems to ensure that their money was going toward the right kind of poor. They shifted their charity work to a development model and emphasized market-based solutions to poverty, such as employment, upgrading skills, and microenterprises. While this trend was pervasive among the organizations I visited, what this meant in practice and the extent to which the organizations shifted their priorities in line with market-based solutions varied greatly. Some associations remained charities but adopted private-sector expertise and the language of neoliberal development. Other organizations simply changed their names to development associations rather than charitable ones. However, name changes were just one indicator of an *ideological* change: along with the consensus regarding the failure of government provision of social services came a newer consensus that the inclusion of the private sector as a development actor was the way forward. The work these organizations did under the banner of development depended upon the education of those involved, their relationship to the West, their view of international aid, and their interpretation of Islam.

An Islamic notion of social solidarity led many well-to-do businesspeople to feel obliged to give to the poor. Business leaders became more involved in charitable work, bringing their private-sector expertise to bear on the sector. Islamic charities became more involved in development, shifting money toward income-generating projects, and in order to receive aid recipients had to become productive. These associations implemented market-based solutions as part of their charity work. However, their identification as charities and the way they drew on religious discourse marked them as distinct from other development actors. The partial and incomplete participation of Islamic charities in development exposes the contingency of neoliberalism. Neoliberalism may work through other entities and in political processes, but this attachment does not leave it intact. Just as neoliberal development changed Islamic charities, the slipperiness created by Islamic associations between charity and development changed (at times even challenged) neoliberalism. One charitable entrepreneur exhibited some of the contradictions of pious neoliberalism when he said: "Everyone is so focused on the short term only and it is an increasingly negative cycle, but I wish it were a positive cycle instead. . . . I think the way we go about implementing *zakat* is wrong—people use so much selectivity when it comes to religion. They take what they like. . . . If we did it right, we would not have this problem with poverty." While he lamented the state of Egypt's charitable landscape, he remained hopeful that Egyptians could one day figure out how to apply *zakat* as a tool for development. According to this entrepreneur, the "right way" to do *zakat* involved a systematic, coordinated approach. Pious neoliberals seeking to do *zakat* in the "right way" produce a new paradigm of Islamic development.

· CHAPTER 6 ·

Islamic "Life Makers" and Faith-Based Development

A sad young man sits alone in a dark room filled with cobwebs. There may be a prayer mat, as he may be praying, or there may be playing cards, games, or some other worthless things. Anyway, he is a sad young man sitting alone in his room. We came to him and asked him why he was sitting alone in a dark room, we gestured him toward the light and convinced him to get out with us, to venture into life, to be successful and help us in "Making Life." This was actually what the first three introductory episodes were about. When the young man tried to get up, he could not. He found that his hands were chained by negativity and lack of responsibility. His feet were chained by carelessness, and there was a very heavy chain around his neck, it was the lack of a goal in life! We told him that he would not be able to get up unless he frees himself from all these chains and shackles! We started the first phase, the current one, which is freeing ourselves from the chains. The chains started to break. He got up and freed his hands and found himself moving, and he wanted to get out of his room, but we stopped him, and that is the second phase. How will he succeed in life, gain self-confidence and discover his talents? He sprang ahead filled with hope, determination and a sense of success. He even tore down the door instead of merely opening it. He found a world full of light, a country that needs to be built. He was pleased with himself, but he was alone. Suddenly he found many young men and women, just like him, coming out from their dark rooms, and they all joined him in "Making Life." We told them to coexist like one team, and succeed together. This will be the third phase, and this is how we will make life.

This is a story presented in a lecture by Amr Khaled, the most prominent character in a transnational Islamic revival that calls on youth to establish faith-based development organizations (FBDOs) across the Middle East.[1] He preaches in colloquial Arabic and Egyptian slang, coupling motivational speeches filled with emotional stories of Prophet Mohammed with a participatory call-and-response model. Khaled uses stories like this one to foster an Islamic revival (*nahda*). His sermons inspired many youth to become involved in *khayr* through volunteerism. His website is the third most popular Arabic site in the Middle East and in 2005 it got more hits worldwide than Oprah Winfrey's site.[2] He is known as "the cool preacher, the Islamist in jeans who knows how to talk to young people in a language they understand."[3] In his lecture on youth and the summertime, he asked, "Does Islam allow having fun? Yes! We want you to be merry, we want you to have fun and to laugh. We want you to play, swim, and be happy, but without sinning!" He uses sayings of the Prophet to mobilize youth to give charity. "The Prophet (SAWS)[4] says 'charity eliminates Allah's anger the same way water extinguishes fire.' This means that by opening your closet and giving away the clothes, Allah (SWT)[5] will forgive all your bad deeds, because you gave away and spent for charity."[6] Khaled's appeal lies in how seamlessly he blends religion, self-reliance, and business principles—a clear articulation of pious neoliberal subjectivity. He particularly appeals to the well-to-do Egyptians who desire a spiritual and fulfilling life that does not shun materialism and consumerism. For Khaled and his followers, the best model of success is capitalism melded with Islamic social values.

Using management science and self-help rhetoric, Khaled calls upon Muslims to "do something good" and, in the process, promotes volunteerism and entrepreneurship as religious acts. His approach embodies pious neoliberalism, the discursive combination of religion and economic rationales that encourages individuals to be proactive and entrepreneurial in the interest of furthering their relationship to God. The production of pious neoliberal subjectivities is partially undertaken by FBDOs; the organizations featured here couple self-help and management-science rhetoric with religion in their quest to participate in the development process in Egypt. Combined, the language espoused by Khaled and the work of the FBDOs discussed here embodies pious neoliberal subjectivity. This chapter illustrates how Khaled and four Islamic development associations cultivate these subjectivities.

I focus on Khaled for several reasons. First, Khaled, through his "Life Makers" program, has inspired a broad movement of FBDOs that stretches far beyond Cairo. The founders of the organizations discussed here enact the precise kinds of projects Khaled espouses in his lectures. Khaled is far from the sole impetus for these organizations; however, several interviewees did mention Khaled as a key inspiration for their foray into FBDOs. Second, both the language used by the leaders and the language of Khaled's Life Makers movement are part of a new discourse that emphasizes the compatibility of Islam and neoliberal ways of thinking and being. I discuss the Life Makers movement because it exemplifies the attitudes and motivations of numerous FBDOs in Egypt and across the Middle East. Khaled is an important figure in the growth of FBDOs writ large, but he does not have an explicit connection to the organizations. Rather, he and these organizations together constitute the milieu within which pious neoliberalism emerges.[7] The faith-based development projects that these organizations implement constitute pious neoliberalism in various ways, promoting volunteerism, industrial development, human development, and a much broader definition of piety than most other charitable organizations in Egypt.

There is a strong semblance between the pious neoliberal ideology espoused by Khaled (in his Life Makers lectures) and that of many of the young FBDO leaders I interviewed. I draw attention to the processes of subject formation invoked through Khaled's program by tracing "those practices that try to shape, sculpt, mobilize and work through the choices, desires, aspirations, needs, wants and lifestyles of individuals and groups."[8] The examples I employ demonstrate how individual acts of piety become acts of polity. Khaled became a celebrity across the globe as a champion of Islamic FBDOs. Many journalists hypothesize that his popularity and iconic status for Islamism in Egypt led the Mubarak regime to perceive of him as a security risk. Khaled left Egypt for the United Kingdom in 2002 out of a proclaimed fear of persecution. Despite his departure, his website, television shows, and cassette tapes continued to circulate widely and have left a profound mark on FBDOs in Egypt. The Khaled phenomenon also opened up a space for numerous other pop-preachers, such as Mustafa Hosni, Moez Masoud, and Khaled al-Gendy.[9] Since the Egyptian uprising of 2011, Khaled frequently returns to Cairo as part of his efforts to foster a *nahda* in Egypt.

Shapers of Destiny: "Life Makers" and the Making of Responsible Subjects

Khaled, calling his project "faith-based development," stated in an interview, "The first piece of the puzzle I am completing was faith; after that I moved onto development." In a series of forty-six lectures and a movement he called "Life Makers," Khaled outlined the steps, skills, and benchmarks for creating a *nahda* (Figure 25).[10] The main objective of Life Makers is to encourage people to be productive, useful, and influential individuals and to take on effective and beneficial roles in serving their country. Khaled promotes a parallel focus on personal piety and volunteerism, "We must never forget the part of faith and worship while carrying out a practical project. We must seek help by praying, fasting, and worshiping alongside every voluntary act we do." Khaled focuses on individual subjecthood and an individual's role in society, shifting seamlessly between responsibility to oneself, to the nation, and foremost to God. This scaling of responsibility emerges in his definition of Life Makers as "selfless people who are concerned about the welfare of their countries. . . . People toiling, not for their own good, but for Allah (SWT) and their religion."[11] He encouraged

Figure 25. Egypt's Islamic televangelist Amr Khaled delivers a speech to a crowd of followers. Photograph by "Iraqidude" from Wikipedia's *Creative Commons.*

individual subjects to take after the prophet, who learned "the art of management, the art of governing, and the art of war."[12] The Life Makers series
is about the production of pious neoliberal subjects.

Khaled's Islamic development movement focused on productivity and
self-reliance. The goals of the Life Makers program include, "1. Creating a
generation that has a useful, effective and dynamic role in their communities. 2. Instilling hope and optimism among the youth. 3. Increasing our
perseverance in Allah's path and in resisting sin."[13] The Life Makers action
plan includes two stages. The first one is "implanting in oneself the value
of success," which includes belonging to Islam, feeling responsible, being
positive, being diligent and exerting effort, realizing the value of time, pos-
sessing intellectual depth, seeking excellence, safekeeping resources, appre-
ciating art and beauty, and having a goal in life. The second is "instilling
confidence in oneself," which includes having willpower, discovering talents, innovation and creativity, organized thinking, realizing the value of
knowledge and work, taking initiative, working with examples and models,
setting priorities, making use of social intelligence, learning the art of communication, overcoming challenges, cultivating perseverance, acquiring a
clear vision, and planning.[14] While the majority of these traits are "soft" skills,
Khaled scripts these skills as part of what it means to be a good Muslim.
He outlines the responsibilities of a Muslim, "There is something in Islam
called individual duty and something called collective duty. . . . The individual duty is what every individual should do on his own, like praying and
fasting. Nobody else can do these duties for you as long as you're alive. . . .
The collective duty is a command which is imperative upon all Muslims,
but if only one performs it, it will be sufficient. However if no one performs it then the whole *ummah* is in great sin."[15] Khaled uses "collective
duty" to enforce the notion of individual responsibility and encourages
individuals to be as useful as possible. He asks, "How can we change the
whole 24 hours into profit and energy? How can we invest the 24 hours in
the best way?" His answer is by learning how to participate in the "fruitful
week," which includes working productively every day, worshiping more
than the minimum, engaging in daily fitness, and socializing.[16] Khaled's
emphasis on productive time resonates with Max Weber's considerations
on time: "Waste of time is thus the first and in principle the deadliest of
sins. . . . Loss of time through sociability, idle talk, luxury, even more sleep
than is necessary for health, six to at most eight hours, is worthy of absolute
moral condemnation."[17]

Khaled admires the West for its advances in literacy, scientific research, and industrial ethics, as well as its ability to cultivate educated and focused subjects. He uses statistics in his speeches, including the United Nations Development Program indices and figures that depict the Arab world as "behind" the West.[18] In contrast, he sees the West as immoral and declared that the Muslim world needs to turn to Islam in order to have its own renaissance: "We do not want to lead a life like those living in the West. They have immense problems and the material lives they are leading have taken the best out of them. The best model is the Muslim model, if it is put into practice properly."[19]

By emphasizing business and entrepreneurship, Khaled presents the "dreams of achievement" in science and industry and the importance of microenterprise, artisan crafts, and industrial development as the path to prosperity and a means of gaining access to heaven. Khaled envisions a world where, "every businessman would build a training centre for his industry. These training centres would mainly be for unemployed youth, where they would be trained in various crafts, instead of remaining idle without work. If every businessman were to open a small training centre, call the youth to start training and promise to employ the best trainees in his factory, this would help them, as well as the society. Moreover, it would contribute to solving the problem of unemployment."[20] He sees microenterprise, artisan crafts, and technological and industrial development as the path to prosperity and heaven: "As for the *thawab* (reward) you will get, listen to this saying of the Prophet (SAWS), 'He who leads a way for seeking knowledge, Allah will forward for him a way that leads to paradise.' Every time you sit at your PC to learn, this is a way to paradise."[21] Khaled also encourages youth to be proactive and productive. He said that "when you think of something good that could be done and you are able to do it, then you do it yourself without even mentioning it to anyone . . . the garbage in the streets. Get rid of it yourself. The pothole in front of your house. Fill it yourself . . . at your college if the laboratory is lacking some instruments, collect some money from your colleagues and buy those instruments . . . making use of every minute of your life."[22] In an effort to explain how to be productive, Khaled gives examples of what he sees as models of success: university students changing old prayer mats at the college mosque with new ones at their own expense, students repairing the facilities on campus, painting their campus, and making visits to the elderly, or an engineer who opened a training center.[23] Testimonials demonstrate the benefits of participating in Life Makers: "My friends and I started to think of a project that will benefit Islam and our communities.... I gained increased self-confidence, new management skills, and a feeling of responsibility."[24]

Khaled has had an immense effect on Egyptian religious life, an effect that has very visible manifestations. Through his sermons, he inspired numerous (particularly upper class) women to wear the veil and youths to become involved in the *nahda* through FBDOs. Khaled has inspired the establishment of several organizations both within larger NGOs and across college campuses. His language illustrates one way Islam is being narrated in relation to neoliberalism, the result being the cultivation of pious neo-liberal subjects. The discourse and actions of these four FBDOs illustrate how pious neoliberalism unfolds on the ground. With the exception of Resala, and in contrast to the other associations discussed in this book, these organizations were founded as development organizations rather than charities. They are a part of cluster III *"tanmiya Islamiyya"* or Islamic development (see Figure 5 in the Introduction).

The often Western-educated middle- and upper-middle-class followers of Amr Khaled merge their religiosity with management science. Because these groups aim to attract upper-middle-class youths to volunteer, they have broadened their definitions of religious practices. They embrace the West, literally and figuratively. Many work in multinational corporations, speak fluent English, and have traveled abroad extensively. These Khaled followers look to Cairo's gated communities and extravagant shopping malls as markers of Egypt's modernization as well as beacons of success. These pious neoliberals forge their own narrative of progress, blending an economic-development agenda focused on efficiency and productivity with what they see as Islamic social values. They use *zakat* and *sadaqa* to fund development projects rather than as a form of charity, a move that requires a more fluid vision of Islam. Rather than draw on discourses of social justice and income equality, their narration draws on self-help and management science. The first organization, Resala, is a charity rather than a development organization, but I have included it in this chapter for several reasons. First, the organization was begun by a group of youths, like the other organizations discussed in this chapter. Second, the organization is focused on volunteerism and responsibility and illustrates how volunteerism has become a dominant expression of *sadaqa*. Third, it is one of the largest and the fastest-growing Islamic associations in Egypt. In just over a decade, Resala established more than thirty branches, with offices in almost every Egyptian governorate. Finally, the language espoused by Resala staff noticeably expressed pious neoliberal subjectivities.

Resala: Inspiring Volunteerism

Resala, which means "message" in Arabic, was established in 1999 by a group of student activists from the College of Engineering at Cairo University (Figure 26).[25] The group began by performing community service around campus, organizing blood drives, painting the walls of buildings, and preparing Ramadan food bags for campus service workers. In December 2000, a relative of one of the organizers offered to donate a piece of land in the Faisal neighborhood of Cairo on the condition that they make the ground floor a mosque and have a project up and running within three years. The students did a feasibility study and found out that the building they envisioned would cost 200,000 LE to build.[26] They fund-raised extensively and had a facility built in nine months with an actual value of 750,000 LE (mostly from in-kind donations). The main project was a medical center with examination and treatment services. They also have an orphanage, a hospital, and a school in Maadi. Medical care was a key concern that Nadia, one active volunteer, noted because, "People have medical needs, and if they go to the government public hospitals, by the time they reach their turn they could die. So we provide the equivalent of private services for a small symbolic fee."[27] They also have an orphanage in their Maadi branch that houses 170 orphans, 24 of whom are school age. They recently started a school so the orphans, the blind, disabled, and deaf who use their services could all attend under their supervision. They waited over three years for the permits. The pharmaceutical company Seif donated 4 million EGP in land in Maadi for Resala to build the hospital and they fund-raised more than 21 million EGP to finish it. The hospital covers a full range of specializations and surgeries.

Volunteerism lies at the heart of the organizational structure, which has a paid staff of only thirty employees and more than forty thousand volunteers. Dr. Abdelazeem Sherif, the man largely behind the organization's success, is a visionary leader and role model. Twice a week he parades around Resala's offices delivering recruitment speeches to groups of potential volunteers. According to Dr. Sherif, "It is volunteers who run this organization. Our enthusiasm and belief in God keep us strong. . . . Resala opened the door to charitable work and people came. They are the gems

Figure 26. Resala is one of the largest voluntary organizations in Egypt. Its vans move supplies and services to the informal settlements and villages where it is most needed. Photograph by the author.

of the country." One evening I heard him present the rewards of volunteerism to a full house of potential recruits:

> Ask yourself, what did you do in the service of the nation? Islam is about helping people, caring about others through social solidarity. Volunteers are actually the ones who gain the most of all. What better way to build yourself a house in heaven? It is the poor who allow us to go to heaven. . . . How much do you trust in the rewards of volunteerism? In the afterlife, and the current life, the rewards are endless. . . . You will gain success. You will gain happiness! Feelings of *usefulness* and *self-satisfaction!* Respect, people's love! . . . Lots of people who donate their time increase their salaries afterward from the connections they make. . . . Your good deeds are returned to you. . . . You can give, money, efforts, anything. And if you don't have either, come and we'll help you. (public speech, Dr. Sherif, August 24, 2006, emphasis mine)

Resala calls attention to the rewards of volunteerism (usefulness, success, satisfaction, social networks, salaries, etc.) and links those rewards in the current life to rewards in the hereafter (your good deeds will be returned to you). Individuals may volunteer in the interest of furthering their relationship to God, but material benefits are equally motivating. The linking of material and spiritual benefits is one of the hallmarks of pious neoliberalism; it also facilitated the formation of a halal lifestyle market. In this narration of Islam, being a good Muslim entails producing and consuming. Dr. Sherif shares Khaled's attitude toward productivity, necessary skills, and the motivations for charitable work. He also speaks a similar language to Khaled, combining a very polished and professional look and speaking in sophisticated language that simultaneously emphasizes religion and efficiency. Religion was not just mentioned in the recruitment speeches (through invocations) but was also embedded in the organizational structure. Recruitment sessions were timed to allow evening prayers on the ground floor of the mosque and all the women I met in Resala wore the veil. In my discussion with Dr. Sherif about what inspires his work in Resala, he told me about his time living in Kingston, Ontario, where he, like Khaled, took some inspiration from the West. He said, "I had a real awe of the volunteerism and charitable work in the West, the size, and the extent is amazing. I made lots of comparisons between the West and here, and did lots of reading in my effort to understand how the sector became so established and so mature."[28]

Dr. Sherif's emphasis on size and stature as well as Resala's strong focus on youth volunteerism differentiates it from other Islamic charities.[29] Resala's goal is to create a model that can eventually be exported outside Egypt and its dreams of achievement correspond with Khaled's progress narrative. As Dr. Sherif said: "Look at all we've accomplished in the first six years. What do you think will happen in the next six years, God willing? We'll be even bigger than McDonalds!"[30] Resala mobilizes the financial support of the upper middle class and the energy and enthusiasm of the younger generation to bring a new focus on volunteerism among youth and promote civic engagement. The organization has rendered volunteerism and community engagement "cool" and visible; it has grown at an unprecedented rate and its visibility in public and privatized spaces contrasts with the mosque-based character of most charities in Egypt. The organization has grown from being a Cairo phenomenon to having a presence in nearly every governorate in the country, usually in large and impressive buildings residing on two hundred to four hundred square meters of land (Figure 27). Its size and visible presence in most social clubs and shopping malls in Cairo are evidence of the organization's success. Finally, Resala was one of the first organizations to move *da'wa* work outside the mosque and into everyday spaces like malls and sporting clubs. In contrast to most Islamic NGOs in Egypt, Resala is mobile—it brings its resources to the poor (in their neighborhoods) as opposed to having the poor come to them. As such, Resala is producing a new geography of giving that changes spatial relations between the classes and allows for new spaces of interaction to occur in Egypt.

Al-Buraq: High-Tech Development

Al-Buraq was established because the chairman of the board, an IBM computer executive in his early thirties, entered a Ministry of Communications and Technology entrepreneurship contest and won. Al-Buraq used the contest proceeds to launch a development center, a hybrid venture-capital investment company, and an incubator/knowledge academy for high-tech start-up companies. Al-Buraq's mission is "to provide the right environment, resources and support to nurture ideas" for small start-up companies with "a culture built around high quality, innovation, and ethics." Although this

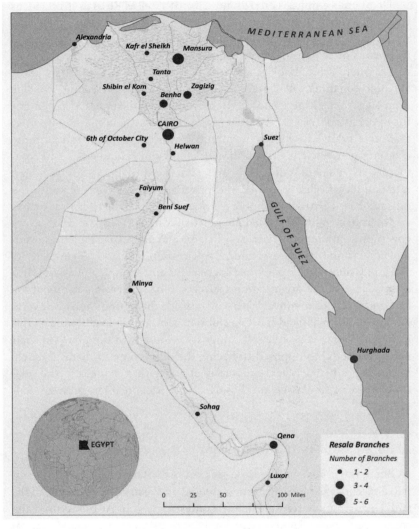

Figure 27. The Resala Charity Association has branches in nearly every governorate of Egypt. Map by Nuala Cowan.

sounds more like the start-up business model that became famous in the United States in the 1990s rather than a development organization, the founders claim to be engaged in development work and fall in line with the development trend of encouraging social entrepreneurship. One of the founders, Ahmed, a twenty-one-year-old engineering student at a public university, identified their organization as developmental: "Yes, we aren't really addressing the poor. We want to address able people and let them work in the high tech-industry. Then it will trickle down to the rest of society. This isn't just microenterprise, but development. We want to raise the level of society."[31] The founders of al-Buraq believe that fostering employment in the skilled sector will trickle down to the poor. Ahmed's statement about poverty is remarkably similar to those made by the proponents of welfare reform in the United States in the 1980s. Their model "gives the poor an opportunity to help themselves" rather than rely on "handouts." Rather than work with the poor directly, they apply engineering, science, industrialization, and productivity to stimulate SMEs (small and medium enterprises).

The organization's strong connections with wealthy businessmen and the corporate sector have shaped its approach to development. Drawing on the discourse of corporate social responsibility (CSR) enabled the organization to fund-raise one million EGP to support eleven different projects. The reliance on CSR instead of *zakat* allows the organization to move beyond the categories of eligible *zakat* recipients in the Quran and thus allow for the transition of charitable monies toward development. Opening up development work to CSR funding also facilitates the inclusion of private-sector expertise, language, and practices into development. The project also corresponds with one of Khaled's dreams for industry—"to have a yearly prize sponsored by a large businessman or a country for the best industrial invention in the Arab world."[32] According to the al-Buraq Development Center proposal, the idea behind the incubator is to help start-up companies by providing professional, technical, and financial assistance to further a business's chances of success. The proposal for the venture-capital investment company and incubator contains a mission statement, goals, and milestones, with an operational model, specific target measures, analysis, tools, and activities, sources of sustainability, and exit criteria, in addition to potential strategic partners, and the famous SWOT analysis (strengths, weaknesses, opportunities, threats) from business schools' analytical toolbox. Just as Khaled emphasized in his sermons, the organization is goal-oriented; it aims for at least 40 percent of the selected start-up projects to be operational and to spin off at least fifteen successful companies in the first five years. The organization's focus on business enterprise and productivity as well as its use of business-school models is emblematic of neoliberal development ideology.

Ahmed not only saw his organization as developmental but faith-based as well. He said that the group had an unspoken agreement that "God was motivating their work." In addition to donning all the visible markers of piety for men, including a long beard, frequent recitation of Islamic aphorisms, the avoidance of eye contact, and not shaking hands with women, he spoke knowledgeably about the Muslim Brotherhood's ideology and networking strategies. He emphasized the importance of religion as a motivation to "do good" but also was very focused on "benchmarks and measurements of success." He described al-Buraq as "religious but not antimodern; we are interested in what works, we believe in the value of secular knowledge." Al-Buraq's combination of faith with a business orientation is illustrative of pious neoliberalism. The members are driven by an unwavering faith and a desire to please God. They see themselves as entrepreneurs who combine religiosity with a desire to do something good for their nation, which fulfills the first goal of the Life Makers program—"creating a generation that has a useful, effective and dynamic role in their communities." Al-Buraq members espouse the neoliberal conviction that they can address poverty without working directly with the poor. Their seamless combination of the language of management science (with an emphasis on business skills and productivity) with a proclamation of faith, an unspoken agreement that their work is for God, is precisely the kind of coupling that constitutes pious neoliberalism.

Gayth: Fulfilling the Dreams

I met Yousef for our interview at an upscale café in Heliopolis to discuss Gayth, an organization that operates inside a larger social welfare organization called Ikhtar Osra. Yousef was a serious young man in his early twenties with a discerning disposition. He spoke knowledgeably about Amr Khaled and the *nahda* that he envisioned. He described the *nahda* as a public discourse in which people talk about their will to improve the place they live by bringing a different level of enthusiasm toward development.

He said, "Once upon a time the Muslim world was teaching Europe and was far more developed scientifically. There is a desire for us to reach this level again." This idea resonated precisely with the rhetoric of Amr Khaled, but what differentiated Yousef was his belief that "too many people are trying to do development in Egypt but in a wrong way. . . . It is very easy to focus on *human development,* but not many people are thinking about industrial development, and they need to complement one another" (emphasis mine).[33]

Yousef and his friends, engineering students at the publicly funded Ain Shams University, founded Gayth in early 2005 as a development project that would create employment while at the same time meeting a need of their own—the production of circuits. At first, they were a group of about ten students who researched the necessary requirements to create a project that would employ needy and uneducated individuals in the high-tech sector. It was a small project in which approximately thirty students from their college participated. The goal of Gayth was to employ Egyptian families in the production of electronic circuits that could be used in their engineering labs as well as in some industrial settings. Given that these students did not have the wealth and resources to set up their own NGO, they decided it was more practical to become part of a larger organization. They explored the possibility of support from several larger NGOs and Ikhtar Osra was the first organization to offer support. The students performed the research, design, and marketing of circuits and then trained individuals to do simple tasks in an assembly-line fashion. Doing so allowed them to produce something that requires great expertise (a circuit) without actually having to teach the workers any technical knowledge (engineering). Ikhtar Osra provided a steady stream of individuals in need of employment who could work on Gayth's assembly line. Electrical engineering students initially created the circuits for use in their projects, but then the students began to design components that could function in commercial products, such as the circuits in an automated light switch. Through this project, Gayth worked to fulfill another one of the "dreams" that Khaled articulated in his lectures: "to locally manufacture all electronic circuits used in mobile phones, computers, television sets and video recorders."[34] Knowledge is most valued when it is applied to solve real-world problems and technology plays a key role in the promotion of pious neoliberal subjectivities.

Several other components of Gayth 's project produce pious neoliberal subjects. Gayth focused on job creation through industrial development. The organization was not interested in teaching women how to sew, as most welfare-oriented organizations do. Instead, it was training people to work in specialized, unskilled, but in-demand jobs that have the potential to raise income levels. The organization's business-oriented planning documents included research design, followed by a strategic plan, marketing research, and financial analysis. The founders took courses at Zidny to improve their business and leadership skills and to recruit other students. In my interview with Yousef, he repeatedly used terms such as "best practices," "self-sustaining," and "systematic," and employed a constant reevaluation of the organization at every level, admitting that the project was a work in progress and that they were learning along the way. Yet when I asked him about the obstacles they face, he said, "We are lucky we have our faith to help us through struggles, trust in God, and a scientific approach. We learn from our experiences and work systematically." Although they mostly applied business skills to development, Yousef also stated that what held them together was a "moral contract that is based on a religious belief." He explained that it is an unspoken agreement but still a common bond, which he attributed to the influence of Amr Khaled. He said Khaled was "the inspiration, part of public discourse that people are trying to improve the place they live in and bring enthusiasm toward development." This ethos of people doing whatever they can, however small, to improve their country is similar to the hopefulness of the 2011 uprising. In some ways, the uprising capitalized upon the insight and idealism of the youth-led development associations and was a scaled-up expression of this "do what you can" phenomenon that had begun years earlier.

Zidny: Human Development Training

The offices of Zidny were on the top floor of a newly renovated three-story building next to the largest mosque in Nasr City, Rabi'a al-'Adawiyya. Zidny, translated as "give me more," began as a group of five young people with jobs in multinational corporations (MNCs) who received human development training as part of their professional work and wanted to spread the skills they gained to youth who had yet to begin their careers. Their offices were part of the Rabi'a al-'Adawiyya complex, which includes the mosque, a ten-story medical center, a meeting room, a *zakat* committee, a youth committee, and Zidny (Figure 28). As one of the largest mosque complexes in Cairo, it is a key node in the geography of giving in Egypt. Hassan, the public relations representative and co-founder of Zidny, told

Figure 28. Zidny is housed in the mid-rise building to the left of Rabiʿa al-ʿAdawiyya's zakat committee. Photograph by the author.

me the organization's story: "We started about the same time as Life Makers, Resala, and al-Buraq. It took us about three years to get off the ground, but we found a real niche in human development and NGO consulting. We came before [Life Makers] by seven months, although we did co-sponsor some team-building activities with them. The first one was an activity with Amr Khaled."[35]

Zidny conducted professional-development training seminars for college students. It launched its first event in January 2000 and expected two hundred students to attend; in the end, two thousand attended. The NGO offered condensed sessions designed around the summer months, when youths usually roam the streets, smoke, hang out with friends, and watch movies. Their target market was youths seeking MNC employment, college students, and secondary school students. The goal was to turn these youths into "productive citizens" by teaching leadership, communication, time management, and business skills to the largest number of youth possible. Demand was highest from female students in public universities studying engineering, medicine, or business administration because they do not have the resources in their universities to support professional development programs. Responsibilization, a hallmark of neoliberalism, leads individuals to pursue supplemental educational programs to ensure their success instead of addressing the structural problems.

Zidny was self-sustaining; funding for the programs came from attendee fees. In a neoliberal era, NGOs increasingly face pressure to become financially sustainable via income-generating projects. They generate a great deal of revenue (an average of 1,000 LE a day) with an average of six hundred to a thousand attendees in each course, paying 50 LE per course or 120 LE per workshop. In addition, their operating costs were minimal since volunteers ran the courses and they paid a room rental fee of only 300 LE. The organization grew to support ten full-time staff and twenty-five volunteer leaders as it expanded its offerings to youth in secondary schools.

Zidny was directly engaged in the goals of the Life Makers program: to empower youth by giving them the skills to succeed (in a neoliberal world). It offered courses in time management, communication skills, creative thinking, and business applications and their instructors were consultants and trainers from the largest MNC training center in the Middle East, who volunteered their time with Zidny. The time-management course included planning, leadership, and self-learning; the communications course includes the principles of *emotional intelligence* and *social metrics*; the creative thinking course provides trainees with a toolkit for problem solving; the final course, business skills, included banking, management skills, financial skills, and working the stock market. The curriculum included popular American self-help books such as *The Seven Habits of Highly Effective People* by Stephen R. Covey, *How to Win Friends and Influence People* by Dale Carnegie, *Men Are from Mars, Women Are from Venus* by John Gray, *Emotional Intelligence: Why It Can Matter More Than IQ* by Daniel Goleman, and Michael Porter's *Competitive Advantage: Creating and Sustaining Superior Performance.*

In my separate interviews with two founding members (Hassan and Moustafa), each spoke of the influence Khaled had on their work and the importance of efficient management skills. Moustafa stated:

> The new style of *da'wa* encourages the civic role of individuals and volunteerism and has had a big influence on the way people think about charitable work. . . . Look at Sama', al-Buraq, Zidny, we are all individuals with similar values working in this vein.[36]

Both mentioned Amr Khaled and Life Makers several times and used references from the Life Makers program, but neither of them had directly mentioned Islam, so I decided to ask Hassan if he considered Zidny to be an Islamic association. His response was indicative of a specific scripting of management science as Islamic:

> It seems people don't see that planning and organizing is Islamic. That's the thing about Islamic organizations; they don't have an accurate idea of what is Islamic. . . . I think the organizations that are following the traditional Islamic approach are missing a big opportunity. They aren't picking up on the learning that can be done from a skills-based model. And that's missing in Islam. . . . I think Amr Khaled really changed things. Before him there wasn't this same space for interpretation. . . . Islam isn't just about *Shari'a.* We try to be a model of what Islam truly is by implementing what works and doing it well, honestly, and in a way that makes a difference.[37]

In line with Khaled's management-science approach, Hassan said that a strategic and skilled-based approach is what it means to be Islamic. To be a good Muslim, one must be productive. Having business skills was scripted as Islamic just as Khaled scripted thinking as Islamic "Thinking is an Islamic obligation: we are committing a sin if we do not think, did you know that?"[38] Pious neoliberalism here entails attaching piety to efficiency and professionalism. At the end of our interview, Hassan told me: "I am a firm believer in development over charity. Five to ten years from now, civil society organizations will play an even larger role in society. . . . What we need in the sector is professionalization. Things are very positive in many ways, even though we have a long way to go."[39] Zidny founders strongly believed in the paradigm of FBDO, supported the rise of the private sector as a development actor, and spoke disparagingly about charity as "handouts." They displayed a markedly optimistic sense of the future, and focused on youth development, which resonated strongly with the first two goals of the Life Makers program. Their approach, while understatedly faith-based, relies on an understanding that to do something successfully is to do something with faith and professionalism.

To demonstrate their level of professionalism, Moustafa described an NGO club that Zidny initiated, which included specialized classes on NGO management. The project emerged out of demand from other NGO leaders who had already attended more basic courses. Approximately three hundred to four hundred highly educated professionals from Nasr City, mostly twenty- or thirty-something, had attended the workshops, and the NGO club evolved out of the synergy of so many individuals with similar goals and interests meeting in the Zidny offices. Moustafa used a great deal of business rhetoric as he explained Zidny's growth and the development of this NGO club; he used terms such as "skill upgrading," "self-development," "capacity building," "leadership," and "specialization." When I inquired about club, which was the first time I had heard of formal cross-organizational cooperation, he elaborated:

> All NGOs came here to learn as individuals looking for self-development. They met here and began cooperating more because of the meetings here. You know, networking, cooperating on joint ventures works, but acquisitions don't work because there is a serious lack of teamwork. They have the same motivations (spiritual needs) but different strategies being employed. The services are different and difficult because individuals have a certain way of thinking about out their work, and each one thinks

his strategy is best. . . . But the idea is to create an environment that is conducive to cooperation. . . . We created the environment, they came, people connected, and it took off from there naturally.[40]

Zidny's professional development program and NGO club cultivated pious neoliberal subjects with an implicitly Islamic ethic of self-reliance. Zidny managed to create a space for cooperation between associations despite the deterrence of state security. One of the first trends in the voluntary sector since the fall of Mubarak has been the establishment of hundreds of specialized NGO coalitions, opening up a space for collaboration that never existed during the Mubarak years.[41]

Development in Egypt and in the Hereafter

FBDOs are an expression of pious neoliberalism—a discourse produced by a new breed of religious leaders and organizations who combine religion and neoliberalism in a way that encourages individuals to be proactive and entrepreneurial in the interest of furthering their relationship to God. The coupling of piety and material gain is not unique to Islam; it can be generalized to other religions, although the manifestation varies in relation to the specific context. Pious neoliberalism also links volunteerism and faith. The rhetoric of individual responsibility, proactiveness, self-help, choice, and accountability resonates across cultures and places as market-based solutions have become the retort to the escalation of social ills. The malleability of the neoliberal project to varying cultural contexts is marked by the success of global discourses to produce a consensus around shifting responsibility for social ills onto individuals. Holding individuals responsible then moves the gaze away from state or societal failures and to the inescapable conclusion that failure to succeed in the neoliberal world is a result of individual shortcomings. FBDOs in Egypt illustrate how neoliberalism diffuses globally and yet morphs in relation to specific geographical context as it operates through other political projects, in this case religion.

In Egypt, pious neoliberals offer a locally produced solution to escalating social problems by linking Islam and development. Despite variances across these organizations, there are strands of similarity in how religion and economy are scripted together. Upper-middle-class, highly educated, religious technocrats produce a discourse that lauds piety and wealth. Faith-based development is shaped by an Islamic notion that charity is a key expression of one's dedication to God, as well as by an equally important neoliberal discourse of self-reliance and management science. The values of productivity, efficiency, and individual responsibility are part of neoliberalism and focused on material change now, yet the motivations and orientation of FBDOs is focused on the afterlife. Amr Khaled and the members of these organizations believe that Islamic social values blended with Western efficiencies constitute the best of both worlds. This blending leaves neither Islamism nor neoliberalism intact. Islamic neoliberalism entails the removal of two important characteristics of preceding Islamist movements: income redistribution in line with an understanding of social justice as equity, and an anti-western political fury articulated by many Islamist circles. Islam inspires the participants in FBDOs. However, unlike their more traditional counterparts, they endorse a Western model of economic development and its associated narrative of progress. Rather than provide "handouts," they focus on job creation and development programs that make the poor self-reliant and entrepreneurial. They use *zakat* and *sadaqa* to fund their initiatives, which requires an alternative interpretation of the categories of *zakat* recipients and an expanded notion of *sadaqa* that emphasizes volunteerism. These organizations inspire volunteerism, emphasize productivity, and expand the meaning of and spaces for *da'wa* throughout Cairo. Their work quashes culturalist claims that Islam and modernity are antithetical. Thus, a space of compatibility emerges between Islam and neoliberalism, a space that is increasingly visible throughout Cairo. This narrative of Islam is not an alternative to neoliberalism but instead is an iterative product of a dialectic relationship between religion and neoliberalism.

Each FBDO discussed in this chapter exposed a different iteration of pious neoliberalism. Resala marshaled the financial support of the upper middle class and the efforts of youth, rearticulating the importance of volunteerism by linking it to the cultivation of one's relationship to God as well as tangible awards in their current life. Al-Buraq worked to stimulate entrepreneurship in the knowledge economy, arguing that industrial ethics and innovation were important components of Islamic development. Zidny combined an emphasis on skills, specifically business skills and management science, as part and parcel of what it means to be an Islamic association. These groups promote various scales of responsibility as individuals become self-optimizing for themselves, in the interest of the nation, and to strengthen their relationship to God. FBDOs spread *da'wa* outside formal religious spaces and into everyday spaces. Islamic development associations are much more mobile than Islamic charities because they moved *da'wa* and social-service provision out of the middle-class hubs and into otherwise isolated neighborhoods. In addition, FBDOs have important consequences for the pathways of development and change; in Cairo, it has changed the spatial divide between rich and poor, with more upper-middle-class volunteers venturing into informal settlements. It has also led to the formation of NGO clusters and the inclusion of faith-based messages in spaces of consumption, fostering the halal marketplace. FBDOs are part of an Islamic revival that carves out religious spaces in everyday life, further normalizing the coupling of religion and economy.

FBDOs have shifted the attitudes of many youth toward pious neoliberal ways of thinking and being. These organizations, regardless of their size and number, became key spaces where pious middle and upper-middle class Egyptian youths articulated their religiosity and expressed their social values. Fostering private businesses, promoting entrepreneurial subjectivity, and focusing on upgrading skills for the poor have become neoliberal *and* Islamic modes of being. Voluntary organizations played a key role in the expansion of neoliberalism and Islamism simultaneously; they facilitated a space where the professionalized development industry and rising religiosity could meet. The on-the-ground development initiatives of FBDOs promoted pious neoliberal subjectivities—the combination of "Western efficiency" with "Islamic morality." FBDOs around the globe combine piety and capitalism regardless of their specific faith as they enact good deeds in this world while "building a house in heaven."

Conclusion

PIOUS NEOLIBERALISM is both the product and generator of particular political economic arrangements between the state, the private sector, and individuals. In Egypt, the neoliberal authoritarian police state created the prime context within which pious neoliberalism could flourish. As the Egyptian state became more market-oriented and Egyptian society became more visibly pious, pious neoliberalism produced new practices, institutions, and subjectivities, including an Islamic framework for development, a halal lifestyle market, private foundations, and subjects who were disciplined by religion and the market simultaneously. This book has highlighted the inseparability of charity from the economy and in turn the inseparability of the economy from cultural and political forces, including religion.[1] Charity and economy are not discrete categorical imperatives; they are mutually constitutive. Charity is an important but undercounted part of the economy and political-economic arrangements shape charitable practices.

Pious neoliberalism in Egypt was a product of the neoliberal authoritarian police state. The government of Hosni Mubarak decimated the overstretched welfare state, privatized state-owned industries to the benefit of the military and a small elite class, and pursued economic growth without regard for escalating inequality. The neoliberal economy widened inequalities and devastated social cohesion. In the midst of a decaying welfare state and a neoliberal economy, Islamic charity came to play an enormous economic role—helping the poor meet their basic needs while enabling the wealthy to purify their money. Islamic charities came to play this role in response to state interventions that marginalized both Islamists and the poor. The government saw religion as a threat to its legitimacy and pursued invasive practices of governing (which existed long before 9/11, particularly when it came to the surveillance and monitoring of Islamic groups). Decades of the state's meddling in the affairs of Islamic associations had numerous unintended consequences: Islamism expanded in everyday life spaces; Islamists gained legitimacy as they called for free and fair elections; the Egyptian public came to believe, just as Mubarak-era fearmongers had preached, that all Islamic practices were undertaken by the Muslim Brotherhood. The state's attempt to undermine organized Islam and co-opt religion into the state apparatus actually gave Islamists more legitimacy. While I argue that most Islamic associations were independent from the Muslim Brotherhood, the Brotherhood undeniably benefited from the discursive association (perpetuated by the Mubarak regime and secularists alike) between Islam and the Brotherhood. The government's fixation on the Brotherhood as a political/security threat furthered the Brotherhood's legitimacy while enabling it to receive credit for the work of numerous independent, locally operating Islamic associations. An authoritarian police state complemented neoliberalism as a form of governing, challenging the Eurocentric assumption that neoliberal governmentality occurs primarily in an advanced liberal context.[2] Liberal and illiberal forms of governing actually merged with one another, illustrating the connection between political economy and apparatuses of security.[3] Nonstate actors produced their own regime of truth alongside of and in tension with the state's authoritarian yet neoliberal government. In this case, authoritarianism enabled pious neoliberalism.

Pious neoliberalism is not only produced but also is *productive*.[4] Islamic charities were spaces of economic activity, producers of subjectivity and spaces of governing. Islamic associations are examples of the spaces where personal conduct coalesced with political or civic conduct. Faith was mobilized as an apparatus of governing. By governing, I mean that charity is a critical site of subject formation and an apparatus for managing the population. Decentering the state, I focused on how Islamic associations constituted a different scale and logic of governing, one that worked through both faith and the market. Individuals discipline the subjects they seek to help and in turn are also disciplined by the associations for which they volunteer.

Pious neoliberalism is one way to understand this transformation.[5] The combination of a neoliberal development ethic with Islamic charity blurred the boundaries between charity and development, between social welfare and capitalism, as well as between the voluntary, private, and public sectors.[6] Private-sector players entered into the *gam'iyyat* as professionals and deployed a different approach to Islamic charity that entailed giving conditionally, employing social research systems, and engaging in a discourse of Islamic development. Islamic charity administrators adopted the

language of free-market development as they merged private-sector expertise with Islamic concepts of social solidarity (*takaful*), trusteeship (*amanah*),
and obligations to aid the poor (*zakat*). They were often Western-educated
and emphasized the value of science, measurement, efficiency, and accountability. At the same time, they saw religiosity as a necessary component of
their work and scripted efficiency and self-actualization *as* Islamic. Faith is
entirely compatible with a neoliberal economic rationale, as neoliberalism
and Islamism were never polar opposites. At the same time, neoliberal
development is not all-encompassing, complete, or inevitable.[7] The combination of neoliberalism and Islamism in fact left neither intact. The Egyptian government pursued economic liberalization for over thirty years, yet
the process was partial, incomplete, and continues to be deeply contested.
The welfare state has not been entirely dismantled; a social welfare ethos
resides side by side with the emergence of an Islamic ethic of self-reliance.
A strong culture of giving is institutionalized through Ramadan and continues to be the driving force behind charity. While most individuals and
charities continue to give direct aid to the eight categories of *zakat* recipients outlined in the Quran, they reinterpreted and reevaluated the precise
meaning of these categories. In the case of Islamic economics, practitioners minimized the significance of charity as components of an Islamic economic system and emphasized Islamic banking and finance. Interpretation
(*ijtihad*) provided the elasticity to transform Islamic economics away from
mediating social concerns (mainly poverty) and instead toward maximiz-
ing profits.[8] Pious neoliberalism, then, exposes the contradictions and limits of both neoliberal development and Islamism.

Pious Neoliberalism and the Egyptian Uprising

The limits of authoritarian-neoliberal tactics of governing were tested on
January 25, 2011, as millions of Egyptians took to the streets demanding
an end to more than thirty years of dictatorship. The world was stunned
as it watched peaceful revolutionaries in Tahrir Square chant "Freedom,
bread, social justice" and demand their economic and political rights. The
immediate scholarly response to these protests highlights the secular bias
that dominates academia and the internalization of the truism that secularism, development, and democracy go hand in hand. Pundits and scholars alike insisted—in fact celebrated—that the protests were secular in
nature. The implicit assumption is that only secular subjects would fight

for freedom, social justice, democracy, or human rights, or that Islam is somehow incompatible with these values. As the pictures of thousands of people kneeling on the ground in prayer with tanks aimed at them can attest, religion was an important component of the protestors' subjectivity and "in between shouting for their economic and political freedoms, Egyptians prayed in the streets" (Figure 29).[9] The ruling military council and the protesters alike participated in this polity; neither took advantage of the prayer to advance on the other. The image of the protestors paused for prayer, with Christians circled around Muslims kneeling on the ground in prayer, invokes what Asef Bayat calls a "different kind of religious polity, one which both wishes to promote pious sensibilities and takes democracy seriously."[10] Religion was an important part of Egyptians' subjectivity, regardless of their faith.[11]

The Egyptian uprising, then, is a stark reminder that the neat boxes we create to understand subjectivities are not so neat—the people who took to the streets for those eighteen days were "not guided by any singular organization, ideology or personality."[12] In the days following Mubarak's

Figure 29. Protestors in Tahrir Square pause for prayer during the Egyptian uprising of 2011. Photograph by Ahmad Faheem.

departure, revolutionaries were not united by much, but they *were* united in their call for a liberal technocratic government. A technocratic government consists of economists, statisticians, scientists, and development "experts" who produce knowledge informed by their professional experiences in order to shape and validate governing practices. The technocrat is engaged in "forms of thought, knowledge, expertise, strategies, means of calculation or rationality" that value efficiency, market rationality, and transparency.[13] Much as numerous charity administrators emphasized to me the importance of efficiency, planning, and development—various technologies of governmentality that were embedded within their organizations—Egypt's young revolutionaries employed a similar language. The revolutionaries did not get the kind of secular technocratic government many envisioned, but they did get a technocratic government nonetheless. Even after the 2013 ousting of Mohamed Morsi, one point of continuity was that Egypt would continue to be ruled by "experts."[14] Pious neoliberal subjectivity played an important role in both the Egyptian uprising and the political aftermath.

Pious Neoliberalism in Post-Mubarak Egypt

Pious neoliberalism offers a framework for undoing false dichotomies and understanding the complexity of political subjectivities. The blurring of the boundaries between faith, economy, and governing discussed in this book as pious neoliberalism permeated Egypt before the uprising, and it remains relevant still. My interlocutors were deeply involved in what they saw as building a better world. The struggles they had, their hopes, dreams, and values, are indicative of the kinds of subjectivities that permeated Egypt before and after the uprising. These individuals are pious (neo)liberals, people who maintained that religion , a market-based economy and democracy could go hand in hand. It is this combination of piety with faith in liberalism and the market that constitutes a pious neoliberal subject. This book has focused on Islamic charity in Mubarak-era Egypt in order to highlight the inseparability of economic, social, and political acts, but the layering of these spheres is all the more apparent in post-Mubarak Egypt.

The first post-Mubarak political party to rule Egypt revealed the salience of the term "pious neoliberalism." In the wake of the 2012 election of the Muslim Brotherhood's Freedom and Justice Party (FJP), Islamists and secularists both contemplated how the Brotherhood's rise to power would affect the Egyptian economy. Secularists worried that the Brotherhood would disrupt Egypt's capitalist economy by instituting an Islamic economic system—one that would impose Islamic guidelines on companies, including banning *riba* (usury), forcing Egyptians to pay *zakat* (alms), and prohibiting businesses from engaging in un-Islamic activities, particularly selling alcohol, maintaining beaches with scantily clad Western tourists, and other activities associated with tourism/leisure spaces. Islamists, by contrast, argued that they would not radically alter the Egyptian economy, that the fears of such practices had been exaggerated, and that what distinguished their economy was adherence to Islamic principles that prevent corruption while protecting workers and the poor. Both groups presented extreme narratives of what an Islamic economy might look like; in reality, the economy that the Islamists sought to craft was a pious neoliberal one.

Devised by a team of technocrats, the FJP emphasized the importance of the private sector, respect for private property, competition, and a culture of self-reliance as part of their political platform. Encouraging capitalist economic development, the party advocated for the development of productive small and medium enterprises (SMEs) as the solution to poverty, supported the continued privatization of state-owned industries, and a reduction of subsidies that disproportionately affect the poor.[15] It called for increased efficiency of management and transparency and proposed a regressive Value Added Tax (VAT). Once elected, President Mohamed Morsi requested a $4.8 billion loan from the IMF that would have required further entrenchment of neoliberal policies (including reducing subsidies) and pursued a total of $44 billion in private- and public-sector investments.[16]

Although the economic platform of the FJP was decidedly capitalist—supporting private ownership, businesses, and market-based solutions—it was also Islamic. The party made no mention of banning fixed-interest rates, but called for the "gradual replacement of usurious institutions and transactions with Islamic ones" and passed new regulation for the Islamic banking sector, including permitting the issuance of *sukuk* (Islamic bonds).[17] In response to fears that an Islamic-led government would reduce international tourism, the FJP vowed to increase tourism by introducing a halal tourism market to supplement the existing one.[18] The FJP also invoked Islamic piety to call for the protection of the poor; used Islamic concepts like *takaful* and *amanah* to define "the deserving" citizen, and supported both state-sponsored welfare programs and microloans for the poor.[19] The Brotherhood, then, was crafting a new pious neoliberal economy, one that selectively drew upon Islamic economic principles *and* a globalized, neo-liberal discourse of development.

The FJP platform also brought renewed relevance to the concept of Islamic development—Morsi won Egypt's first democratic election on an Islamic development platform called the Nahda (Renaissance) Project, which resonates with the version of Islamic development described in this book. The project promised to rebuild Egyptian individuals, society, and the state through an emphasis on economic development, empowerment, and human-resource development. The Nahda sought to restore *waqf*, encourage volunteerism, and promote the growth of civil society. Their faith-based development program promised to draw upon the success of the private sector to fuel civil society and in return educate Egyptians to meet the needs of the private-sector job market. The Nahda was to provide equal opportunity to all Egyptians by fostering small and medium enterprises; it pledged to enhance technical support, financial studies, and other tools in its pursuit of a market-based solution to poverty.[20]

The discourses of Islamic development endorsed by the FJP, including self-reliance, volunteerism, and entrepreneurship, bring us full circle back to Amr Khaled. In 2012 Khaled referred to the introduction of his "Life Makers" program as the equivalent of "standing in Tahrir Square ten years ago." Development, faith, and economy remain central to his program: "The economy!! . . . How are you going to feed these people . . . solve people's problems. . . . The life of the human being is part of his transition to ethics, and to faith, and to civilization, and to the revival!"[21] Khaled sees human development as part of faith, but faith is also what drives Khaled and the Life Makers program.[22] In a satellite television interview on the talk show *Al-Nahar,* Khaled linked faith, nationalism, and political change and described five traits as indispensable to the Nahda: morals (*akhlaq*), faith (*iman*), thought (*fikr*), skills (*maharat*), and on-the-ground projects (*mashru'at al-ard*). During the Mubarak era and beyond, these five traits embody pious neoliberal subjectivity by combining materiality and faith. Pious neoliberal subjects, then, in their quest for rewards here and in the afterlife, implement Islamic development projects that shape the future of Egypt while building their own house in heaven.

A Geographer's Ethnography of Islamic Economic Practices

THE RESEARCH FOR THIS STUDY is based on fieldwork conducted in Cairo from 2006 to 2010 with one final follow-up visit in 2012. My fieldwork included more than one hundred semistructured interviews, daily observations inside associations, and discourse analyses of brochures and collected documents.[1] Much of my expertise draws upon twelve months of fieldwork that I conducted from December 2005 to December 2006, with short annual follow-up visits from 2008 to 2010. During 2006, I was affiliated with the Saleh Kamel Center for Islamic Economics at al-Azhar University and was officially supervised by the head of the center, Dr. Mohamed Abdel Halim Omar.[2] Dr. Omar invited me to attend several relevant conferences and panel discussions and opened numerous doors for my research that otherwise would not have been available to me. For example, I was the first and only woman permitted to attend a quarter-long series of lectures (in Arabic) on Islamic economics intended for sheikhs from Muslim-majority countries, culminating in my receipt of a certificate from al-Azhar University. Because of my research clearance with the Egyptian government and my Egyptian ID card, I also had access to numerous organizations and two essential government entities: the Ministry of Social Solidarity and the Ministry of Endowments.

In the field, I observed and interviewed ministerial staff, association administrators, Islamic scholars, charity workers, local volunteers, aid recipients, bankers, and philanthropists about Islamic charity and development in Egypt. I conducted observations at several mosques and charities, including the oldest Islamic charity in Cairo, the Islamic Charitable Association, the largest Islamic organization in Egypt, al-Gam'iyya al-Shar'iyya, and the first women's-run *zakat* committee at Salah al-Din Mosque. I interviewed the founders of newer and less-established organizations such as the Egyptian Food Bank, Resala, and Zidny. I performed in-depth research on a total of twenty charitable organizations and conducted individual interviews with the leaders of many more. The majority of interviews were conducted in Arabic.[3] While I am fluent in Arabic, my (American) accent revealed my non-native status. As an Egyptian-American woman with funding from a U.S. institution during a time of intense suspicion toward the United States, I found some interviewees were very uncomfortable with my project.[4] To facilitate access, from August through December 2006, an Egyptian-male research assistant accompanied me on interviews. I found that his presence made everyone feel more comfortable. He did not serve as an interpreter per se, but sometimes his cultural awareness allowed him to ask questions with more political savvy, particularly since he was able to gauge each individual's reception to our presence. On a few appropriate occasions—for example, when we interviewed an imam— after coaching him, the assistant conducted the entire interview, while I recorded the exchange. I believe that in addition to his phenomenal interview skills, his gender, nationality, accent, beard, and demeanor facilitated interactions, particularly with government officials and imams.

While conducting research in Egypt, I was often asked how my identity (particularly as a geographer and an Egyptian American) related to the study of Islamic charity and development. As a geographer, I told them that I analyze how and why particular economic and cultural practices occur in particular places. Working interdisciplinary provided me with a wider analytical lens through which to understand Islamic organizations and how they fit within society. My methodology draws upon a long tradition of feminist epistemologies and methodologies that recognize the inseparability of theory, interpretation, and research practice.[5] The partial and situated nature of knowledge production meant that my gender, class, nationality, appearance, religion, age, and language skills all influenced who spoke to me, what was said, and under what conditions. My insider/outsider stance was relevant to the research process. My "insider" status, as an Egyptian American Muslim, was of great interest to my interviewees and they frequently asked questions of my identity, my interest in Islamic charity, and my upbringing. On numerous occasions, I was asked to explain where and how I was raised in terms of religion, language, educational background, and exposure to Egypt, and my interlocutors asked me in exchange about my personal life and convictions. It also was apparent to me that my Muslim upbringing and my Egyptian identification card allowed me access to opinions that might not have been available to a presumed "outsider." Interlocutors frequently commented that I was like them (*inti zayyina*). Yet, as an American researcher on a Fulbright fellowship in Egypt,

I was very much an outsider, and I was well aware that some of my interlocutors were suspicious of me. Some felt particularly uncomfortable with my interest in Islamic charity and assumed that my interests were at best political and at worst disingenuous. The climate of suspicion was compounded by the pretext of the Global War on Terror as well as the Israeli war on Lebanon, which occurred in the summer of 2006, halfway through my initial fieldwork. At the time, there was a great deal of dismay about U.S. foreign policy circulating in the Egyptian media and Egyptians watched warily as Israeli bombs detonated over Lebanon on their television sets. The War on Terror directly impacted my fieldwork. In one meeting with my Egyptian adviser, Dr. Omar, he voiced his anguish and stated that his desire to help me had diminished because I was an American and he saw the bombing of Lebanon as an American act of war. Yet his willingness to tell me that to my face was indicative of our relationship and my saving grace that day was that he considered me to be a "sister." After many months of working with me, he had come to believe that I was bringing important knowledge about Islam to Americans. Undoubtedly, then, this book is a form of situated knowledge and the interpretations I offer are intimately related to this positionality.

Notes

Introduction

1. Khaled, "LM 1 Life Makers, Episode 1: Introduction, Part 1."
2. "Amr Khalid Tops Forbes."
3. "Mujaddidun."
4. For a discussion of Khaled, see also Echchaibi, "Hyper-Islamism?" 199–214, and Moll, "Islamic Televangelism."
5. Warde, *Islamic Finance*.
6. Maurer, "Re-Formatting the Economy," 54–66.
7. Tuğal, *Passive Revolution*, 267.
8. Larner, "Neo-Liberalism," 5–25. While the term neoliberalism has been used widely and at times imprecisely and with little nuance, geographers have always argued that neoliberalism is neither "monolithic in form, nor universal in effect." See Peck and Tickell, "Neoliberalizing Space," 380. Context-specific, empirical studies of neoliberalism can avoid these mistakes, illuminating the messiness, particularities, and multiplicities of neoliberalism. See Larner, "Neo-Liberalism, Policy, Ideology," 5–25; Larner, "Neoliberalism?" 509–12; Peck et al., "Postneoliberalism and Its Malcontents," 94–116; Peck, *Workfare States*; Peck, "Neoliberalizing States."
9. Peck, *Workfare States*; Peck, "Neoliberalizing States"; Peck and Tickell, "Neoliberalizing Space," 380.
10. See Brenner et al., "Variegated Neoliberalization," 182–222; Mitchell, "Neoliberal Governmentality," 389–407; Sharma, "Crossbreeding Institutions," 60–95; Gupta and Ferguson, "Spatializing States," 981–1002.
11. Examples of texts that apply a governmentality perspective to the project of development include Li, *The Will to Improve*; Gidwani, *Capital, Interrupted*; Dunn, *Privatizing Poland*; Ong, *Neoliberalism as Exception*; Tsing, *Friction*; Ferguson, *Global Shadows*; Mitchell, *Rule of Experts*; Sharma, *Logics of Empowerment*.
12. Dean, "Foucault, Government, and the Enfolding."
13. For a discussion of how neoliberalism fits into existing NGO relations, see O'Reilly, "The Promise of Patronage," 179–200.
14. The work of numerous scholars suggests an observable pattern of pious neoliberalism across religions. See Elisha, "Moral Ambitions of Grace," 154–89; Mian, "Prophets-for-Profits," 2143–61; Beaumont and Dias, "Faith-Based

Organisations," 382–92; Hackworth, "Neoliberalism, Social Welfare," 319–39; Bornstein, *The Spirit of Development*.

15. See Hackworth, *Faith Based*, for a discussion of the convergence of neoliberalism with neoconservatism and the U.S. Christian Right.

16. Gökariksel and Secor, "New Transnational Geographies," 6–12; Karaman, "Neoliberalism with Islamic Characteristics"; Atasoy, *Islam's Marriage with Neoliberalism*.

17. Adas, "The Making of Entrepreneurial," 113–24.

18. On the merging of Islam and neoliberalism in Turkey, see also Tuğal, *Passive Revolution*, 306; Gökarıksel and Secor, "New Transnational Geographies," 6–12; Tepe, "Politics between Market and Islam," 107–35; Turam, *Between Islam and the State*, 223.

19. Osella and Osella, "Muslim Entrepreneurs," S202–21.

20. See Hefner, *Civil Islam*, 286; Rudnyckyj, *Spiritual Economies*; Rudnyckyj, "Spiritual Economies," 104–41.

21. Hefner discusses the compatibility of Islamism and democracy as "civil Islam," while Rudnyckyj contrasts "market Islam" as the compatibility of Islam and capitalism (Hefner, *Civil Islam*; Rudnyckyj, "Market Islam in Indonesia," S183–201).

22. For example, during the Arab Spring of 2011, despite Tunisia being the actual impetus for many countries, political commentators pointed to Egypt as a measure of how the rest of the countries might proceed.

23. Moaddel, *Islamic Modernism, Nationalism, and Fundamentalism*, 403–31.

24. The phrase "technologies of rule" is from Rose, "Governing 'Advanced' Liberal Democracies," 41.

25. Hamza, "The State, Foreign Aid and the Political Economy of Shelter in Egypt", 77–96; Bibars, *Victims and Heroines*; Nassar and El Laithy, *Proceedings of the Conference on Socioeconomic Policies*.

26. Ismail, *Political Life in Cairo*.

27. Hart, "Geography and Development"; Geiger and Wolch, "A Shadow State?" 351–66; Cheshire and Lawrence, "Neoliberalism, Individualisation, and Community," 435–45.

28. http://egypt.usaid.gov/en/aboutus/Pages/budgetinformation.aspx. I do not address internationally based or funded NGOs or Coptic associations, which have both been widely covered by other scholars. For information on Coptic organizations, see Labib, "Charity Versus Social Development"; for information on international Islamic organizations, see Benthall and Bellion-Jourdan, *The Charitable Crescent*. Coptic charities are among the strongest and well funded and are of great importance. Christians give in the form of *ushur*, or tithe, traditionally 10 percent of their wealth, and are also active in volunteer activities. Little differences have been found between Muslim and Christian attitudes toward giving. See El Daly, *Philanthropy in Egypt*.

29. Escobar, *Encountering Development*; Pred and Watts, *Reworking Modernity*; Watts, "Development and Governmentality," 6–34; Crush, *Power of Development*; Mitchell, *Rule of Experts*; Ilcan and Lacey, *Governing the Poor*.

30. Lawson, *Making Development Geography*; Hart, "Geography and Development," 812–22; Gupta and Ferguson, "Spatializing States," 981–1002; Wainwright, *Decolonizing Development*; Rankin, "Governing Development: Neoliberalism," 18–37; Li, *The Will to Improve*; Hoffman, "Autonomous Choices and Patriotic Professionalism," 550–70; Watts, "Development and Governmentality," 6–34; Comaroff and Comaroff, *Millennial Capitalism*.

31. Tyndale, *Visions of Development*; Dwyer, "Veiled Meanings," 5; Hefferan et al., *Bridging the Gaps*; Selinger, "The Forgotten Factor," 523–43; Hefferan, "Finding Faith in Development," 887–89. Geographical studies analyzing FBOs tend to address Christian-oriented organizations and/or Western contexts. See, for example, Hackworth, *Neoliberalism, Social Welfare, and the Politics of Faith in the United States*; Beaumont, "Introduction UCSIA Dialogue Series 11"; Beaumont, "Workfare, Associationism, and the 'Underclass,'" 249–78; Hackworth *Faith Based*. The broader literature on FBD is focused on Christian organizations and rarely extends beyond Africa or Latin America. On Africa, see Bornstein, *The Spirit of Development*; Hope and Timmel, *A Kenyan Experience*; on Latin America, see Olson, "Common Belief, Contested Meanings," 393–405; Wilson, "Neoliberalism, Indigeneity, and Social Engineering," 127–44; Hefferan et al., *Bridging the Gaps*. Clarke and Jennings, *Development, Civil Society, and Faith-Based Organizations*, includes three chapters on Islamic FBOs, two of which are focused on the Middle East. See Clark, "FBOs and Change," 145–70; Harb, "Faith-Based Organizations," 214–39; Kroessin and Mohamed, "Saudi Arabian NGOs," 187–213. These scholars also highlight how the work of Islamic organizations is not fundamentally distinct from their Western counterparts.

32. Clarke, "Faith Matters," 835–84; Berger, "Religious Nongovernmental Organizations," 15.

33. Bayat, "Activism and Social Development," 1–28; Clark, *Islam, Charity, and Activism*; Abdelrahman, *Civil Society Exposed*; Ibrahim, *An Assessment of Grass Roots*; Sullivan, *Private Voluntary Organizations*.

34. The Emergency Law expired and was replaced by a Supreme Council of the Armed Forces (SCAF) decree on May 30, 2012, but as of October 2012 a new draft law, called the "Protecting Society from Dangerous People" Bill, was being drafted by the Egyptian cabinet. See "Egypt: Hidden Emergency Law," All Africa. In 2013, after protests broke out on the two-year anniversary of January 25, 2011, Morsi reinstituted the Emergency Law in three cities.

35. FIDH, "The Emergency Law in Egypt," 178.

36. Ibrahim, "Islamic Activism and Political Opposition," 53–68.

37. Thousands of Islamists, including nonviolent Brotherhood members in

addition to militant Islamists, were subject to imprisonment, torture, and abuse under the Emergency Law.

38. Schielke, "Policing Ambiguity," 539–52; Hirschkind, *The Ethical Soundscape*; Abu-Lughod, *Dramas of Nationhood*, and; Abu-Lughod, *Local Contexts of Islamism*; Wise, "'Words from the Heart'"; Bayat, *Making Islam Democratic*.

39. Many scholars document the rise of Islamism. See, respectively, Hoodfar, "Return to the Veil," 105–26; Gaffney, *The Prophet's Pulpit*; Zaied, "Daʿwa for Dollars"; Bayat, *Making Islam Democratic*; Mahmood, *Politics of Piety*; Starrett, "The Political Economy of Religious Commodities in Cairo," 51; Hirschkind, *The Ethical Soundscape*; Abu-Lughod, *Dramas of Nationhood*; Anderson, "New Media, New Publics," 888–906; Starrett, "Islam in the Digital Age," 268–71; Ghannam, *Remaking the Modern*.

40. My interview subjects consistently used the phrase "human development" (*tanmiya bashariyya*). Initially, I did not ask about development but used words like *gamm'iyya* (association) or *khayr* (good deeds), *zakat,* and *sadaqa*. People repeatedly made a point of referring to their work as human development.

41. The production of modernity is intertwined with "tradition" because "modernizing forces continuously re-appropriate elements that have been categorized as non-modern, such as religious elements in order to produce their own effectiveness" (Mitchell, "Introduction," xi–xxvii).

42. Roy, "Subjects of Risk," 131–55.

43. Mitchell, *Rule of Experts*; Denis, "Cairo as Neo-Liberal Capital?" 47–73.

44. Sabry, "Poverty Lines in Greater Cairo."

45. See Abaza, *Changing Consumer Cultures,* for a discussion of the explosion of shopping malls and cafés as part of neoliberal development in Egypt.

46. The Gini coefficient of 35.2 indicates a high degree of income inequality and disparities in the beneficiaries of economic growth. See United National Development Program (UNDP), *Egypt Human Development Report,* [2005]).

47. Slackman, "Egypt's Problem and Its Challenge."

48. Mitchell, *Rule of Experts,* discusses the role of speculative capital in the development of "Dreamland" and other gated communities on the outskirts of Cairo. An interesting new phenomenon that has yet to be studied is the geography of mosque development in Cairo's new suburbs.

49. Abaza, *Changing Consumer Cultures*.

50. "Table of the Merciful" is the name given to free *iftar* (the meal at which one breaks fast) distribution during Ramadan. Large tables and chairs are set up on street corners, in tents, and in vacant lots and are open to all at sundown.

51. Gupta and Ferguson, "Beyond 'Culture.'"

52. For details of my methodology and fieldwork, see the appendix.

53. Labib, "Charity Versus Social Development."

54. These three clusters are a starting point from which to understand Islamic

charitable organizations; they are not all-inclusive, nor are they static. These categories work as a backdrop or framework for situating the organizations in relation to one another, but they are not a replacement for attention to the multiplicities, contradictions, and overlapping practices that destabilize these categories. This typology helped me to recognize the presence of multiple and intersecting variables in an integrated form. I do not know of any other attempts to map the sector in such a way.

1. The Economy of Charity

1. Benthall, "Financial Worship."

2. Mallat, "Tantawi on Banking in Egypt," 431, offers a detailed analysis of Tantawi's fatwa.

3. Sullivan, "Extra-State Actors and Privatization," 135–55. Bayat, "Political Economy of Social Policy."

4. Aly, "Privatization in Egypt."

5. Ibid.

6. Sullivan, *Private Voluntary Organizations in Egypt.*

7. Harik and Sullivan, *Privatization and Liberalization.*

8. Wilson, "Islam and Business," 109–23.

9. Aly, "Privatization in Egypt." The Muslim Brotherhood is a banned political party in Egypt. Founded in 1928 by Hasan Al-Banna, the organization has evolved to become the largest opposition party in Egypt. Because of its slogan, "Islam Is the Answer," it represents the Islamization of Egyptian society and advocates for the transformation of Egypt from a secular state to an Islamic one. The history of the Brotherhood is discussed further in chapter 2.

10. Tripp, *Islam and the Moral Economy,* 198.

11. Benthall, "Financial Worship," 27–42.

12. See also Powell, "Zakat," 94–95; Oran and Rashid, "Fiscal Policy in Early Islam," 75–101; Quraishi, "The Institution of Zakat," 77–81.

13. Benthall and Bellion-Jourdan, *The Charitable Crescent.* In India, Sayyid Abu' A'la Mawdudi (1903–1979), the founder of *Jama'at al Islami* (Party of Islam), promoted the idea of Islamic economics as part of "a broad campaign to preserve the religious identity and traditional culture" of India's Muslims at the end of the colonial era, a time when Muslims were anxiously asserting their identity" (Kuran, "The Genesis of Islamic Economics").

14. Çizakça, *Islamic Capitalism,* 3.

15. Wilson, "Islam and Business," 109–23; Naqvi, *Ethics and Economics,* 176.

16. Zubair Hasan, "Distributional Equity in Islam," 54.

17. Ibid.

18. Maurer, "Re-Formatting the Economy," 54–66.

19. Zubair Hasan, "Distributional Equity in Islam," 57.

20. Iqbal, *Distributive Justice and Need Fulfillment.*

21. Emara, "Islam: 'A Guide for the Perplexed.'" Marriage expenses are included in the list of basic necessities because it is considered an important obligation for Muslims and is the only acceptable context for sexual relations. Hoodfar's study of marriage in Egypt found that marriage is not only an important social event but also a necessary part of self-realization and adulthood (Homa Hoodfar, *Between Marriage and the Market*). Several *hadith* (the sayings of the prophet and the second most sacred source of religious guidance after the Quran) indicate the central role of marriage to leading a pious life.

22. Iqbal, *Distributive Justice and Need Fulfillment,* 16.

23. Hasan, "Distributional Equity in Islam," 39–41.

24. Qutb, *Social Justice in Islam,* 49.

25. Ibid, 48.

26. Ibid, 48–49.

27. Ibid, 305–6.

28. Emara, "Islam: 'A Guide for the Perplexed,'" 239.

29. Shujaat, *Social Justice in Islam.*

30. During Nasser's rule, the Brotherhood supported industrialization, nationalization, and state regulation of the economy. Khadduri, *The Islamic Conception of Justice.*

31. El Daly, *Philanthropy in Egypt.*

32. Mostafa, "The Third Pillar."

33. This definition of social justice shared by the Muslim Brotherhood and liberals alike is perhaps one more reason why distributive justice was never sought during the Mubarak era and was quickly sidelined in the post-Mubarak years.

34. For a discussion of the first *waqf* in Egypt, see Sabra, *Poverty and Charity in Medieval Islam.*

35. Clark, *Islam, Charity, and Activism,* 236; Hassan and Lewis, "Islamic Finance," 151–60; Benthall and Bellion-Jourdan, *The Charitable Crescent;* El Daly, *Philanthropy in Egypt.*

36. The trademarks of Egyptian *waqf* developed during the Mamluk era (1250–1517), the Ottoman Empire (1517–1798), and Mohamed Ali's Dynasty (1805–1952), which includes the British occupation from 1882 to 1922 and culminated with King Farouk I, who reigned from 1936 to 1952. For a broad discussion of the history of waqf, see Hoexter, "Waqf Studies," 474–95.

37. However, not all scholars agree that money qualifies, on the basis that utilizing money decreases its value, and one condition for creating a *waqf* is that the extraction of benefit does not decrease its value (Omar, "Nezaam Al Waqf Al Islamy").

38. Ibid.

39. Ibid. See Çizakça, "Waqf in History," 43–73; Çizakça, *A History of Philanthropic Foundations,* 288, for a discussion of innovative *awqaf* funding streams as part of the contemporary *waqf* revival in several Muslim-majority countries.

40. Omar, "Nezaam Al Waqf Al Islamy."

41. Douara, "Philanthropy and Development." Sections of my description of *waqf* appear in Ibrahim, "Introduction."

42. See, for example, Surat 34, verse 39, and Surat 2, verses 271–72, in the Quran.

43. Omar, "Al-Qard al-Hassan."

44. Ibid.

45. Gibson-Graham, *A Postcapitalist Politics.*

46. The prohibition of *riba* is also widely agreed upon, but the definition of what constitutes *riba* is not (Emara, "Islam: 'A Guide for the Perplexed'").

47. Kuran, "Islamic Redistribution through Zakat," 275–93.

48. Emara, "Islam: 'A Guide for the Perplexed'"; Dean and Khan, "Muslim Perspectives on Welfare," 193–209.

49. Ismail, "Kayfa Tozakky Maalak Wa Tigaaratak." See also Qaradawi, *Fiqh al Zakah.* There is a specific *nisab* for each type of *zakat,* but generally Muslims calculate *zakat* as two and a half percent of their net income, which must be paid on money, merchandise, profit derived from harvest, livestock, stocks and shares, and bonds and securities. In addition, 20 percent of all extracted resources are subject to *zakat* after deducting the cost of extraction

50. Ismail, "Kayfa Tozakky Maalak Wa Tigaaratak."

51. Ibid; Sami Hasan, "Muslim Philanthropy and Social Security."

52. Kuran, "Islamic Redistribution through Zakat."

53. Benthall, "Financial Worship," 27–42.

54. Iqbal, *Distributive Justice and Need Fulfillment,* 378; Wilson, "Islam and Business," 109–23; Kuran, "Islamic Redistribution through Zakat."

55. Benthall and Bellion-Jourdan, *The Charitable Crescent,* 42–43.

56. Benthall, "Financial Worship," 27–42.

57. Baron, "Orphans and Abandoned Children," 13–34.

58. http://www.dar-alifta.org/ViewFatwa.aspx?ID=1281&text=*zakat.*

59. Chowdury. "Is Zakat Permissible for Islamic Dawah Organisations?" http://muslimmatters.org/2007/10/24/the-permissibility-of-zakat-for-islamic -dawah-organizations-a-detailed-analysis/.

60. In this century, many jurists including Muhammad Abduh, Rashid Rida, Maulana Mawdudi, Amin Ahsan Islahi, and Yusuf al-Qaradawi argue that the phrase "in the cause of God" covers a wide variety of areas. See http://www.islam icity.com/Articles/articles.asp?ref=IC0212-1797.

61. See Powell, "Zakat," 61; 91–96. See also fatwas by Ali Gomaa on using *zakat* to pay for: health expenses of the poor, http://www.ali-gomaa.com/?page=fatwas &fatwa_details=416; to support the cancer institute, http://www.ali-gomaa.com/

?page=fatwas&fatwa_details=384; and relieving debtors, http://www.ali-gomaa .com/?page=fatwas&fatwa_details=404.

62. For examples, see Ali Gomaa's website, http://www.ali-gomaa.com/?page= fatwas&fatwa_cat=10.

63. Fatwa 168/622, http://www.dar-alifta.org/ViewFatwa.aspx?ID=316&text =*zakat*.

64. http://www.dar-alifta.org/ViewFatwa.aspx?ID=509&text=*zakat*. See also http://beta.57357.com/2009/two-recent-fatwasadvisory-opinionby-daar-el -iftaa-and-sheikh-el-kardawy-approve-hospital-57357%E2%80%99s-collection -of-*zakat*-sadaka-and-*waqf*-for-the-benefit-of-scientific-research.

65. PlusNews, "Positive Fatwas."

66. Alalwani, "Fatwa on Zakat for CSID."

67. Abdul Salam, "Zakat: Institution for Poverty Alleviation."

68. Currie, "Who Can be Added."

69. http://www.dar-alifta.org/ViewFatwa.aspx?ID=55&text=*zakat*.

70. El Daly, *Philanthropy in Egypt*, 209–12.

71. Ibid., 205.

72. Interview, Cairo, December 11, 2006. See also Powell, "Zakat," 85, for another discussion of how *zakat* is used for job creation.

73. Interview, Cairo, March 22, 2006.

74. Hackworth, *Faith Based*.

75. Data regarding the state of Islamic banking in Egypt was obtained from Dr. Mohamed Abdel Halim Omar, director of Saleh Kamel Center for Islamic Economics, interview, Cairo, January 2, 2006.

76. Nabil, "Islamic Banking Loses Patrons."

2. Managing Poverty and Islam

1. Janine A. Clark, *Islam, Charity, and Activism* argues that economic and political factors are critical to understanding Islamic associations in Egypt: "Islamic social institutions, therefore, must be put in the context of a changing economy, the growth of the state, and the rise of the middle classes" (11). She posits that Islamic institutions have mushroomed in order to fill the gaps left as a result of political liberalization and economic restructuring in the Middle East.

2. I use the term "Islamist" to refer to those who mobilize Islam as a basis from which to gain political power and legitimacy, often through the pursuit of a *shari'a*-based Islamic state. This definition of Islamist includes groups like the Muslim Brotherhood, but it excludes most of the organizations that I discuss in this book, whose primary purpose is to engage in acts of charity or development. Chapter 3 discusses the connection between *da'wa* and Islamic charity.

3. Mitchell, "Society, Economy and the State Effect," 169.

4. Moaddel, *Islamic Modernism, Nationalism, and Fundamentalism,* 403–31.

5. Lisa Pollard, *Nurturing the Nation,* covers the various techniques of governance mobilized during the period 1805–1923, while Timothy Mitchell, *Colonizing Egypt,* discusses colonial techniques of rule mobilized by Europeans to govern Egypt.

6. Ener, *Managing Egypt's Poor.*

7. Ibid., 33.

8. Rose, "Governing 'Advanced' Liberal Democracies," 144.

9. Ener argues that the outcome of these strategies of social control was that the poor actively sought social assistance (whether from state or private entities) and began to demand more social services from the state (Ener, *Managing Egypt's Poor,* 17).

10. Ibid., 137.

11. Clark, *Islam, Charity, and Activism,* 45.

12. Ibid., 9.

13. Kandil, *Defining the Nonprofit Sector;* Ibrahim, "Islamic Activism and Political Opposition," 53–68.

14. See Pollard, *Nurturing the Nation,* 43, on the emergence of public social and cultural institutions.

15. Ibrahim, *An Assessment of Grass Roots Participation,* 40; Beattie, *Egypt during the Nasser Years,* 244–49.

16. Ener, *Managing Egypt's Poor.*

17. Abdelrahman, *Civil Society Exposed;* Sullivan, *Private Voluntary Organizations.*

18. Alexander, *Nasser: His Life and Times.*

19. Ismael, *Middle East Politics Today,* 483–94.

20. Milton-Edwards, *Contemporary Politics in the Middle East.*

21. Bayat, "The Political Economy of Social Policy," 135–55; Lippman, *Egypt After Nasser.*

22. Ismael, *Middle East Politics Today;* Wahba, "Private and Public Economic Bases," 73.

23. Bayat, "The Political Economy of Social Policy," 135–55.

24. Howaidy, "The Productive Families Project," 4–6, quoted in Sullivan, *Private Voluntary Organizations in Egypt,* 49–50.

25. Sullivan, *Private Voluntary Organizations in Egypt,* 34.

26. Moustafa, "Conflict and Cooperation."

27. Sharp, *U.S. Foreign Assistance.*

28. Bayat, "The Political Economy of Social Policy in Egypt," 135–55.

29. Lippman, *Egypt After Nasser.*

30. Wahba, "Private and Public Economic Bases"; Nakashima, *The Political Understanding of Al-'Infitah Al-'Iqtisadi.*

31. Milton-Edwards, *Contemporary Politics in the Middle East.*

32. USAID began sponsoring projects in Egypt in 1975. U.S. assistance, only a small portion of which is development aid, solidified through the 1979 peace treaty with Israel. Egypt is the second largest recipient of American foreign aid worldwide. Gamal Essam El-Din, "USAID's New Strategy in Egypt."

33. Ibid.

34. Bayat, "The Political Economy of Social Policy in Egypt," 135–55.

35. Kandil, *Defining the Nonprofit Sector,* 1–2.

36. Abdo, *No God but God,* 209–14.

37. Al-Awadi, *In Pursuit of Legitimacy.*

38. Abdelrahman, *Civil Society Exposed,* 105.

39. Sullivan, "Extra-State Actors and Privatization in Egypt"; Hamza, "The State, Foreign Aid, and the Political Economy of Shelter in Egypt," 77–96.

40. Peck, "Geography and Public Policy," 392–405.

41. Bayat, "The Political Economy of Social Policy in Egypt," 135–55.

42. Data from the International Monetary Fund, World Economic Outlook Database, April 2007. Estimates start after 2005. See also Ismael, *Middle East Politics Today,* 483–94.

43. Sullivan, "Extra-State Actors and Privatization in Egypt."

44. Ismael, *Middle East Politics Today,* 483–94.

45. Ibid. After the 2011 uprising, activists demanded the jailing of corrupt businessmen and the seizure of their funds.

46. GDP (in USD billions) increased steadily from $35.9 billion in 1986 to $67.6 billion in 1996 and from $89.7 billion in 2005 to $107.5 billion in 2006. World Bank Group, *Egypt, Arab Republic Data Profile,* [2007]). The GDP per capita (2007–8) was 10,246 LE (UNDP, 2010). At the same time, the average Egyptian's standard of living fell and unemployment reached nearly 20 percent. Individual income went from $670 a year in the 1960s to $610 in the early 1990s. Ismael, *Middle East Politics Today.*

47. Bayat, "The Political Economy of Social Policy in Egypt," 135–55.

48. Slackman, "Egypt's Problem and Its Challenge."

49. Egypt Information Services, *Yearbook 2007 (Social Solidarity).*

50. Elyachar, *Markets of Dispossession.*

51. Interview, Cairo, December 15, 2007.

52. Some of my interlocutors told me that because data are not collected, it is impossible to know the nature of the jobs; for example, many temporary jobs are counted as multiple jobs if they are renewed.

53. Sharp, *U.S. Foreign Assistance to the Middle East.* Because they include grants, debt forgiveness, and technical support, the numbers for economic development are inflated. These figures hide the reality that the United States gave much more

military aid than economic aid, and that much of this economic assistance was indirect aid funneled into a prosperous development industry dominated by Westerners.

54. See http://www.egyptindependent.com/news/new-draft-law-would-limit -scope-work-ngos; http://www.icnl.org/research/monitor/egypt.html; http:// www.reuters.com/article/2013/02/25/us-egypt-ngos-idUSBRE91O0TZ 20130225.

55. Roy, *Poverty Capital*.

56. For a critical discussion of the project of development, see Watts, "Development and Governmentality"; Peet and Hartwick, *Theories of Development*; Escobar, *Encountering Development*; Rahnema and Bawtree, *The Post-Development Reader*; Lawson, *Making Development Geography*; Crush, *Power of Development*.

57. Clark, *Islam, Charity, and Activism*; Bayat, *Making Islam Democratic*; Abdelrahman, *Civil Society Exposed*.

58. Often, Islamic groups are classified into militants, conservatives, and moderates (Ismail, *Political Life*, and Beinin and Stork, *Political Islam*). While I find these distinctions overly simplistic, I employ them out of a practical need to differentiate the groups I studied from others associated with acts of violence. Although sometimes Islamic organizations participate in political Islam, calling for an Islamic state based on *shari'a*, I distinguish them from Islamic associations. In contrast, Islamic associations, particularly of the kind I studied, are not part of political Islam despite an interest in Islamizing society.

59. Mahmood, *Politics of Piety*, 75.

60. Gupta, "Blurred Boundaries," 211.

61. For a more thorough discussion of the state's relationship to Islamism, see Ibrahim, *Islamic Activism and Political Opposition in Egypt*, 53–68; Bayat, "Activism and Social Development in the Middle East," 1–28.

62. Beattie, *Egypt during the Nasser Years*, 244–49.

63. The Free Officers was a group of revolutionary army officers who were committed to ending King Farouk's monarchy and eventually established the republic in 1952.

64. Alam, *Religion and State*, 79.

65. Alexander, *Nasser: His Life and Times*.

66. Alam, *Religion and State*, 83–85.

67. Ibid, 87.

68. Moustafa, *Conflict and Cooperation*, 3–22.

69. Alam, *Religion and State*, 103. As Egypt re-created its constitution after the 2011 uprising, Article 2 once again generated huge controversy, especially among liberals calling for a secular state.

70. Moustafa, "Conflict and Cooperation," 3–22.

71. Sonbol, "Egypt."

72. Beattie, *Egypt during the Sadat Years.*

73. Sullivan, *Private Voluntary Organizations in Egypt.*

74. Cantori, "Religion and Politics in Egypt," 77.

75. Bayat, "Radical Religion and the Habitus"; Beattie, *Egypt during the Sadat Years.*

76. Alam, *Religion and State.*

77. Moustafa, "Conflict and Cooperation," 3–22.

78. Al-Awadi, *In Pursuit of Legitimacy,* 262.

79. Moustafa, "Conflict and Cooperation," 3–22.

80. Sullivan, *Private Voluntary Organizations in Egypt;* Ibrahim, *Egypt, Islam, and Democracy.*

81. El-Tawil, "Egypt's Democratic Margin," 135.

82. Moustafa, "Conflict and Cooperation," 3–22.

83. El-Tawil, "Egypt's Democratic Margin," 135.

84. Ibid.

85. Atia, "Innocent Victims," 1–24. Law 162 of 1958 was renewed again on April 30, 2006, for an additional three-year term and then finally expired on May 13, 2012. Morsi temporarily reinstated it in three cities for one month in January 2013 after protests broke out. Egypt's Emergency Law was adopted in response to the assassination of Anwar Sadat in 1981. Under the law, the government has free rein to arrest suspected security threats and detain them without charges. In addition, the law has been used to try civilians in military courts, imprison dissenters, and restrict free speech. For an explanation of the various articles of the Emergency Law and the associated human rights abuses, see http://www.fidh.org/spip.php?article1397.

86. Bayat, *The Political Economy of Social Policy,* 135–55.

87. Ibid.

88. Al-Awadi, *In Pursuit of Legitimacy.*

89. Bayat, *The Political Economy of Social Policy,* 135–55.

90. Interview, Cairo, October 21, 2006.

91. Alam, *Religion and State;* Abdo, *No God but God,* 209–14; Ibrahim, *Egypt, Islam, and Democracy;* Bianchi, *Unruly Corporatism.*

92. Aly, "Privatization in Egypt," 3.

93. The results of the 2012 parliamentary election were nullified; parliament was dissolved and as of February 2013 elections were rescheduled for April or May 2013.

94. Instead of liberalizing the NGO law, Morsi's government proposed an even more draconian law.

95. Abdelrahman, *Civil Society Exposed,* 132–34, 143.

96. For a thorough discussion of the 1999 NGO law and the long struggle by

associations to change the 1964 law, see Fouad, Ref'at, and Murcos, "From Inertia to Movement."

97. ICNL, "Implementing Regulation for Law 84 of 2002."

98. Youssef, "Dawr al-ittihad al-'amm lil-gam'iyyat wa-l-mu'assasat al-ahliyya fi al-tadamun al-igtima'i."

99. Interview, Cairo, January 28, 2006.

100. See, for example, the work of Amani Kandil, Sara Bin-Nafissa, Maha Abdelrahman, Asef Bayat, Denis Sullivan, and Diane Singerman for different categorizations of the third sector in Egypt.

101. Kandil, "Al-'amal al-khayri wa-l-tanmiya fi Misr."

102. Sullivan, *Private Voluntary Organizations*, 11, 133.

103. Undoubtedly, numerous NGOs operate without registering and are therefore difficult to document. Government estimates and independent estimates vary greatly. Abdelrahman indicates that data for the year 1995 are inaccurate. The 1995 official estimate was 14,000 NGOs, but other figures indicated that there could have been as many as 19,348 and 28,000 for the same year. Abdelrahman, *Civil Society Exposed*, 6–7.

104. After the 2011 uprising, the number of federations skyrocketed, as NGOs were initially enthusiastic about the opportunity to collaborate. While there certainly has been an increase in communication among groups, many of the new federations quickly dissolved and the climate of fear and isolation has returned.

105. Chiffoleau, "NGOs and the Reform," 167–80; Abdelrahman, *Civil Society Exposed*; Ibrahim, *An Assessment of Grass Roots Participation*.

106. Abdelrahman notes that the Egyptian government's categorization of NGOs, in particular the unitary grouping of "cultural, scientific, and religious" organizations, is a result of the ministry's desire to hide the strength of Islamic organizations (Abdelrahman, *Civil Society Exposed*, 7–9, 43). The government understates the number of Islamic organizations because it is vying with them for legitimacy over religious affairs.

107. The categories are: (1) child care and motherhood; (2) family care; (3) social aid; (4) elderly care; (5) care for the disabled; (6) cultural, scientific, and religious services; (7) local community development; (8) planning and management; (9) prisoner welfare; (10) family planning; (11) international exchange; (12) literacy; (13) social defense; (14) retirees; (15) environmental protection; (16) productive families; (17) consumer protection; and (18) human rights.

108. Ibrahim, *An Assessment of Grass Roots Participation*.

109. Kandil, *Defining the Nonprofit Sector*, 6.

110. Abdelrahman, *Civil Society Exposed*, 6.

111. Abdel-Wahab, *Dalyl al-gam'iyyat al-ahliyya al-tanmawiyya fi muhafazat al-Qahira*.

112. Disclosure of public information was also part of the 2011 uprising. The sector itself may feel empowered to produce such a directory as part of renewed calls for transparency and coordination.

113. The term used in Arabic for development is *tanmiya*. It is distinct from *tatawwur*, which is evolution or process. For example, *tatawwur al isina'a* is industrial production or improvement in the production process. Progress translates as *taqaddum*, whereas modernity is *hadatha*. The verb forms, *tahdith* and *tatwir*, are close in meaning.

114. For an explanation of these categories, see chapter 2. See also Surat 9, verse 63 in the Quran.

115. Abdel-Wahab, interview, Cairo, December 12, 2006.

116. *Takamul* (integration) in this case refers to social integration. The root of this word is *kamula*, or to be complete. *Takamul* usually refers to Muslim unity. A famous hadith states: "The similitude of believers in regard to mutual love, affection, fellow-feeling is that of one body; when any limb of it aches, the whole body aches, because of sleeplessness and fever." Hadith narrated by Nu'man b. Bashir, translated by Sahih Muslim, book 32, no. 6258, "The Book of Virtue, Good Manners, and Joining of the Ties of Relationship." http://www.usc.edu/dept/MSA/fundamentals/hadithsunnah/muslim/032.smt.html#032.6258.

117. Kasbah. "Al-gami'yyat al-ahliyya fi-Misr: al-waqi' wa-l-m'amul fi daw' al-mutghayyirat al-dawliyya wa-l-mahaliyya."

118. My interlocutors consistently used the phrase "human development" (*tanmiya bashariyya*) to describe their work.

119. Bibars, *Victims and Heroines*, 206.

120. Interview, Cairo, October 3, 2006.

121. See Aziza Youssef (Mustafa), "Dawr wizarat al-tadamun al-igtima'i fi taf'yl dawr al-munazzamat ghayr al-hukumiyya wa-l-tansyq ma'aha li-tahqiq al-tadamun al-igtima'i."

122. Greater Cairo includes the combined governorates of Cairo and Giza. Cairo alone has 5,240 organizations; Giza has 2,076.

123. Interview, Cairo, December 12, 2006.

124. Hakm, "Dawr Bank Nasser al-igtima'i fi da'm wa-tanmiyat al-mashru'at al-saghyra."

125. Egypt Information Services, *Yearbook 2007 (Social Solidarity)*.

126. Wilson, "Arab Government Responses," 143–63.

127. Ener, *Managing Egypt's Poor* discusses the shift from poor to poverty, 25.

128. Nassar and El Laithy, *Proceedings of the Conference on Socioeconomic Policies*; Bibars, *Victims and Heroines*.

129. Sharma uses Quangoization to connote the rise of quasi-nongovernmental organizations (Sharma, "Crossbreeding Institutions, Breeding Struggle," 60–95).

130. Bayat, *Activism and Social Development*, 1–28.

131. See Clark, *Islam, Charity, and Activism*; Sullivan, *Private Voluntary Organizations*; Bayat, *Activism and Social Development*, 1–28; Abdelrahman, *Civil Society Exposed*; Ibrahim, *An Assessment of Grass Roots Participation*.

132. Cantori, "Religion and Politics in Egypt," 77–78, 80–81.

3. A Space and Time for Giving

1. Procacci, "Social Economy and the Government of Poverty," 165.

2. See Hafez, "Women Developing Women," 56–73, for a discussion of the female *da'iya* subjectivities.

3. Egyptians refer to children who have lost their father as orphans because presumably (and according to Islam) the father is the breadwinner, responsible for providing for the immediate family. There are also a huge number of orphans in Egypt because adoption is taboo in Muslim societies.

4. See Surat al-Tuwba in the Holy Quran (9:60).

5. Ismail, *Political Life*, 77–80. Cruikshank, *The Will to Empower*, discusses the production of the poor, 34–42.

6. See Hoodfar, *Between Marriage and the Market*.

7. Donation boxes in mosques declined after 9/11 because increased anti-terrorism measures sought to limit anonymous giving (Atia, "Innocent Victims," 1–24).

8. Ghannam, *Remaking the Modern*, 130.

9. Mahmood, *Politics of Piety*, 80, 144.

10. Clark, *Islam, Charity, and Activism*, 14.

11. Interview, Cairo, November 28, 2006.

12. Schielke, "Policing Ambiguity," 539–52; Hirschkind, *The Ethical Soundscape*; Abu-Lughod, *Dramas of Nationhood*; Wise, "'Words from the Heart'"; Bayat, *Making Islam Democratic*.

13. Gaffney, *The Prophet's Pulpit*.

14. Bayat, "Activism and Social Development," 1–28.

15. Ibid.; Wiktorowicz, *Islamic Activism*; Clark, *Islam, Charity, and Activism*; Starrett, "The Political Economy"; Eickelman and Anderson, *New Media in the Muslim World*; Mahmood, *Politics of Piety*.

16. Ismail, "Being Muslim," 614–31.

17. Hirschkind, *The Ethical Soundscape*, 116.

18. Ismail, "Being Muslim," 614–31.

19. I use the term "Islamist" to refer to those who use Islam as a basis from which to gain political power and legitimacy, often through the pursuit of an Islamic state. There are many competing definitions of "Islamist," and such a discussion is beyond the scope of this book. The definition that I employ includes groups such as the Muslim Brotherhood but excludes most of the organizations

I discuss in this book, whose primary purpose is to engage in acts of charity. These individuals were not vying for political power; in fact, they made a point of separating themselves from the Muslim Brotherhood or any political movement. I differentiate between Islamists who advocate for a *shariʿa*-based government and individuals who enact *daʿwa*, i.e., those individuals and organizations that promote the active Islamization of everyday life. Islamist politics, in contrast, entailed "a political ideology articulating the idea of the necessity of establishing an Islamic government, understood as government which implements the shariʿa (Islamic law)" (Ismail, "Being Muslim," 614–31). Islamic associations work primarily as service providers; despite their role in Islamization of the country, they were not primary places for Islamist political mobilization (Bayat, *Making Islam Democratic*, 44). With few exceptions, the organizations that I researched fall under this second category and do not actively support the establishment of an Islamic state, but rather the Islamization of everyday life.

20. Clark, *Islam, Charity, and Activism*, 14.

21. The *American Heritage Dictionary* defines activism as "the use of direct, often confrontational action, such as a demonstration or strike, in opposition to or support of a cause." While it is common for interviewees to urge others to engage in acts of piety, they were not involved in direct or confrontational action and did not engage in protests, advocacy, or campaigns. In short, they are more commonly volunteers than activists.

22. Makhimar, "Al-gamʿiyya al-sharʾiyya wa-l-ʿamal al-khayri."

23. Interview, Cairo, May 16, 2006.

24. The organization is one of the only nongovernmental entities allowed to provide training for imams (Addeh and Fuad, *The Legal Framework of Mosque Building*).

25. Interview, Cairo, August 14, 2006.

26. Ibid.

27. I went to the central office in Cairo several times and faced great difficulty in getting any answers to my questions. Several other researchers of Islamic charities in Egypt have told me that they had the same experience with the organization in terms of secrecy and an inability to gather data on their activities. I would classify it as a Salafi-oriented association.

28. Et-Tahawy, "The Internet Is the New Mosque"; Echchaibi, "Hyper-Islamism?" 199–214.

29. Hirschkind, *The Ethical Soundscape*; Anderson, "New Media, New Publics," 888–906; Abu-Lughod, *Dramas of Nationhood*; Starrett, "Islam in the Digital Age," 268–71; Hefner, *Remaking Muslim Politics*.

30. El-Tawil, "Egypt's Democratic Margin," 141.

31. Ibid.

32. In addition, the class position of the individuals involved in these activities and the nonpolitical nature of their work made them much less susceptible to

government scrutiny. The organizations were by and large independently funded and dealt with the government only in bureaucratic matters.

33. Starrett, *The Political Economy,* 51.

34. Interview, Cairo, December 6, 2006.

35. For many volunteers, participating in these mobile drives was their first exposure to impoverished neighborhoods and as such was quite transformative.

36. See also Schielke, "Being Good in Ramadan," S24–S40, on Ramadan and subjectivity.

37. "Tables of the merciful" do not count as *zakat* but as *sadaqa*: http://www.dar-alifta.org/ViewFatwa.aspx?ID=41&text=waq f.

38. A father is responsible for paying *zakat* on behalf of each of his nonadult children. In the United States, *zakat al-fitr* is equal to $11 USD. The price across the globe is calculated based on the price of a bushel of wheat in the country.

39. El Daly, *Philanthropy in Egypt.*

40. Ibid. In comparison, the Fraser Institute estimates that Americans give 1.32 percent of their income to charity, while Canadians give .64 percent. Gabler, Lammam, and Veldhuis, "Generosity in Canada and the United States," 1, http://www.fraserinstitute.org/uploadedFiles/fraser-ca/Content/research-news/research/publications/generosity-index-2011.pdf.

41. El Daly, *Philanthropy in Egypt,* 141.

42. Ibid., 145.

43. Ibid., 142.

44. Ibid., 197.

45. Interview, Cairo, November 26, 2006.

46. Ibid.

47. Interview, Cairo, December 13, 2006.

48. Ibid.

49. Interview, Cairo, December 11, 2006.

50. Ibid.

51. Interview, Cairo, December 12, 2006.

4. Privatizing Islam

1. "Mashru'at qanun al-awqaf."

2. Ghannam, *Remaking the Modern,* 195–206; Mahmood, *Politics of Piety.*

3. "Egypt Warns Against Using Mosques."

4. Mahmood, *Politics of Piety.*

5. Gaffney, *The Prophet's Pulpit,* 168.

6. Interview, Cairo, August 9, 2006.

7. Interview, Cairo, October 15, 2006.

8. Nasser required that mosques be licensed and under Ministerial Decree

97 of 1962, Nasser gave the Ministry of Endowments supervisory authority over mosques and their imams. See "Mashro'at qanuun al-awqaf."

9. Pioppi, *From Religious Charity*, 4–5. Ironically, Sadat spent his career undoing Nasserist nationalization of industries and yet nationalized private mosques in the name of security. Ministerial Decree 152 of 1973 gave the ministry the authority to assign imams and oversee mosque employees. See Pioppi, *From Religious Charity*, 1–10.

10. Addeh and Fuad, *The Legal Framework of Mosque Building*.

11. Wickham, "Islamic Mobilization." In the literature on mosques, nationalization and annexation are used interchangeably. Although the term used in Arabic is "annexation" (*damm*), not "nationalization" (*ta'mim*), the effect is the same.

12. Addeh and Fuad, *The Legal Framework of Mosque Building*.

13. Ibid.

14. Ibid.

15. Wattad and Rizzuto, "Issues in the News."

16. Mostafa, "Mahmoud Zaqzouq."

17. Atia, "Innocent Victims," 1–24.

18. Khattab, "A Call or a Cause?"

19. Mostafa, "Mahmoud Zaqzouq."

20. Charbel, "Cairo's Unified Prayer."

21. Ibid.

22. Jensen, "Government Looks to Muffle."

23. "Gov't to Keep Closer Tabs."

24. "Ministry Calls for Speeches."

25. Kamel, "Egypt Approves Draft Law."

26. June 22, 2011, http://latimesblogs.latimes.com/babylonbeyond/2011/06/egypt-drafts-for-new-laws-face-criticism.html?dlvrit=99665.

27. Massive private mosques have been built in the sprawling suburbs of Cairo, such as Qattamaya Heights, 6th of October, Rehab, Tag'am'a el-Khamis, and New Cairo. Several foundation managers I spoke to mentioned plans to build mosques in these new areas. Timothy Mitchell discusses Cairo's suburban sprawl and the role of speculative capital in Mitchell, *Rule of Experts*.

28. Benthall, "Financial Worship," 27–42.

29. Kuran, "Islamic Redistribution through Zakat," 282.

30. Singer, *Charity in Islamic Societies*.

31. Benthall, "Financial Worship," 27–42.

32. One *feddan* equals 1.038 acres.

33. Alam provides data regarding the status of *waqf* and the relations between the monarchy and religious institutions during King Farouq's rule (Alam, *Religion and State*).

34. Ener, *Managing Egypt's Poor and the Politics of Benevolence*, xxiii.

35. Omar, "Nizam al-Waqf al-Islami."

36. Interview, Cairo, August 2006.

37. Douara, "Philanthropy and Development."

38. Adelkhah, *Being Modern in Iran.*

39. Çizakça, "Waqf in History," 43–73.

40. Pioppi, *From Religious Charity,* 7; Atia, "The Arab Republic of Egypt," 23–42.

41. Bremer, "Islamic Philanthropy."

42. Toukan, "A New Arab."

43. Interview, Cairo, March 2010.

44. Ibid.

45. Ibid.

46. As part of its community programs, the foundation has a creative partnership program where "social pioneers" come up with an idea to lessen the differences between Maadi and its environs. They also had a partnership with the Egyptian Food Bank for distributing Ramadan bags, but extended the program to a "Ramadan to Ramadan waqf," which covers the nutritional requirements of the poor year-round rather than just during the month of Ramadan.

47. Maadi Community Foundation, "Waqfeyat al-Maadi."

48. Interview, Cairo, September 20, 2006.

49. Ibid.

50. Ibid.

51. August 22, 2011, http://emajmagazine.com/2011/08/22/philanthropy-roadmap-to-rebuilding-egypt/.

52. Interview, Cairo, December 12, 2006.

53. ICNL, "Information about the NGO."

54. 2005, http://www.dinarstandard.com/innovation/ilkone10305.htm. See also World Halal Forum website, www.worldhalalforum.org.

55. Gökariksel and McLarney, "Introduction," 1–18.

56. May 19, 2011, http://dinarstandard.com/leadership/adnan-durrani%E2%80%99s-saffron-road-and-ethical-consumerism/.

57. Shikoh, *Islamic Mobile Phone.*

58. Deeb and Harb, "Piety and Pleasure," 414–27; Deeb and Harb, "Politics, Culture, and Religion," 198–206; Deeb and Harb, "Sanctioned Pleasures." In a 2012 trip to Cairo, I observed the formation of a few "Islamic cafés" that mimic the leisure spaces that Deeb and Harb discuss.

59. Gökarıksel and Secor, "Islamic-Ness," 313–33; Gökariksel and McLarney, Introduction, 1–18.

60. Jones, "Images of Desire," 91–117; Lewis, "Marketing Muslim Lifestyle," 58–90.

61. Hirschkind, *The Ethical Soundscape.*

62. Pollard and Samers, "Islamic Banking and Finance," 313–30; Maurer, *Mutual Life, Limited.*

63. Ibrahim, "The 'Missing Links,'" 55–66.

64. Ibid.

65. Hassan and Lewis, "Islamic Finance," 151–60.

66. Ibid.

67. Benthall, *Financial Worship,* 27–42.

68. Little scholarly attention has documented the lending-circle phenomenon in Egypt. See Singerman, *Avenues of Participation,* 125–29, 154–57, for an exception. However, scholars have discussed similar rotating-credit associations initiated by migrants congregated in ethnic enclaves. See Yoon, "The Changing Significance of Ethnic and Class Resources in Immigrant Businesses," 303–30; Oh, "Economic Incentives, Embeddedness, and Social Support," 623–33. On refugees in camps, see Jacobsen, *The Economic Life of Refugees.* On the rural poor in places such as Kenya, see Gugerty, "You Can't Save Alone," 251–32; Chhetri, "Rotating Credit Associations in Nepal," 449, and Tsai, "Banquet Banking." Roy also found that savings are more important as a development technique than access to capital (Roy, *Poverty Capital*).

69. Interview, Cairo, May 28, 2006.

70. Hossain, "Al-qard al-hasan."

71. Omar, "Al-qard al-hasan li-l-tamwil."

72. Ahmed, "Waqf-Based Microfinance."

73. Interview, Cairo, May 22, 2006.

74. Microfinance has become a big business in Cairo, much like other parts of the Global South. See Elyachar, "Best Practices," 413–26, and *Markets of Dispossession*; Ismail, *Political Life.* For discussions of microfinance in other contexts, see Briggs, "Empowering NGOs," 233–58; Rankin, "Governing Development," 18–37; Kabeer, *The Power to Choose*; Karim, *Microfinance and Its Discontents*; and Roy, *Poverty Capital.*

75. Benthall, *Financial Worship,* 27–42.

76. Ibid.

77. Ahmed, "Waqf-Based Microfinance."

78. A markup can occur through various mechanisms. One is the cost-plus credit sale, in which the credit price is higher than the cash price (with an implicit markup). See El-Gamal, *Islamic Finance,* 213–18.

79. Hossain, "Al-qard al-hasan."

80. Rankin theorizes microcredit through a governmentality approach, asking, "How can microcredit then operate as a governmental strategy though which this particular political rationality is exercised on the social body?" Microcredit has become the favored self-help strategy, allowing the poor to help themselves through the market (Rankin, "Governing Development").

81. Ahmed, "Waqf-Based Microfinance."

82. Interview, Cairo, December 9, 2006.

83. Interview, Cairo, September 26, 2006.

84. As my interest in *qard hasan* grew, I looked for organizations that were providers in Egypt. After extensive research, I found only two organizations engaged in *qard hasan;* most organizations indicated that if they had a *qard hasan* program, it had transitioned to microfinance or in-kind tools for entrepreneurs.

85. *Sha'bi* means popular in the sense of being associated with the common people. It is often used to describe poor neighborhoods or cultural preferences or practices associated with the lower class (for example, a genre of music, or a particular type of wedding, ceremony, or taste in fabric).

86. Interview, Cairo, October 11, 2006.

87. The use of *qard hasan* to relieve debtors seemed to be increasing after the 2011 uprising. In a follow-up visit to Dar al-Orman in 2012, the director told me about a new program the association initiated to support debtors who could not pay and were at risk of going to jail. The association had provided *qard hasan* as emergency loans to 638 debtors as of June 2012.

5. Business with Allah

1. The name al-Zahrawan has a religious connotation; it means "the bright ones" and refers to two suras in the Quran, al-Baqarah and Al 'Imran, which are thought to bring light and guidance to those who read them.

2. Interview, Cairo, November 27, 2006.

3. Interview, Cairo, December 12, 2006.

4. Ibid.

5. Larner and Laurie, "Travelling Technocrats," 218–26.

6. Julia Elyachar discovered the intricate insular networks created between American University of Cairo (AUC) alumni (particularly graduates of the business school), USAID, the Social Fund for Development, and numerous NGOs involved in microenterprise. Elyachar, "Best Practices," 413–26.

7. Rose, in "Governing 'Advanced' Liberal Democracies," 37–65, and *Powers of Freedom,* describes the "know-hows of enumeration, calculation, monitoring, evaluation, management" as "grey sciences." Statistics, once called "moral science," was a critical technology of power that enabled the growth of the nineteenth-century bureaucratic machine (Hacking, "How Should We Do the History of Statistics?" 181–96). See also Porter, *Trust in Numbers,* 310; and Strathern, *Audit Cultures,* 310, for a more thorough discussion of the rise of quantitative analysis, statistics, and accounting practices.

8. Interview, Cairo, December 11, 2006.

9. Interview, Cairo, December 10, 2006.

10. Interview, Cairo, December 13, 2006.

11. The phrase "house in heaven" came up in numerous interviews as a way to describe motivations for pursuing charitable work.

12. Interview, Cairo, December 13, 2006.

13. Interview, Cairo, December 12, 2006.

14. Interview, Cairo, December 11, 2006.

15. The term ʿashwayaʾi means disorganized, scattered, unplanned. It is also the term used to refer to squatter settlements that have proliferated on the outskirts of town. These settlements, such as Manshayat Nasser, with illegally attained water and electricity, are entirely unplanned communities, without any access to government services. The term ʿashwayaʾi has a decidedly negative connotation, then, associated with disorder.

16. Interview, Cairo, December 11, 2006.

17. Homa Hoodfar discusses the economic conditions that frame the marriage problem. Hoodfar, *Between Marriage and the Market.*

18. Interview, Cairo, December 11, 2006.

19. The government, in an effort to reduce Cairo's worsening congestion, has been involved in the creation of several new urbanism-style towns outside Cairo. Many middle- and upper-class families are buying parcels of land in these areas in anticipation of mass movement out of the city and a desire to secure homes for their children. Many have built their own compounds, but several large construction companies have created what are essentially gated communities that act as suburbs.

20. Interview, Cairo, December 11, 2006.

21. Although associations run by businesspeople and former military officers were both extremely transparent, businesspeople seemed more concerned than their military counterparts about competition and sharing proprietary information.

22. Interview, Cairo, December 11, 2006.

23. Wilson, "The Show-Me Sheikh."

24. Clark, *Islam, Charity, and Activism*; Sullivan, *Private Voluntary Organizations in Egypt.*

25. Salvatore, "Social Differentiation, Moral Authority."

26. Sullivan, *Private Voluntary Organizations in Egypt*; Salvatore, "Social Differentiation, Moral Authority."

27. The square is the site in which the contentious battle over the status of Sudanese refugees played out during my first month in Cairo in December 2005. Earlier that fall, Sudanese refuges began a sit-in in the square, located near the regional office of the UN Commissioner for Refugees. The refugees, mostly from Southern Sudan, were protesting against their treatment in Egypt and demanding relocation out of the country. At the end of 2005, there were 18,946 refugees registered with UNHCR in Egypt and 11,000 asylum seekers (Currie, "Who Can Be

Added"). From October to December, thousands of refuges joined the sit-in, becoming squatters in the park, which eventually became a health and safety hazard. On December 29, four thousand Egyptian security forces invaded the square, launched water cannons, and beat protestors, resulting in twenty-seven deaths and hundreds of injuries ("Egypt: A Chronology of the Sudanese Protest Crisis" [*Africa News*, February 8, 2006]). More than two thousand refugees were detained and only released in January 2006. When I approached the square in 2006, it was heavily patrolled with security personnel, and continued to be a symbol of the contentious issue of Sudanese refugees in Cairo.

28. Interview, Cairo, November 15, 2006.

29. Ibid.

30. Ibid.

31. Procacci, "Social Economy" 105–18; Dean, *Governmentality*, 24.

32. Interview, Cairo, November 15, 2006.

33. Sullivan, *Private Voluntary Organizations in Egypt,* 71.

34. Similar to the A-level exams in the UK, Egyptian students are placed in colleges based on their scores on these exams. Engineering and Medicine are the degrees available to those at the top of their class, and are therefore seen as the most prestigious. Whereas for many years, the American University in Cairo was seen as the only legitimate option for those preferring private education, the private university market has exploded in the past few years. The German University, British University, and several other foreign institutions have opened up in the new suburbs of Cairo, further exacerbating the sprawl.

35. Interview, Cairo, November 15, 2006.

36. Ibid.

37. Ibid.

38. Ibid. Zahrawan got around the rules regarding production because it was established after the 2011 uprising.

39. Interview, Cairo, November 15, 2006.

40. Ibid.

41. Ibid. This problem of work ethic, of inefficiency in implementation, could be an explanatory variable for why an increase in the number of organizations has not meant an increase in quality.

42. Interview, Cairo, November 15, 2006.

43. Following on the heels of Timothy Mitchell's attention to the formation of the "expert" (Mitchell, *Rule of Experts*), several scholars draw attention to the linkages between education and the practices of governmentality. Matthew Sparke, for example, argues that the work of bankers and financiers in the Global South is intricately linked to their education in Western-based business schools (Sparke, "Political Geography," 357–72).

44. Interview, Cairo, June 4, 2012.

45. Interview, Cairo, December 9, 2006.

46. www.yumalyateem.com.

47. Interview, Cairo, December 9, 2006

48. Interview, Cairo, June 4, 2012.

49. The Egyptian government, the Social Fund for Development, and the World Bank created the Egyptian Poverty Map in 2006. Using poverty statistics, they created a database of the one thousand poorest villages in Egypt. Many charities and businessmen used this list as a tool to target their giving to the poorest of the poor.

50. Interview, Cairo, December 9, 2006.

51. Interview, Cairo, June 4, 2012.

52. Farnsworth and Holden, "The Business-Social Policy," 473–94; Ryan, "The New Landscape," 127.

53. Interview, Cairo, December 2009. Pro-poor investments are premised on the idea that the poor should be targeted as consumers. See, for example, Prahalad, *The Fortune at the Bottom of the Pyramid.*

54. El Daly, *Philanthropy in Egypt.*

6. Islamic "Life Makers" and Faith-Based Development

1. Khaled, "LM 14 Life Makers, Episode 14: Setting Your Goal in Life."

2. Shapiro, "Ministering to the Upwardly Mobile," 46–77. According to www .alexa.com, www.amrkhaled.net has more reach (number of views) and a higher global rank than www.oprah.com since March 2004. In 2007 www.amrkhaled.net had a ranking of 1,252 globally and forty-ninth in Egypt. The site has since slipped to 14,097 globally and 323rd in Egypt. www.alexa.com.

3. Atia, "Amr Khaled."

4. SAWS is the abbreviation used for *"Salla Allahu 'allayhi wa sallam,"* Peace be upon him. Muslims repeat this after any mention of the prophet.

5. SWT is the abbreviation for *"Subhanahu wa ta'ala,"* which translates as "He who one needs and is the highest above all." This is often repeated after mentioning God's name.

6. Khaled, "LM 13 Life Makers: Preserving Our Resources, Part 2."

7. Similarly, Deeb and Harb, "Politics, Culture, and Religion," 198–206, discuss the concept of a an Islamic milieu or *"hala Islamiyya."*

8. Dean, *Governmentality,* 20.

9. Zaied, "Da'Wa for Dollars."

10. *Nahda* literally means "awakening" in Arabic but is used to refer to an Islamic renaissance. The term is traditionally traced to the nineteenth century, when Rifa' al-Tahtawi and subsequently Jamal al-Din al-Afghani used the term. Al-Afghani is considered one of the most influential figures in the ideology of the Muslim Brotherhood.

11. Khaled, "LM 1 Life Makers: Introduction, Part 1."

12. Ibid.

13. Khaled, "LM 3 Life Makers: Introduction, Part 3."

14. Ibid.

15. Khaled, "LM 35 Life Makers: Small Industries, Part 1."

16. Weber discusses the idea of productive time and the desire to make use of every minute. The similarities between the rhetoric of neoliberal Islamism and Weber's analysis of the protestant ethic in relation to "productive" capitalism is startling (Weber, *The Protestant Ethic*, 271).

17. Ibid. See also Thompson, "Time, Work-Discipline," 56–97.

18. In the first episode of Life Makers, Khaled compares Arab countries to other "underdeveloped" countries, and Western countries, including statistics that measure illiteracy, average yearly income per citizen, patents, number of engineers working in research and development, number of daily newspapers, numbers of translated books, and computer usage.

19. Khaled, "LM 1 Life Makers: Introduction, Part 1."

20. Khaled, "LM 26 Life Makers: Our Dreams for Technology and Industry."

21. Ibid.

22. Khaled, "LM 4 Life Makers: Proactiveness, Part 1."

23. Khaled, "LM 7 Life Makers: Perfection."

24. Khaled, "LM 13 Life Makers: Preserving Our Resources, Part 2."

25. I do not think it is a coincidence that many of the youth initiatives are begun by engineering and medical students; rather there is a hierarchy of professions in Egypt. The top performing students are often the most motivated overall. Based on their performance in exams in their senior year of high school, the top performing students are given first choice in these two highly competitive university programs.

26. In 2006 the exchange rate was $1 USD = 5.74 LE.

27. Interview, Cairo, February 4, 2006.

28. Interview, Cairo, August 24, 2006.

29. Historically, volunteers in Islamic charities are retirees or homemakers.

30. Interview, Cairo, August 24, 2006.

31. Interview, Cairo, December 3, 2006.

32. Khaled, "LM 26 Life Makers: Our Dreams for Technology and Industry."

33. Interview, Cairo, August 15, 2006.

34. Ibid.

35. Interview, Cairo, October 31, 2006.

36. Interview, Cairo, December 6, 2006.

37. Interview, Cairo, October 31, 2006.

38. Khaled, "LM 16 Life Makers: Utilizing Our Minds." The emphasis on thinking as religious practice is also present in Weber's discussion of the Protestant Ethic: "Inactive contemplation is also valueless, or even directly reprehensible

if it is at the expense of one's daily work. For it is the less pleasing to God than the active performance of His will in a calling" (Weber, *The Protestant Ethic*, 271).

39. Interview, Cairo, October 31, 2006.

40. Interview, Cairo, July 6, 2006.

41. From March 2013 onwards, the trend of coalitions and collaboration among NGOs was in decline because of a new draft NGO law. See http://www.al-monitor.com/pulse/originals/2013/03/egypt-ngo-trial-morsi-repression.html.

Conclusion

1. Mitchell, *Colonising Egypt*, 218; Gibson-Graham, *The End of Capitalism*, 299; Goede, *Virtue, Fortune, and Faith*; Mitchell, *Rule of Experts*, 413.

2. Governmentality literature comes out of a focus on Western "advanced liberal." See Rose, "Governing 'Advanced' Liberal Democracies," 144; Dean, "Foucault, Government, and the Enfolding of Authority," 209–30.

3. Hindess, *Discourses of Power*, 183, and Dean, *Governing Societies*, 228, discuss liberal and illiberal forms of governance as coexisting. Clark, "FBOs and Change," also examines Islamic charities under authoritarianism. Hoffman's *Patriotic Professionalism in Urban China*, Sharma's *Logics of Empowerment*, Rudnyckyj's *Spiritual Economies*, and Ong's *Neoliberalism as Exception* all highlight the emergence of neoliberalism in illiberal or authoritarian contexts.

4. In *Rule of Experts*, Timothy Mitchell traces the project of economic reform in Egypt, pointing to the productions and exclusions that make the economy possible (413).

5. Other scholars offer conceptions such as "Spiritual Economies" or "Market Islam" or "Islamic-Neoliberal" ethic or assemblage to discuss the same phenomenon. See Rudnyckyj, "Market Islam in Indonesia," S183–201; Rudnyckyj, "Spiritual Economies," 104–41; Gökarıksel and Secor, "New Transnational Geographies," 6–12; Karaman, "Neoliberalism with Islamic Characteristics."

6. The increased involvement of the private sector in development not only privileges particular concepts of poverty but also is a risky endeavor. Since the 2011 uprising, several Egyptian charities have reported running out of money because businessmen no longer provide them with funds, which, until then, constituted the majority of their administrative budgets.

7. The concept of "McJihad" captures the notion that Islamism and capitalism are co-constitutive (Mitchell, "McJihad," 1–18).

8. See Maurer, "Re-Formatting the Economy," 54–66.

9. Hussain, "A Muslim Revolution in Egypt."

10. Bayat, "Egypt and the Post-Islamist."

11. The political aftermath of the Egyptian uprising symbolizes the merger of religion and politics that can be observed across the globe and across religions.

Hackworth, *Faith Based*, 172, discusses the merger of neoliberalism and neoconservatism of the American Right.

12. Bayat, "Egypt and the Post-Islamist."

13. Dean, *Governmentality*, 31.

14. I am evoking Timothy Mitchell, *Rule of Experts*, 413.

15. Gamal, "The Brotherhood's One-Percent."

16. Hussein, "Mind the Gap."

17. El-Tablawy and Namatalla, "Egypt's Lawmakers Approve Sukuk for Islamic Bond Issues."

18. Freedom and Justice Party, "Dr. Morsi's Electoral Program." Despite the rhetoric, the continued political instability pummeled the tourism market.

19. Widespread inequality is one of the most prominent social problems facing Egypt; it was one of the major factors of the 2011 Egyptian uprising. Money circulates in the hands of a few, while the majority of people live in poverty. For decades, Islamists (in particular) pointed to the rising gap between haves and have-nots as evidence of the corrupt nature of a secular Egypt. They gained a reputation as caring for the poor by providing them with charity, such as bags of food, blankets, and clothing. A discursive attachment of economic justice to Islam worked in the interest of Islamist political parties.

20. This is not unique to the FJP; throughout the book I have highlighted the point that many of my interlocutors also articulated their understanding of social justice not as income equality but as equal opportunity. Prior to the ousting of Mohamed Morsi in July 2013, the Egyptian economy was on the brink of collapse, the value of the pound was near an all-time low, the country was at a political standstill, new parliamentary elections were delayed, protests continued, and the country was gripped with escalating crime, violence, social disintegration, and insecurity.

21. Translation my own, Al-Nahar interview with Amr Khaled, January 19, 2012. http://www.youtube.com/watch?v=993i1FuxSCQ.

22. While Khaled was not part of the FJP's Nahda Project, he implicitly supported it and used the phrase to promote faith-based development. Evidently, Islamic charity is also a path to politics. Amr Khaled returned to Egypt after the Egyptian uprising and began his own development-oriented political party called the Egypt Party (*Hizb Misr*). The party builds on his Islamic "Life Makers" FBDO by focusing on youth and development.

Appendix

1. Qualitative methods constitute the core of my research because they offer an in-depth glimpse into processes that otherwise remain opaque. I use ethnographic methods because they illuminate the informal spaces of interaction that constitute the everyday lives of individuals; Herbert, "For Ethnography." By

using ethnographic methods, I am able to shed light on the linkages between the macrologies and micrologies of everyday life and the ways that different axes of power coagulate so as to form multiple and competing power relations (Katz, "All the World Is Staged: Intellectuals and the Projects of Ethnography").

2. The initial fieldwork was conducted while on a Fulbright grant, which required the approval of the Egyptian Ministry of Higher Education, as well as the IRB (minimal-risk) committee at the University of Washington. One requirement of the Egyptian Ministry of Higher Education is that all foreign researchers seeking research permits be affiliated with a state-sponsored university. The role of this affiliate was to facilitate the research process and he was assigned to me by the Fulbright commission to oversee my research. During the second half of my field stay, I served as a fellow at the American University in Cairo's Gerhart Center for Philanthropy and Civil Engagement. Follow up trips between 2008 and 2012 were supported by IMES at GWU.

3. Interviews were semistructured and lasted approximately one hour, allowing considerable flexibility to pursue areas of interest. Interviewees were given an informational sheet introducing the project and asking for their consent; no written consent was required for interviews conducted in Egypt. Interviews were not recorded due to in-country restrictions strictly dictated through the Fulbright Commission. Instead, I transcribed verbatim on-site during the interviews, using simultaneous translation and transliteration.

4. Islamic charity is difficult to study because the majority of giving does not occur through institutions but between individuals. A recent survey of philanthropy found that most Egyptians prefer to give secretly and through individuals rather than through institutions, motivated largely by religious invocations to give in secrecy. See Marwa El Daly, *Philanthropy in Egypt*. By 78.6 percent, Egyptians prefer to assist relatives with their donations and 36.3 percent of people would prefer to assist someone living in the same neighborhood, preferences that also resonate with religious direction regarding charitable giving.

5. For a discussion of feminist methodologies in geography, see Cope, "Feminist Epistemology in Geography," 43–57; Silvey and Lawson, "Placing the Migrant," 121; Moss, "Taking on, Thinking about, and Doing Feminist Research in Geography," 1–21; Winchester, "Qualitative Research and Its Place in Human Geography"; Deutsch, "Positionality and the Pen: Reflections on the Process of Becoming a Feminist Researcher and Writer"; Einagel, "Telling Stories, Making Selves," 223–35. For a discussion of situated knowledge and positionality in ethnographic research, see England, "Getting Personal: Reflexivity and Feminist Research," 80–89; Falconer and Kawahata, "Toward a More Fully Reflexive Feminist Geography," 103–16; Haraway, "Situated Knowleges," 287; Katz, "All the World Is Staged," 495–510; McKay, "Negotiating Positionings"; Rose, *Feminism and Geography*; Valentine, "People Like Us," 116–27.

Glossary of Arabic Terms

ʿabaya	Long, traditional overcoat.
ʿadala	Justice.
ʿadala igtimaʿi yya	Social justice.
ʿalim (pl. ʿulama')	Religious scholar or leader, including an imam.
ʿamal khayriyya	Good deeds or works, often used to refer to charitable practices.
aʿmal saliha	Good deeds or works, often used to refer to charitable practices.
ʿamal tatawwuʿi (or simply tatawwuʿiyya)	Voluntary work, voluntarism.
amanah	Trusteeship.
amn al-dawla	State security.
ʿashwa'i	Unauthorized, haphazard in conception and planning. Also refers to squatter settlements.
ʿashwa'iyyat	Informal settlements, slums.
ʿata' igtimaʿi	Philanthropy.
daʿi/ daʿiya	A preacher, or one who implements *daʿwa.*
daʿwa	Call of God, propagation of the religion, preaching.
Eid al-Adha	Feast of the Sacrifice (also called Eid al-Kabeer).
Eid al-Fitr	Feast at the end of Ramadan (also known as Eid al-Sughayyir).
fatwa (pl. fatwas)	Religious edict or legal opinion, usually an interpretation issued by an authorized sheikh to address specific questions regarding matters

	that derive from Muslims living in a different time and place than the prophet. Anglicized plural is *fatawas*.
fi sabil Allah	On the path of God, in God's way; something done to please God.
fiqh	Islamic jurisprudence or inferences based on *shari'a*.
gallabiyya	A loose long garment, the common traditional dress in Egypt, most commonly worn by those from the countryside or of modest means or origins.
gami'	Mosque.
gami'a	University. Can refer to a university, a mosque, an organization, or rotating-credit association.
gam'iyya (pl. gam'iyyat)	Gathering, assembly, or association/society. Also used to refer to nongovernmental organizations and rotating-credit associations.
gam'iyya ahliyya	People's association.
gam'iyya khayriyya	Welfare or benevolence association or society.
gam'iyya tanmawiyya	Community development associations.
hadith (pl. ahadith)	Historically transmitted report of Prophetic traditions; the documented oral traditions related to the words and deeds of Prophet Mohammed recorded by his companions and family members. Considered the second source for Muslims after the Quran.
hagg (fem. hagga)	An honorific title and form of address; designates an individual who has completed the pilgrimage to Mecca.
hajj	The pilgrimage to Mecca, one of the five pillars of Islam.
halal	Permitted; when combined with meat, it refers to meat prepared in compliance with the Quran.

haram	Forbidden.
al-hamdulillah	"Thanks be to God"; frequently used as an expression of satisfaction. Used both in good situations (as gratitude for God) and in less fortunate situations (as resignation).
Hay'at al-Awqaf al-Masriyya	Egyptian Endowment organization.
iftar (sa'im)	Breakfast for a fasting person.
al-Ikhwan (al-Muslimun)	The Muslim Brotherhood, Islamist group founded in Egypt in 1928 by Hassan Al-Banna.
imam	A religious leader who also leads prayer.
infitah	Open-door policy.
irshad dini	Religious instruction.
ijtihad	Literally, exerting one's best effort, diligence. Independent reasoning or judgment, juristic inference; interpretation.
jihad	Fighting in the name of or for the protection of Islam.
khayr	Good deeds.
khayr wa-khalas	Good deeds seeking only credit from God with little concern for material change.
khutba (diniyya)	A religious speech or sermon commonly given at a Friday congregational prayer.
kushk	Street kiosk.
lagnat al-zakat (pl. ligan al-zakat)	*Zakat* committee; part of a mosque dedicated to the collection and distribution of *zakat*.
ma'idat al-rahman	"Table of the Merciful," the name given to free *iftar* distribution during Ramadan.
masagid ahliyya	Privately funded mosques.
masarif al-zakat	The categories eligible for *zakat* disbursements outlined in the Quran.

mu'assasa (igtima'iyya) (pl. mu'assasat)	Establishment or a (social) foundation.
mudaraba	Partnership where one party provides the capital and the other the labor.
muezzin	Prayer callers.
mufti	An Islamic scholar or jurist capable of issuing *fatwas*.
mugtama' madani	Civil society.
mujaddidun	The reformers.
musharaka	Partnership.
nahda	Renaissance, revival.
nisab	Minimum amount of money that a Muslim must have after meeting his needs (over the course of one year) in order to be obliged to pay *zakat*. Determined as 98 grams of gold or sliver.
qard	Loan of fungible property.
qard hasan	Interest-free loan.
riba	Usury, a major prohibition in Islam and the subject of debate in Islamic economics.
sadaqa (pl. sadaqat)	Any good deed done voluntarily. For example, charity, voluntary giving, volunteerism.
sadaqa gariya	A specific type of ongoing *sadaqa* whose benefits are indefinite. Usually consisting of donations made to generate benefits beyond the lifetime of someone who has passed away. *Waqf* is one type of *sadaqa gariya*.
sadaqa khayriyya	Voluntary deed assisting in mosque maintenance and upkeep.
sadaqa tatawwu'iyya	Voluntary charity.
sakk (pl. sukuk)	Bond or certificate.
Sakk al-Udhiya	Sacrificial bond.

sawab	Godly rewards/points.
sha'b	The people, the nation.
sha'bi (fm. sha'biyya)	Popular, national, folklore, grassroots; something close to the people. Often used in reference to a neighborhood (*'ahya' sha'biyya,* or popular traditional neighborhood). Commonly used to mean "popular" in the meaning of populism.
shari'a	Laws derived from Islamic jurisprudence with the Quran or *hadith* as their foundation.
sheikh (pl. sheikhs)	An old man or elder, a chief or head. Commonly used as title of respect for someone's piety.
Sunna	Path or example of the Prophet Mohammed. Usually refers to his actions and words, including habits and religious practices narrated through *ahadith* (see *hadith*). Also refers to actions voluntary taken as an act of piety.
Surat al-Tawba	Quranic verses that protect the eight categories of *zakat* recipients.
tadamun igtima'i	Social solidarity.
takaful	Social solidarity, reciprocal responsibility, or mutual guaranty. Now used as insurance in Islamic economics.
takamul	Integration.
tanmiya	Development.
tanmiya bashariyya	Human development.
tanmiya Islamiyya	Islamic development.
tanmiya khayriyya	Charitable development.
taqaddum	Progress.
tatawwur	Evolution, process.
thawab	Rewards from God for good deeds.
'ulama'	Muslim legal scholars.
umma	Global community of Muslims.

al-Usar al-Muntiga	"Productive Families" program.
usul al-fiqh	Principles of legal science.
waqf (pl. awqaf)	Islamic endowment or trust.
zakat	Almsgiving; one of the five pillars of Islam and considered a religious duty and social obligation. There are many categories of *zakat* on each specific type of wealth.
zakat al-fitr	Alms on feast.
zakat al-mal	Alms given in relation to capital savings. Several different percentages and proportions are used, but in Egypt it usually refers to 2.5 percent of net income paid by Muslims each year to assist the poor. To be spent on the *masarif al-zakat*.

Bibliography

"Amr Khalid Tops Forbes Arabia Preachers' Earning List with $2.5m Net Income."
AME Info. http://www.ameinfo.com/147875.html.

"Egypt Warns Against Using Mosques for Launching Protests." *Egypt Independent (Al-Musry Al-Youm)*, January 27, 2011.

"Egypt: Hidden Emergency Law." All Africa. http://allafrica.com/stories/2012 09201151.html.

"Egypt: A Chronology of the Sudanese Protest Crisis." *Africa News*, February 8, 2006.

"Govt to Keep Closer Tabs on Nation's Mosques." *Egypt Independent (Al-Musry Al-Youm)*, August 3, 2010.

"Mashru'at qanun al-awqaf." *Halaqat al-'amal hawla istikmal al-qanun al-istirshadi li-l-waqf.* Cairo: Markaz Salah Abdullah Kamel li-l-Iqtisad al-Islami. Gami'at al-Azhar. July 29–30, 2008.

"Ministry Calls for Speeches for National Unity in All Mosques." *Egypt Independent (Al-Masry al-Youm)*, March 10, 2011.

"Mujaddidun: Not Your Typical Reality Show." http://www.masress.com/en/dailynews/64055.

"Positive Fatwas: Using Religious Rulings in the AIDS Struggle," PlusNews IRIN, http://www.plusnews.org/Report.aspx?ReportId=75728.

Abaza, Mona. *Changing Consumer Cultures of Modern Egypt: Cairo's Urban Reshaping.* Social, Economic, and Political Studies of the Middle East and Asia, vol. 101. Boston: Brill, 2006.

Abdelrahman, Maha M. *Civil Society Exposed: The Politics of NGOs in Egypt.* Library of Modern Middle East Studies, vol. 40. New York: Tauris Academic, 2004.

Abdo, Geneive. *No God but God: Egypt and the Triumph of Islam.* New York: Oxford University Press, 2000.

Abdel-Wahab, Ayman Al-Sayyid. *Dalyl al-gam'iyyat al-ahliyya al-tanmawiyya fi muhafazat al-Qahira.* Cairo: Markaz al-Ahram li-l-Dirasat al-Siyasiyya wa al-Istiratigiyya, 2003.

Abdul Salam, Oladosu Abdul Ganiyya. "Zakat: Institution for Poverty Alleviation." *Nigerian Tribune.* http://tribune.com.ng/index.php/eyes-of-islam/26882 -zakat-institution-for-poverty-alleviation.

Abu-Lughod, Lila. *Dramas of Nationhood: The Politics of Television in Egypt*. The Lewis Henry Morgan Lectures, vol. 2001. Chicago: University of Chicago Press, 2005.

———. *Local Contexts of Islamism in Popular Media*. ISIM Papers, vol. 6. Leiden: Amsterdam University Press, 2006.

Adas, E. B. "The Making of Entrepreneurial Islam and the Islamic Spirit of Capitalism." *Journal for Cultural Research* 10, no. 2 (2006): 113–24.

Addeh, Damas, and Sayida Fuad. *The Legal Framework of Mosque Building and Muslim Religious Affairs in Egypt: Toward a Strengthening of State Control*: Arab West Report, 2011.

Adelkhah, Fariba. *Being Modern in Iran*. London: C. Hurst and Company, 1999.

Ahmed, Habib. "Waqf-Based Microfinance: Realizing the Social Role of Islamic Finance." Paper written for the International Seminar on Integrating Awqaf in the Islamic Financial Sector, in Singapore. Islamic Research and Training Institute, Islamic Development Bank, Jeddah, Saudi Arabia. March 6, 2007.

Alam, Anwar. *Religion and State: Egypt, Iran, and Saudi Arabia: A Comparative Study*. New Delhi: Gyan Sagar Publications, 1998.

Alalwani, Taha Jabir. "Fatwa on Zakat for CSID." Center for the Study of Islam and Democracy, http://www.csidonline.org/index.php?option=com_content&task=view&id=148&Itemid=73.

Al-Awadi, Hesham. *In Pursuit of Legitimacy: The Muslim Brothers and Mubarak, 1982–2000*. New York: Tauris, 2004.

Al-ʿawady, Rifʿaat al-Sayid. "Al-zakat wa ʿilga mushkilat al-faqr." *Dawr dur al-zakat wa-l-waqf fi-al-takhfif min hadd al-faqr*. June 25–29 2005. Markaz Salah Abdullah Kamel li-l-Iqtisad al-Islami. Gamiʿat al-Azhar.

Alexander, Anne. *Nasser: His Life and Times*. Cairo: American University in Cairo Press, 2005.

Aly, Abdel Monem Said. "Privatization in Egypt: The Regional Dimensions." In *Privatization and Liberalization in the Middle East*. Edited by Iliya Harik and Denis J. Sullivan (Bloomington: Indiana University Press, 1992).

Anderson, Jon. "New Media, New Publics: Reconfiguring the Public Sphere of Islam." *Social Research* 70, no. 3 (Fall 2003): 888–906.

Atasoy, Y. *Islam's Marriage with Neoliberalism: State Transformation in Turkey*. New York: Palgrave Macmillan, 2009.

Atia, Mona. "The Arab Republic of Egypt." In *From Charity to Social Change: Trends in Arab Philanthropy*. Edited by Barbara Ibrahim and Dina Sherif. New York: American University in Cairo Press, 2008.

———. "Innocent Victims: An Accounting of Anti-Terrorism in the Egyptian Legal Context." *UCLA Journal of Islamic and Near Eastern Law* 9, no. 1 (2010): 1–24.

Atia, Tarek. "Amr Khaled: A Preacher's Puzzle." *Al-Ahram Weekly*, issue 765. http://weekly.ahram.org.eg/2005/765/profile.htm.

Baron, Beth. "Orphans and Abandoned Children in Modern Egypt." In *Interpreting Welfare and Relief in the Middle East,* vol. 103. Edited by Nefissa Naguib and Inger Marie Okkenhaug. Boston: Brill, 2008.

Bayat, Asef. "Activism and Social Development in the Middle East." *International Journal of Middle East Studies* 34 (2002): 1–28.

———. *Making Islam Democratic: Social Movements and the Post-Islamist Turn.* Stanford Studies in Middle Eastern and Islamic Societies and Cultures. Stanford: Stanford University Press, 2007.

———. "The Political Economy of Social Policy in Egypt." In *Social Policy in the Middle East: Economic, Political, and Gender Dynamics.* Edited by Massoud Karshenas and Valentine M. Moghadam. New York: Palgrave Macmillan, 2006.

———. "Radical Religion and the Habitus of the Dispossessed: Does Islamic Militancy Have an Urban Ecology?" *International Journal of Urban and Regional Research* 31, no. 3 (2007): 579–90.

———Bayat, Asef. "Egypt and the Post-Islamist Middle East." *Jadaliyya* (February 10, 2011): http://www.jadaliyya.com/pages/index/603/egypt-and-the -post-islamist-middle-east.

Beattie, Kirk J. *Egypt during the Nasser Years: Ideology, Politics, and Civil Society.* Boulder: Westview Press, 1994.

———. *Egypt during the Sadat Years.* New York: Palgrave, 2000.

Beaumont, Justin. "Introduction UCSIA Dialogue Series 11." Antwerp: UCSIA, 2007.

———. "Workfare, Associationism, and the 'Underclass' in the United States: Contrasting Faith-Based Action on Urban Poverty in a Liberal Welfare Regime." In *European Churches Confronting Poverty: Social Act Against Social Exclusion.* Edited by H. Noordegraaf and R. Volz. Bochum: SWI Verlag, 2004.

Beaumont, Justin, and Candice Dias. "Faith-Based Organisations and Urban Social Justice in the Netherlands." *Tijdschrift Voor Economische En Sociale Geografie (Journal of Economic & Social Geography)* 99, no. 4 (September 2008): 382–92.

Beinin, Joel, and Joe Stork. "On the Modernity, Historical Specificity, and International Context of Political Islam." In *Political Islam: Essays from Middle East Report.* Edited by Beinin and Stork. Berkeley: University of California Press, 1997.

Benthall, Jonathan. "Financial Worship: The Quranic Injunction to Almsgiving." *Journal of the Royal Anthropological Institute* 5 (1999): 27–42.

———, and Jérôme Bellion-Jourdan. *The Charitable Crescent: Politics of Aid in the Muslim World.* New York: I. B. Tauris, 2003.

Berger, Julia. "Religious Nongovernmental Organizations: An Exploratory Analysis." *Voluntas: International Journal of Voluntary & Nonprofit Organizations* 14, no. 1 (March 2003): 15.

Bianchi, Robert. *Unruly Corporatism: Associational Life in Twentieth-Century Egypt.* New York: Oxford University Press, 1989.

Bibars, Iman. *Victims and Heroines: Women, Welfare, and the Egyptian State.* London: Zed Books, 2001.

Bornstein, Erica. *The Spirit of Development: Protestant NGOs, Morality, and Economics in Zimbabwe.* Stanford: Stanford University Press.

Bremer, Jennifer. "Islamic Philanthropy: Reviving Traditional Forms for Building Social Justice." Paper presented at the annual meeting of the Center for the Study of Islam and Democracy, Washington, D.C. May 26, 2004.

Brenner, Neil, Jamie Peck, and Nik Theodore. "Variegated Neoliberalization: Geographies, Modalities, Pathways." *Global Networks* 10, no. 2 (April 2010): 182–222.

Briggs, Morgan. "Empowering NGOs: The Microcredit Movement through Foucault's Notion of Dispositif." *Alternatives* 26, no. 3 (2001): 233–58.

Cantori, Louis J. "Religion and Politics in Egypt." In *Religion and Politics in the Middle East.* Edited by Michael Curtis. American Academic Association for Peace in the Middle East. Boulder, Colo.: Westview Press, 1981.

Charbel, Jano. "Cairo's Unified Prayer Call Not So Unified." *Egypt Independent (Al-Musry Al-Youm)*, August 20, 2010.

Cheshire, Lynda, and Geoffrey Lawrence. "Neoliberalism, Individualisation, and Community: Regional Restructuring in Australia." *Social Identities* 11, no. 5 (September 2005): 435–45.

Chhetri, Ram. "Rotating Credit Associations in Nepal: Dhikuri as Capital, Credit, Saving, and Investment." *Human Organization* 54, no. 4 (1995): 449.

Chiffoleau, Sylvia. "NGOs and the Reform of the Egyptian Health System: Realistic Prospects for Governance or Pipe Dream?" In *NGOs and Governance in the Arab World.* Edited by Sarah Ben Néfissa, Nabil Abd al-Fattah, Sari Hanafi, and Carlos Milani. New York: American University in Cairo Press, 2005.

Chowdhury, Tawfique. "Is Zakat Permissible for Islamic dawah Organizations?" http://muslimmatters.org/2007/10/24/the-permissibility-of-zakat-for-islamic-dawah-organizations-a-detailed-analysis/.

Çizakça, Murat. *A History of Philanthropic Foundations: The Islamic World from the Seventh Century to the Present.* İstanbul: Boğaziçi University Press, 2000.

———. "Waqf in History and Its Implications for Modern Islamic Economies." *Islamic Economic Studies* 6, no. 1 (1998): 43–73.

———. *Islamic Capitalism and Finance: Origins, Evolutions, and the Future.* Northampton, Mass.: Edward Elgar, 2011.

Clark, Janine A. "FBOs and Change in the Context of Authoritarianism: The Islamic Center Charity Society in Jordan." In *Development, Civil Society, and Faith-Based Organizations: Bridging the Sacred and the Secular.* Edited by G. Clarke and M. Jennings. London: Palgrave Macmillan, 2008.

———. *Islam, Charity, and Activism: Middle-Class Networks and Social Welfare in*

Egypt, Jordan, and Yemen. Indiana Series in Middle East Studies. Bloomington: Indiana University Press, 2004.

Clarke, Gerard. "Faith Matters: Faith-Based Organizations, Civil Society, and International Development." *Journal of International Development* 18 (2006): 835–48.

———, and Michael Jennings. *Development, Civil Society, and Faith-Based Organizations: Bridging the Sacred and the Secular*. Edited by Michael Jennings. New
York: Palgrave Macmillan, 2008.

Comaroff, Jean, and John L. Comaroff. *Millennial Capitalism and the Culture of
Neoliberalism*. Durham: Duke University Press, 2001.

Cope, Meghan. "Feminist Epistemology in Geography." In *Feminist Geography
in Practice: Research and Methods*. Edited by Pamela J. Moss. Malden, Mass.:
Blackwell Publishers, 2002.

Cruikshank, Barbara. *The Will to Empower: Democratic Citizens and Other Subjects*. Ithaca: Cornell University Press, 1999.

Crush, Jonathan. *Power of Development*. New York: Routledge, 1995.

Currie, Lorraine. "'Who Can be Added': The Affects of Refugee Status and Third
Country Resettlement Processes on the Marriage Strategies, Rites, and Cus-
toms of the Southern Sudanese in Cairo." *Refuge* 24, no. 1 (Winter 2007).

Dean, Hartley, and Zafar Khan. "Muslim Perspectives on Welfare." *Journal of
Social Policy* 26, no. 2 (1997): 193–209.

Dean, Mitchell. "Foucault, Government, and the Enfolding of Authority." In *Foucault and Political Reason: Liberalism, Neo-Liberalism, and Rationalities of Government*. Edited by Andrew Barry, Thomas Osborne, and Nikolas S. Rose.
Chicago: University of Chicago Press, 1996.

———. *Governmentality: Power and Rule in Modern Society*. Thousand Oaks, Calif.:
Sage Publications, 1999.

Deeb, Lara, and Mona Harb. "Piety and Pleasure: Youth Negotiations of Moral
Authority and New Leisure Sites in Al-Dahiya." *Bahithat: Cultural Practices of
Arab Youth* 14 (2010): 414–27.

———. "Politics, Culture, and Religion: How Hizbullah Is Constructing an Islamic
Milieu in Lebanon." *Review of Middle East Studies* 43, no. 2 (2010): 198–206.

———. "Sanctioned Pleasures: Youth, Piety, and Leisure in Beirut." *Middle East
Report* 245 (2007).

———. *An Enchanted Modern: Gender and Public Piety in Shiʻi Lebanon*. Princeton Studies in Muslim Politics. Princeton: Princeton University Press, 2006.

de Goede, Marieke. *Virtue, Fortune, and Faith: A Genealogy of Finance*. Border-
lines, vol. 24. Minneapolis: University of Minnesota Press, 2005.

Denis, Eric. "Cairo as Neo-Liberal Capital? From Walled City to Gated Commu-
nities." In *Cairo Cosmopolitan: Politics, Culture, and Urban Space in the New
Globalized Middle East*. Edited by Diane Singerman and Paul Amar. New York:
American University in Cairo Press, 2006.

Department of Islamic Affairs and Islamic Activities. "Egypt: Endowments Ministry to Place Another 498 Mosques under Umbrella." May 12, 2008. http://www.dicd.gov.ae/vEnglish/detailnewspage.jsp?articleID=6373&newsType=4&pageFlag=0.

Deutsch, Nancy L. "Positionality and the Pen: Reflections on the Process of Becoming a Feminist Researcher and Writer." *Qualitative Inquiry* 10, no. 6 (2004): 885–902.

Douara, Deena. "Philanthropy and Development Conference Presents New Research, Calls for Waqf Revival." *Daily Star Egypt,* March 2, 2007. http://www.masress.com/en/dailynews/104060.

Dunn, Elizabeth C. *Privatizing Poland: Baby Food, Big Business, and the Remaking of Labor.* Culture and Society after Socialism. Ithaca: Cornell University Press, 2004.

Dunne, Michele Durocher. *Democracy in Contemporary Egyptian Political Discourse.* Discourse Approaches to Politics, Society, and Culture, vol. 6. Philadelphia: J. Benjamins, 2003.

Dwyer, Claire. "Veiled Meanings: Young British Muslim Women and the Negotiation of Differences." *Gender, Place & Culture: A Journal of Feminist Geography* 6, no. 1 (March 1999): 5.

Echchaibi, Nabil. "Hyper-Islamism? Mediating Islam from the Halal Website to the Islamic Talk Show." *Journal of Arab & Muslim Media Research* 1, no. 3 (November 2008): 199–214.

Egypt Information Services. *Yearbook 2007 (Social Solidarity)*: SIS Publications, Egyptian Government, 2007.

Eickelman, Dale F., and Jon W. Anderson. *New Media in the Muslim World: The Emerging Public Sphere.* Indiana Series in Middle East Studies. 2nd ed. Bloomington: Indiana University Press, 2003.

Einagel, Victoria Ingrid. "Telling Stories, Making Selves." In *Subjectivities, Knowledges, and Feminist Geographies: The Subjects and Ethics of Social Research.* Edited by L. Bondi. Lanham, Md.: Rowman and Littlefield, 2002.

El Daly, Marwa. *Philanthropy in Egypt: A Comprehensive Study on Local Philanthropy in Egypt and Potentials of Directing Giving and Volunteering Towards Development.* Cairo: Center for Development Studies (CDS), 2007.

El-Din, Gamal Essam. "USAID's New Strategy in Egypt." *Al-Ahram Weekly,* March 3–9, 2005.

El-Gamal, Mahmoud A. *Islamic Finance: Law, Economics, and Practice.* New York: Cambridge University Press, 2006.

Elisha, Omri. "Moral Ambitions of Grace: The Paradox of Compassion and Accountability in Evangelical Faith-Based Activism." *Cultural Anthropology* 23, no. 1 (February 2008): 154–89.

El-Tabwaly, Tarek, and Ahmed A. Namatalla. "Egypt's Lawmakers Approve Sukuk for Islamic Bonds." *Bloomberg Businessweek,* March 19, 2013. http://www .businessweek.com/news/2013-03-19/egypt-s-lawmakers-approve-sukuk -for-islamic-bond-issues.

El-Tawil, Hosam. "Egypt's Democratic Margin." In *Development in the Age of Liberalization: Egypt and Mexico.* Edited by Dan Tschirgi. Cairo: American University in Cairo Press, 1996.

Elyachar, Julia. "Best Practices: Research, Finance, and NGOs in Cairo." *American Ethnologist* 33, no. 3 (2006): 413–26.

———. *Markets of Dispossession: NGOs, Economic Development, and the State in Cairo.* Politics, History, and Culture. Durham: Duke University Press, 2005.

Emara, Nancy Fathy. "Islam: 'A Guide for the Perplexed': Study and Evaluation of an Attempt of Application: Alleviating Poverty in Tafahna Al-Ashraf." Master's thesis, American University in Cairo, 2003.

Encyclopædia Britannica Online. "Egypt: Year in Review 1998." http://www .britannica.com.proxygw.wric.org/EBchecked/topic/180386/Egypt-Year -In-Review-1998.

Ener, Mine. *Managing Egypt's Poor and the Politics of Benevolence, 1800–1952.* Princeton: Princeton University Press, 2003.

England, Kim V. L. "Getting Personal: Reflexivity and Feminist Research." *Professional Geographer* 46 (1994): 80–89.

Escobar, Arturo. *Encountering Development: The Making and Unmaking of the Third World.* Princeton Studies in Culture/Power/History. Princeton: Princeton University Press, 1995.

Et-Tahawy, Abdallah. "The Internet Is the New Mosque: Fatwa at the Click of a Mouse." *Arab Insight: Emerging Social and Religious Trends* 21 (Winter 2008).

Falconer, Karen, and Hope Kawahata. "Toward a More Fully Reflexive Feminist Geography." In *Feminist Geography in Practice: Research and Methods.* Edited by Pamela J. Moss. Malden, Mass.: Blackwell Publishers, 2002.

Farnsworth, Kevin, and Chris Holden. "The Business-Social Policy Nexus: Corporate Power and Corporate Inputs into Social Policy." *Journal of Social Policy* 35, no. 3 (2006): 473–94.

Ferguson, James. *Global Shadows: Africa in the Neoliberal World Order.* Durham: Duke University Press, 2006.

FIDH. "The Emergency Law in Egypt." La Fédération Internationale des Droits de l'Homme (FIDH). http://www.fidh.org/THE-EMERGENCY-LAW-IN-EGYPT.

Fouad, Viviane, Nadia Ref'at, and Samir Murcos. "From Inertia to Movement: A Study of the NGO Law." In *NGOs and Governance in the Arab World.* Edited by Sarah Ben Nefissa, Nabil Abd al-Fattah, Sari Hanafi, and Carlos Milani. Cairo: American University in Cairo Press, 2005.

Gabler, Nachum, Charles Lammam, and Niels Veldhuis. "Generosity in Canada and the United States: The 2011 Generosity Index." *Fraser Alert* (Fraser Institute, 2011), 1.

Gaffney, Patrick D. *The Prophet's Pulpit: Islamic Preaching in Contemporary Egypt.* Comparative Studies on Muslim Societies, vol. 20. Berkeley: University of California Press, 1994.

Geiger, R., and J. Wolch. "A Shadow State? Voluntarism in the Los Angeles Metropolitan Region." *Environment & Planning D: Society & Space* 4 (1986): 351–66.

Ghannam, Farha. *Remaking the Modern: Space, Relocation, and the Politics of Identity in a Global Cairo.* Berkeley: University of California Press, 2002.

Gibson-Graham, J. K. *The End of Capitalism (as We Knew It): A Feminist Critique of Political Economy.* Cambridge, Mass.: Blackwell Publishers, 1996.

————. *A Postcapitalist Politics.* Minneapolis: University of Minnesota Press, 2006.

Gidwani, Vinay K. *Capital, Interrupted: Agrarian Development and the Politics of Work in India.* Minneapolis: University of Minnesota Press, 2008.

Gökarıksel, Banu, and Anna Secor. "Islamic-Ness in the Life of a Commodity: Veiling-Fashion in Turkey." *Transactions of the Institute of British Geographers* 35, no. 3 (July 2010): 313–33.

————. "New Transnational Geographies of Islam, Capitalism, and Subjectivity: The Veiling-Fashion Industry in Turkey."*Area* 411 (2009): 6–12.

Gökariksel, Banu, and Ellen McLarney. "Introduction: Muslim Women, Consumer Capitalism, and the Islamic Culture Industry." *Journal of Middle East Women's Studies* 6, no. 3 (Fall 2010): 1–18, 200–202.

Gran, Peter. *Islamic Roots of Capitalism: Egypt, 1760–1840.* Cairo: American University in Cairo Press, 1999.

Gugerty, Mary Kay. "You Can't Save Alone: Commitment in Rotating Savings and Credit Associations in Kenya." *Economic Development & Cultural Change* 55, no. 2 (2007): 251–82.

Gupta, Akhil. "Blurred Boundaries: The Discourse of Corruption, the Culture of Politics, and the Imagined State." In *The Anthropology of the State: A Reader,* vol. 9. Edited by Aradhana Sharma and Akhil Gupta. Malden, Mass.: Blackwell Publishers, 2006.

Gupta, Akhil, and James Ferguson. "Beyond 'Culture': Space, Identity, and the Politics of Difference." *Cultural Anthropology* 7, no. 1 (February 1992): 6–23.

————. "Spatializing States: Toward an Ethnography of Neoliberal Governmentality." *American Ethnologist* 29, no. 4 (2002): 981–1002.

Hacking, Ian. "How Should We Do the History of Statistics?" In *The Foucault Effect: Studies in Governmentality: With Two Lectures by and an Interview with Michel Foucault.* Edited by Graham Burchell, Michel Foucault, Colin Gordon, and Peter Miller. Chicago: University of Chicago Press, 1991.

Hackworth, Jason. *Neoliberalism, Social Welfare, and the Politics of Faith in the United States*. Toronto: Center for Urban and Community Studies, 2007.

Hackworth, Jason R. *Faith Based: Religious Neoliberalism and the Politics of Welfare in the United States*. Geographies of Justice and Social Transformation, vol. 11. Athens: University of Georgia Press, 2012.

Hafez, Sherine. "Women Developing Women: Islamic Approaches for Poverty Alleviation in Rural Egypt." *Feminist Review* 97 (2011): 56–73.

Hakm, Nabil. "Dawr Bank Nasser al-igtimaʿi fi daʿm wa-tanmiyat al-mashruʾat al-saghyra." Bank Nasser Al-Igtimaʿi. Unpublished manuscript, n.d.

Hamza, Mohamed. "The State, Foreign Aid and the Political Economy of Shelter in Egypt." In *Market Economy and Urban Change: Impacts in the Developing World*. Edited by Roger Zetter and Mohamed Hamza. Sterling, Va.: Earthscan, 2004.

Haraway, Donna Jeanne. "Situated Knowledges: The Science Question in Feminism and the Privilege of Partial Perspective." In *Simians, Cyborgs, and Women: The Reinvention of Nature*. London: Free Association Books, 1991.

Harb, Mona. "Faith-Based Organizations as Effective Development Partners? Hezbollah and Post-War Reconstruction in Lebanon." In *Development, Civil Society, and Faith-Based Organizations: Bridging the Sacred and the Secular*. Edited by G. Clarke and M. Jennings. London: Palgrave Macmillan, 2008.

Harik, Iliya, and Denis J. Sullivan. *Privatization and Liberalization in the Middle East*. A Midland Book. Bloomington: Indiana University Press, 1992.

Hart, Gillian. "Geography and Development: Critical Ethnographies." *Progress in Human Geography* 28, no. 1 (2004): 91–100.

———. "Geography and Development: Development/s Beyond Neoliberalism? Power, Culture, Political Economy." *Progress in Human Geography* 26, no. 6 (December 2002): 812–22.

———*Unfolding Neoliberalisms*. Seattle: University of Washington Colloquium Series, 2005. (Lecture).

Hasan, Sami. "Muslim Philanthropy and Social Security: Prospects, Practices, and Pitfalls." Paper presented at the 6th ISTR Biennial Conference, Bangkok.

Hasan, Zubair. "Distributional Equity in Islam." In *Distributive Justice and Need Fulfilment in an Islamic Economy*. Edited by Munawar Iqbal. Leicester, UK: Islamic Foundation; Islamabad, Pakistan: International Institute of Islamic Economics, 1988.

Hassan, Amro. "Draft Laws for Mosques and Churches Face Criticism." Los Angeles Times, June 22, 2011. http://latimesblogs.latimes.com/babylonbeyond/2011/06/egypt-drafts-for-new-laws-face-criticism.html?dlvrit=99665.

Hassan, M. Kabir, and Mervyn K. Lewis. "Islamic Finance: A System at the Crossroads?" *Thunderbird International Business Review* 49, no. 2 (2007): 151–60.

Hefferan, Tara. "Finding Faith in Development: Religious Non-Governmental

Organizations (NGOs) in Argentina and Zimbabwe." *Anthropological Quar*
terly 80, no. 3 (2007): 887–89.

———, Julie Adkins, and Laurie A. Occhipinti. *Bridging the Gaps: Faith-Based*
Organizations, Neoliberalism, and Development in Latin America and the Carib-
bean. Lanham, Md.: Lexington Books, 2009.

Hefner, Robert W. *Civil Islam: Muslims and Democratization in Indonesia.* Princeton Studies in Muslim Politics. Princeton: Princeton University Press, 2000.

———. *Remaking Muslim Politics: Pluralism, Contestation, Democratization.* Princeton: Princeton University Press, 2005.

Herbert, Steve. "For Ethnography." *Progress in Human Geography* 24, no. 4 (2000):
595–613.

Hirschkind, Charles. *The Ethical Soundscape: Cassette Sermons and Islamic Coun-*
terpublics. Cultures of History. New York: Columbia University Press, 2006.

Hirst, Paul Q., and Grahame Thompson. *Globalization in Question: The Interna-*
tional Economy and the Possibilities of Governance. 2nd ed. Malden, Mass.: Polity
Press, 1999.

Hobsbawm, E. J., and T. O. Ranger. *The Invention of Tradition.* Past and Present
Publications. New York: Cambridge University Press, 1983.

Hoexter, M. *Waqf* Studies in the Twentieth Century: The State of the Art. *Jour-*
nal of the Economic and Social History of the Orient 41, no. 4 (1998): 474–95.

Hoffman, Lisa. "Autonomous Choices and Patriotic Professionalism: On Governmentality in Late-Socialist China." *Economy and Society* 35, no. 4 (November 2006): 550–70.

———. *Patriotic Professionalism in Urban China: Fostering Talent.* Philadelphia:
Temple University Press, 2010.

Hoodfar, Homa. *Between Marriage and the Market: Intimate Politics and Survival*
in Cairo. Comparative Studies on Muslim Societies, vol. 24. Berkeley: University of California Press, 1997.

———. "Return to the Veil: Personal Strategy and Public Participation in Egypt."
In *Working Women: International Perspectives on Labor and Gender Ideology.*
Edited by Nanneke Redclift and M. Thea Sinclair. London; New York: Rout-
ledge, 1991.

Hope, Ann, and Sally Timmel. *A Kenyan Experience for Faith-Based Transforma-*
tive Action. New York: Palgrave Macmillan, 2003.

Hossain, Mohammad Delwar. "Al-Qard al-Hasan: A Practical Approach." Unpublished Manuscript.

Hussein, Marwa. "Mind the Gap: It's Harming Egypt's Economic Growth, Says
UN." Ahram Online, September 13, 2012. http://english.ahram.org.eg/News
Content/3/12/52717/Business/Economy/Mind-the-gap,-its-harming-Egypts
-economic-growth,-.aspx.

Ibrahim, Badr El Din A. "The 'Missing Links' between Islamic Development Objectives and the Current Practice of Islamic Banking: The Experience of the Sudanese Islamic Banks (SIBs)." *Humanomics* 22, no. 2 (2006): 55–66.

Ibrahim, Barbara. "Introduction: Arab Philanthropy in Transition." In *From Charity to Social Change: Trends in Arab Philanthropy.* Edited by Barbara Ibrahim and Dina Sherif. New York: American University in Cairo Press, 2008.

Ibrahim, Saad Eddin. *An Assessment of Grass Roots Participation in the Development of Egypt.* Cairo Papers in Social Science, vol. 19, monograph 3. Cairo: American University in Cairo Press, 1997.

———. *Egypt, Islam, and Democracy: Critical Essays, with a New Postscript.* New York: American University in Cairo Press, 2002.

———. "Islamic Activism and Political Opposition in Egypt." In *Egypt, Islam, and Democracy: Critical Essays, with a New Postscript.* Edited by Saad Eddin Ibrahim. New York: American University in Cairo Press, 2002.

ICNL. "Implementing Regulation for Law 84 of 2002 (Ministry of Social Affairs Decision 178 of 2002)." International Center for Not-for-profit Law. http://www.icnl.org/research/library/files/Egypt/law178-2002-Ar.pdf.

Ilcan, Suzan, and Anita Lacey. *Governing the Poor: Exercises of Poverty Reduction, Practices of Global Aid.* Montreal: McGill-Queen's University Press, 2011.

Iqbal, Munawar. *Distributive Justice and Need Fulfillment in an Islamic Economy.* Leicester, UK: Islamic Foundation; Islamabad, Pakistan: International Institute of Islamic Economics, 1988.

Isma'il, Muhammad Bakr. "Kayfa Tuzakki Malaka wa-Tigarataka" [How to give zakat on your money and your trade]. Professor of Quranic Studies and Interpretation at al-Azhar University, Dar al-Manar, Cairo.

Ismail, Salwa. "Being Muslim: Islam, Islamism, and Identity Politics." *Government and Opposition* 39, no. 4 (2004): 614–31.

———. *Political Life in Cairo's New Quarters: Encountering the Everyday State.* Minneapolis: University of Minnesota Press, 2006.

Ismael, Tareq Y. *Middle East Politics Today: Government and Civil Society.* Gainesville: University Press of Florida, 2001.

Jacobsen, Karen. *The Economic Life of Refugees.* Bloomfield, Conn.: Kumarian Press, 2005.

Jensen, Jon. "Government Looks to Muffle the Clamor of Cairo's Mosques." *Global Post*, September 5, 2010.

Jones, Carla. "Images of Desire: Creating Virtue and Value in an Indonesian Islamic Lifestyle Magazine." *Journal of Middle East Women's Studies* 6, no. 3 (Fall 2010): 91–117, 201.

Kabeer, Naila. *The Power to Choose: Bangladeshi Women and Labour Market Decisions in London and Dhaka.* New York: Verso, 2000.

Kamel, Mansour. "Egypt Approves Draft Law on Unified Places of Worship." *Egypt Independent (Al-Musry Al-Youm)*, June 1, 2011.

Kandil, Amani. *Defining the Nonprofit Sector: Egypt*: Johns Hopkins University Institute for Policy Studies, 1993.

———. "Al-ʿamal al-khayri wa-l-tanmiya fi Misr." *Nadwat al-ʿamal al-khayri fi Misr: al-waqiʿ wa-l-mʾamul*. Cairo: Al-Gamʿiyyat al-Khayriyya al-Islamiyya. February 18, 2002.

Karaman, Ozan. (2013) "Neoliberalism with Islamic Characteristics." *Urban Studies*.

Karim, Lamia. *Microfinance and Its Discontents: Women in Debt in Bangladesh*. Minneapolis: University of Minnesota Press, 2011.

Kasbah, Moustafa Dassouki. "al-gamiʿyyat al-ahliyya fi-Misr: al-waqiʿ wa-l-maʿmul fi dawʾ al-mutghayyirat al-dawliyya wa-l-mahaliyya." *Nadwat al-taqyim al-iqtisadi wa-l-igtimaʿi li-l-gamʿiyyat al-khayriyya al-ahliyya fi Gumhuriyyat Misr al-ʿArabiyya*, vol. 1. October 29–30, 1997. Cairo: Markaz Salah Abdullah Kamel lil Iqtissad al-Islami. Gamiʿat al-Azhar.

Katz, Cindi. "All the World Is Staged: Intellectuals and the Projects of Ethnography." *Environment & Planning D: Society & Space* 10 (1992): 495–510.

Khadduri, Majid. *The Islamic Conception of Justice*. Baltimore: Johns Hopkins University Press, 1984.

Khaf, Monzer. "Islamic Banks: The Rise of a New Power Alliance of Wealth and Shariʿa Scholarship." In *The Politics of Islamic Finance*. Edited by Rodney Wilson and Clement M. Henry. Edinburgh: Edinburgh University Press, 2004.

Khaled, Amr. "LM 1 Life Makers, Episode 1: Introduction, Part 1" (lecture, Cairo, 2004).

———. "LM 13 Life Makers, Episode 13: Preserving Our Resources, Part 2" (lecture, Cairo, 2004).

———. "LM 14 Life Makers, Episode 14: Setting Your Goal in Life" (lecture, Cairo, 2004).

———. "LM 16 Life Makers, Episode 16: Utilizing Our Minds" (lecture, Cairo, 2004).

———. "LM 26 Life Makers, Episode 26: Our Dreams for Technology and Industry" (lecture, Cairo, 2004).

———. "LM 35 Life Makers, Episode 35: Small Industries, Part 1" (lecture, Cairo, 2004).

———. "LM 4 Life Makers, Episode 4: Proactiveness, Part 1" (lecture, Cairo, 2004).

———. "LM 7 Life Makers, Episode 7: Perfection" (lecture, Cairo, 2004).

———. "LM3 Life Makers, Episode 3: Introduction, Part 3" (lecture, Cairo, 2004).

Khattab, Azza. "A Call or a Cause?" *Egypt Today* 27, no. 6 (June 2006).

Kroessin, Mohammed R., and Abdulfatah S. Mohamed. "Saudi Arabian NGOs in Somalia: 'Wahabi' Daʿwah or Humanitarian Aid?" In *Development, Civil Society, and Faith-Based Organizations: Bridging the Sacred and the Secular.* Edited by G. Clarke and M. Jennings. London: Palgrave Macmillan, 2008.

Kuran, Timur. "The Genesis of Islamic Economics: A Chapter in the Politics of Muslim Identity." *Social Research* 64, no. 2 (1997): 301–38.

———. "Islamic Redistribution through Zakat: Historical Record and Modern Realities." In *Poverty and Charity in Middle Eastern Contexts.* Edited by Michael David Bonner, Mine Ener, and Amy Singer. Albany: State University of New York Press, 2003.

Labib, Gihan Wasfy. "Charity Versus Social Development: The Grassroots Approach of the Coptic Church and Monasticism." Master's thesis, American University in Cairo, 2005.

Larner, Wendy. "Neo-Liberalism: Policy, Ideology, Governmentality." *Studies in Political Economy* 63 (Autumn 2000): 5–25.

———. "Neoliberalism?" *Environment & Planning D: Society & Space* 21, no. 5 (2003): 509–12.

Larner, Wendy, and Nina Laurie. "Travelling Technocrats, Embodied Knowledges: Globalising Privatisation in Telecoms and Water." *Geoforum* 412 (2010): 218–26.

Lawson, Victoria A. *Making Development Geography.* Human Geography in the Making. New York: Hodder Arnold, 2007.

Lewis, Reina. "Marketing Muslim Lifestyle: A New Media Genre." *Journal of Middle East Women's Studies* 6, no. 3 (Fall 2010): 58–90, 201.

Li, Tania. *The Will to Improve: Governmentality, Development, and the Practice of Politics.* Durham: Duke University Press, 2007.

Lippman, Thomas W. *Egypt After Nasser: Sadat, Peace, and the Mirage of Prosperity.* New York: Paragon House, 1989.

Lombardi, Clark B. *State Law as Islamic Law in Modern Egypt: The Incorporation of the Sharia into Egyptian Constitutional Law.* Boston: Brill, 2006.

Maadi Community Foundation. "Waqfeyat al-Maadi." http://www.waqfeyatalmaadi-cf.org/.

al-Mahdy, Husayn. "Dawr al-istithmar fi tanmiyat al-'amal al-Islami." Unpublished manuscript, n.d.

Mahmood, Saba. *Politics of Piety: The Islamic Revival and the Feminist Subject.* Princeton: Princeton University Press, 2005.

Makhimar, Fouad Ali. "Al-gam'iyya al-shar'iyya wa-l-'amal al-khayri." *Nadwat al-'amal al-khayri fi Misr: al-waqi' wa-l-ma'mul.* Cairo: Al-Gam'iyyat al-Khayriyya al-Islamiyya. February 18, 2002.

Mallat, Chibli. "Tantawi on Banking in Egypt." In *Islamic Legal Interpretation: Muftis and Their Fatwas.* Edited by Muhammad Khalid Masud, Brinkley Messick, and David S. Powers. Cambridge, Mass.: Harvard University Press, 1996.

Maurer, Bill. *Mutual Life, Limited: Islamic Banking, Alternative Currencies, Lateral Reason.* Princeton: Princeton University Press, 2005.

———. "Re-Formatting the Economy: Islamic Banking and Finance in World Politics." In *Islam in World Politics.* Edited by Nelly Lahoud and Anthony H. Johns. New York: Routledge, 2005.

Mayer, Ann Elizabeth. "Islamic Banking and Credit Policies in the Sadat Era: The Social Origins of Islamic Banking in Egypt." *Arab Law Quarterly* 1, no. 1 (1985): 32–50.

McKay, Deirdre. "Negotiating Positionings: Exchanging Life Stories in Research Interviews." In *Feminist Geography in Practice: Research and Methods.* Edited by Pamela J. Moss. Malden, Mass.: Blackwell Publishers, 2002.

Mian, Nadia A. "'Prophets-for-Profits': Redevelopment and the Altering Urban Religious Landscape." *Urban Studies (Sage Publications)* 45, no. 10 (September 2008): 2143–61.

Milton-Edwards, Beverley. *Contemporary Politics in the Middle East.* 2nd ed. Malden, Mass.: Polity, 2006.

Mitchell, Katharyne. "Neoliberal Governmentality in the European Union: Education, Training, and Technologies of Citizenship." *Environment & Planning D: Society & Space* 24, no. 3 (June 2006): 389–407.

Mitchell, Timothy. *Colonizing Egypt.* Berkeley: University of California Press, 1991.

———. "Introduction." In *Questions of Modernity.* Edited by Timothy Mitchell. Minneapolis: University of Minnesota Press, 2000.

———. "McJihad: Islam in the U.S. Global Order." *Social Text* 20, no. 4 (2002): 1–18.

———. *Rule of Experts: Egypt, Techno-Politics, Modernity.* Berkeley: University of California Press, 2002.

———. "Society, Economy, and the State Effect." In *The Anthropology of the State: A Reader,* vol. 9. Edited by Aradhana Sharma and Akhil Gupta. Malden, Mass.: Blackwell Publishers, 2006.

Moaddel, Mansoor. *Islamic Modernism, Nationalism, and Fundamentalism: Episode and Discourse.* Chicago: University of Chicago Press, 2005.

Moll, Yasmin. "Islamic Televangelism: Religion, Media, and Visuality in Contemporary Egypt." *Arab Media & Society* no. 10 (2010).

Morrison, John. "The Government-Voluntary Sector Compacts: Governance, Governmentality, and Civil Society." *Journal of Law and Society* 27, no. 1 (March 2000): 98.

Moss, Pamela J. "Taking on, Thinking about, and Doing Feminist Research in Geography." In *Feminist Geography in Practice: Research and Methods.* Edited by Pamela J. Moss. Malden, Mass.: Blackwell Publishers, 2002.

Mostafa, Hadia. "Mahmoud Zaqzouq." *Egypt Today,* January 2005.

———. "The Third Pillar." *Egypt Today,* October 2004. 6.

Moustafa, Tamir. "Conflict and Cooperation between the State and Religious Institutions in Contemporary Egypt." *International Journal of Middle East Studies* 32 (2000): 3–22.

Mustafa , Aziza Youssef. "Dawr wizarat al-tadamun al-igtima'i fi taf'yl dawr al-munazzamat ghayr hukumiyya wa-l-tansyq ma'aha li-tahqiq al-tadamun al-igtima'i." *Nadwat dawr al-munazzamat ghayr al-hukuumiyya fi-l-tadamun al-igtima'i.* May 31, 2006. Cairo: Markaz Salah Abdullah Kamel li-l-Iqtisad al-Islami. Gami'at al-Azhar.

Nabil, Asmaa. "Islamic Banking Loses Patrons." *Daily News Egypt,* June 24, 2012.

Nakashima, Yoichi. *The Political Understanding of Al-'Infitah Al-'Iqtisadi: A Case Study of Economic Liberalization in Egypt.* Yamato-machi, Niigata-ken, Japan: Kokusai Daigaku Ch⁻ut⁻o Kenky⁻ujo, 1987.

Naqvi, Syed Nawab Haider. *Ethics and Economics: An Islamic Synthesis.* Islamic Economic Series, vol. 2. Leicester, UK: Islamic Foundation, 1981.

Nassar, Heba, and Heba El Laithy. *Proceedings of the Conference on Socioeconomic Policies and Poverty Alleviation Programs in Egypt.* Cairo: Jâami°at al-Qâahirah. Markaz al-Buòhâuth wa-al-Dirâasâat al-Iqtiòsâadâiyah wa-al-Mâalâiyah, 2001.

Nielsen, Jorgen S. *Muslims in Western Europe.* Islamic Surveys. 2nd ed. Edinburgh: University of Edinburgh Press, 1995.

Oh, Joong-Hwan. "Economic Incentives, Embeddedness, and Social Support: A Study of Korean-Owned Nail Salon Workers' Rotating Credit Associations." *International Migration Review* 41, no. 3 (2007): 623–56.

Olson, Elizabeth. "Common Belief, Contested Meanings: Development and Faith-Based Organisational Culture." *Tijdschrift Voor Economische En Sociale Geografie (Journal of Economic & Social Geography)* 99, no. 4 (September 2008): 393–405.

Omar, Mohamed Abdel Halim. "Al-qard al-hasan li-tamwil al-'amal al-khayri fi al-gam'iyyat al-Ahliyya fi itar al-tamwil shibh al-rasmy." Al-Azhar University, Cairo. Unpublished manuscript.

———"Nizam al-waqf al-Islami wa-l-nuzum al-mushabiha fi al-'alam al-gharby [Endowment-Foundation-Trust]." Lecture presented at the Second Conference for Waqf, Umm Al-Qura University, Mecca, Saudi Arabia.

Ong, Aihwa. *Neoliberalism as Exception: Mutations in Citizenship and Sovereignty.* Durham: Duke University Press, 2006.

Oran, Ahmad, and Salim Rashid. "Fiscal Policy in Early Islam," *Public Finance* 44, (1989): 75–101.

O'Reilly, Kathleen. "The Promise of Patronage: Adapting and Adopting Neoliberal Development." *Antipode* 42, no. 1 (2010): 179–200.

Osella, Filippo, and Caroline Osella. "Muslim Entrepreneurs in Public Life between India and the Gulf: Making Good and Doing Good." *Journal of the Royal Anthropological Institute* 15 (May 2, 2009): S202–21.

Peck, Jamie. "Geography and Public Policy: Constructions of Neoliberalism." *Progress in Human Geography* 28, no. 3 (June 2004): 392.

———. "Neoliberalizing States: Thin Policies/Hard Outcomes." *Progress in Human Geography* 25, no. 3 (2001): 445–55.

———. *Workfare States.* New York: Guilford Press, 2001.

Peck, Jamie, Nik Theodore, and Neil Brenner. "Postneoliberalism and Its Malcontents." *Antipode,* vol. 41 (2010): 94–116.

Peck, Jamie, and Adam Tickell. "Neoliberalizing Space." *Antipode* 34, no. 3 (June 2002): 380.

Peet, Richard, and Elaine R. Hartwick. *Theories of Development.* New York: Guilford Press, 1999.

Pioppi, Daniela. *From Religious Charity to the Welfare State and Back: The Case of Islamic Endowments (Waqfs) Revival in Egypt.* Rome: Robert Schuman Center for Advanced Studies, 2004.

Pollard, Jane, and Michael Samers. "Islamic Banking and Finance: Postcolonial Political Economy and the Decentring of Economic Geography." *Transactions of the Institute of British Geographers* 32, no. 3 (2007): 313–30.

Pollard, Lisa. *Nurturing the Nation: The Family Politics of Modernizing, Colonizing, and Liberating Egypt, 1805–1923.* Berkeley: University of California Press, 2005.

Porter, Theodore M. *Trust in Numbers: The Pursuit of Objectivity in Science and Public Life.* Princeton: Princeton University Press, 1995.

Powell, Russell. "Zakat: Drawing Insight for Legal Theory and Economic Policy from Islamic Jurisprudence." *Pittsburgh Tax Review* 43, no. 7 (2010): 43–101.

Prahalad, C. K. *The Fortune at the Bottom of the Pyramid.* Upper Saddle River, N.J.: Wharton School Publishing, 2006.

Pred, Allan Richard, and Michael Watts. *Reworking Modernity: Capitalisms and Symbolic Discontent.* Hegemony and Experience. New Brunswick, N.J.: Rutgers University Press, 1992.

Procacci, Giovanna. "Social Economy and the Government of Poverty." In *The Foucault Effect: Studies in Governmentality: With Two Lectures by and an Interview with Michel Foucault.* Edited by Graham Burchell, Michel Foucault, Colin Gordon, and Peter Miller. Chicago: University of Chicago Press, 1991.

Qaradawi, Yusuf. Fiqh al-zakat: dirasah muqaranah li-ahkamiha wa-falsafatiha fi daw' al-Qur'an wa-al-sunnah. *Fiqh al Zakah (Volume I): A Comparative Study of Zakah Regulations and Philosophy in the Light of Quran and Sunnah.* Beirut: Mu'assasat al-Risalah, 1977.

Qurasishi, Marghoob A. The Institution of Zakat and Its Economic Impact on Society. *Proceedings of the Second Harvard University Forum on Islamic Finance: Islamic Finance into the 21st Century.* Cambridge, Mass. Center for Middle Eastern Studies, Harvard University (1999): 77–81.

Qutb, Sayyid. *Social Justice in Islam*. Translated by John B. Hardie. Rev. ed. Oneonta, N.Y.: Islamic Publications International, 2000.

Rahnema, Majid, and Victoria Bawtree. *The Post-Development Reader*. London: Zed Books, 1997.

Rankin, Katharine N. "Governing Development: Neoliberalism, Microcredit, and Rational Economic Woman." *Economy and Society* 30, no. 1 (February 2001): 18–37.

Rose, Gillian. *Feminism and Geography: The Limits of Geographical Knowledge*. Cambridge: Polity Press, 1993.

Rose, Nikolas. "Governing 'Advanced' Liberal Democracies." In *Foucault and Political Reason: Liberalism, Neo-Liberalism, and Rationalities of Government*. Edited by Andrew Barry, Thomas Osborne, and Nikolas S. Rose. Chicago: University of Chicago Press, 1996.

———. "Governing 'Advanced' Liberal Democracies." In *The Anthropology of the State: A Reader,* vol. 9. Edited by Aradhana Sharma and Akhil Gupta. Malden, Mass.: Blackwell Publishers, 2006.

———. *Powers of Freedom: Reframing Political Thought*. Cambridge: Cambridge University Press, 1999.

Roy, Ananya. *Poverty Capital: Microfinance and the Making of Development*. New York: Routledge, 2010.

———. "Subjects of Risk: Technologies of Gender in the Making of Millennial Modernity." *Public Culture* 24, no. 1 (2012): 131–55.

Roy, Delwin A. "Islamic Banking." *Middle Eastern Studies* 27, no. 3 (1991): 427.

Rudnyckyj, Daromir. "Market Islam in Indonesia." *Journal of the Royal Anthropological Institute* 15 (May 2009): S183–201.

———. "Spiritual Economies: Islam and Neoliberalism in Contemporary Indonesia." *Cultural Anthropology* 24, no. 1 (February 2009): 104–41.

———*Spiritual Economies: Islam, Globalization, and the Afterlife of Development*. Ithaca: Cornell University Press, 2010.

Ryan, William P. "The New Landscape for Nonprofits." *Harvard Business Review* 77, no. 1 (1999): 127.

Sabra, Adam Abdelhamid. *Poverty and Charity in Medieval Islam: Mamluk Egypt, 1250–1517*. Cambridge Studies in Islamic Civilization. New York: Cambridge University Press, 2000.

Sabry, Sarah. *Poverty Lines in Greater Cairo: Underestimating and Misrepresenting Poverty*. London: International Institute for Environment and Development, 2009.

Said Aly, Abdel Monem. "Privatization in Egypt: The Regional Dimensions." In *Privatization and Liberalization in the Middle East*. Edited by Iliya Harik and Denis J. Sullivan. Bloomington: Indiana University Press, 1992.

Said Aly, Abdel Monem, Ayşe Öncü, Çağlar Keyder, and Saad Eddin Ibrahim.

Developmentalism and Beyond: Society and Politics in Egypt and Turkey. Cairo: American University in Cairo Press, 1994.

Salvatore, Armando. "Social Differentiation, Moral Authority, and Public Islam in Egypt." *Anthropology Today* 16, no. 2 (April 2000): 12–15.

Sansi Roca, Roger. "'Dinheiro Vivo': Money and Religion in Brazil." *Critique of Anthropology* 27, no. 3 (September 1, 2007): 319–39.

Sarif, Suhaili, and Nor 'Azzah Kamri. "A Theoretical Discussion of Zakat for Income Generation and Its *Fiqh* Issues." *Shariah Journal* 17, no. 3 (2009): 457–500.

Schielke, Samuli. "Being Good in Ramadan: Ambivalence, Fragmentation, and the Moral Self in the Lives of Young Egyptians." *Journal of the Royal Anthropological Institute* 15 (March 2009): S24–40.

———. "Policing Ambiguity: Muslim Saints-Day Festivals and the Moral Geography of Public Space in Egypt." *American Ethnologist* 35, no. 4 (November 2008): 539–52.

Selinger, Leah. "The Forgotten Factor: The Uneasy Relationship between Religion and Development." *Social Compass* 51, no. 4 (December 2004): 523–43.

Shapiro, Samantha M. "Ministering to the Upwardly Mobile Muslim." *New York Times,* April 30, 2006, 46–77.

Sharma, Aradhana. "Crossbreeding Institutions, Breeding Struggle: Women's Empowerment, Neoliberal Governmentality, and State (Re)Formation in India." *Cultural Anthropology* 21, no. 1 (2006): 60–95.

———. *Logics of Empowerment: Development, Gender and Governance in Neoliberal India*. Minneapolis: University of Minnesota Press, 2008.

Sharp, Jeremy M. *U.S. Foreign Assistance to the Middle East: Historical Background, Recent Trends*. Washington, D.C.: Congressional Research Service, 2010.

Sonbol, Amira El-Ashary. "Egypt." In *The Politics of Islamic Revivalism: Diversity and Unity*. Edited by Shireen Hunter (Bloomington: Indiana University Press, 1988).

Rafi-uddin Shikoh. "Islamic Mobile Phone Signals Emergence of Muslim Lifestyle Market." *Dinar Standard,* January 3, 2005. http://www.dinarstandard.com/innovation/ilkone10305.htm.

Shujaat, Mohammad. *Social Justice in Islam*. New Delhi: Anmol Publications, 2004.

Silvey, Rachel, and Victoria Lawson. "Placing the Migrant." *Annals of the Association of American Geographers* 89, no. 1 (March 1999): 121.

Singer, Amy. *Charity in Islamic Societies*. Themes in Islamic History. Cambridge: Cambridge University Press, 2008.

Singerman, Diane. *Avenues of Participation: Family, Politics, and Networks in Urban Quarters of Cairo*. Princeton: Princeton University Press, 1995.

Sklair, Leslie. *Globalization: Capitalism and Its Alternatives*. New York: Oxford University Press, 2002.

Slackman, Michael. "Egypt's Problem and Its Challenge: Bread Corrupts." *New York Times,* January 17, 2008, sec. World.

Smith, Neil. "Contours of a Spatialized Politics: Homeless Vehicles and the Production of Geographical Scale." *Social Text* 33 (1992): 54–81.

Solayman, Hanan. "Philanthropy: Roadmap to Rebuilding Egypt," August 22, 2011, EMAJ magazine (Euro-Mediterranean Academy for Young Journalists), http://emajmagazine.com/2011/08/22/philanthropy-roadmap-to-rebuilding-egypt/.

Sonbol, Amira El-Ashary. "Egypt." In *The Politics of Islamic Revivalism: Diversity and Unity*. Edited by Shireen Hunter. Bloomington: Indiana University Press, 1988.

Sparke, Matthew. "Political Geography: Political Geographies of Globalization (2) —Governance." *Progress in Human Geography* 30, no. 3 (June 2006): 357–72.

Starrett, Gregory. "Islam in the Digital Age: E-Jihad, Online Fatwas, and Cyber Islamic Environments." *History of Religions* 46, no. 3 (February 2007): 268–71.

———. "The Political Economy of Religious Commodities in Cairo." *American Anthropologist* 97, no. 1 (March 1995): 51.

Stepputat, Finn, and Thomas Blom Hansen. *States of Imagination: Ethnographic Explorations of the Postcolonial State*. Politics, History, and Culture. Durham: Duke University Press, 2001.

Strathern, Marilyn. *Audit Cultures: Anthropological Studies in Accountability, Ethics, and the Academy*. New York: Routledge, 2000.

Sullivan, Denis J. "Extra-State Actors and Privatization in Egypt." In *Privatization and Liberalization in the Middle East*. Edited by Iliya Harik and Denis J. Sullivan. Bloomington: Indiana University Press, 1992.

———. *Private Voluntary Organizations in Egypt: Islamic Development, Private Initiative, and State Control*. Gainesville: University Press of Florida, 1994.

———, and Sana Abed-Kotob. *Islam in Contemporary Egypt: Civil Society Vs. the State*. Boulder, Colo.: Lynne Rienner, 1999.

Tepe, Sultan. "Politics between Market and Islam: The Electoral Puzzles and Changing Prospects of Pro-Islamic Parties." *Mediterranean Quarterly* 18, no. 2 (2007): 107–35.

Thompson, E. P. "Time, Work-Discipline, and Industrial Capitalism." *Past & Present* 38, no. 1 (December 1, 1967): 56–97.

Toukan, Dima. "A New Arab Philanthropism Is Emerging." *Daily Star*, May 29, 2009. http://www.dailystar.com.lb/Opinion/Commentary/May/29/A-new-Arab-philanthropism-is-emerging.ashx#axzz2OI4KmhQe.

Tripp, Charles. *Islam and the Moral Economy: The Challenge of Capitalism*. New York: Cambridge University Press, 2006.

Tsai, Kellee S. "Banquet Banking: Gender and Rotating Savings and Credit Associations in South China." *China Quarterly* 161 (March 2000): 142–70.

Tsing, Anna Lowenhaupt. *Friction: An Ethnography of Global Connection*. Princeton: Princeton University Press, 2004.

Tuğal, Cihan. *Passive Revolution: Absorbing the Islamic Challenge to Capitalism*. Stanford: Stanford University Press, 2009.

Turam, Berna. *Between Islam and the State: The Politics of Engagement.* Stanford: Stanford University Press, 2007.

Tyndale, Wendy. *Visions of Development: Faith-Based Initiatives.* Edited by Wendy Tyndale. Burlington, Vt.: Ashgate, 2006.

United National Development Program (UNDP). *Egypt Human Development Report,* 2005.

U.S. Department of State. Bureau of Democracy, Human Rights and Labor. "International Religious Freedom Report." Washington, D.C., 2006.

Valentine, Gill. "People Like Us: Negotiating Sameness and Difference in the Research Process." In *Feminist Geography in Practice: Research and Methods.* Edited by Pamela J. Moss. Malden, Mass.: Blackwell Publishers, 2002.

Wahba, Mourad. "Private and Public Economic Bases: The Egyptian Case." In *Development in the Age of Liberalization: Egypt and Mexico.* Edited by Dan Tschirgi. Cairo: American University in Cairo Press, 1996.

Wainwright, Joel. *Decolonizing Development: Colonial Power and the Maya.* Antipode Book Series. Malden, Mass.: Blackwell Publishers, 2008.

Warde, Ibrahim A. *Islamic Finance in the Global Economy.* Edinburgh: University of Edinburgh Press, 2000.

Wattad, Nizar, and Paola Rizzuto. "Issues in the News: Egypt Will Continue Nationalizing Mosques." *Washington Report on Middle East Affairs* 22, no. 8 (October 2003). http://www.wrmea.org/component/content/article/254 -wrmea-archives/washington-report-archives-2000-2005/october-2003/ 4786-issues-in-the-news.html.

Watts, Michael. "Development and Governmentality." *Singapore Journal of Tropical Geography* 24, no. 1 (March 2003): 6–34.

Weber, Max. *The Protestant Ethic and the Spirit of Capitalism.* Routledge Classics. [Protestantische Ethik und der Geist des Kapitalismus]. New York: Routledge, 1992.

Wickham, Carrie Rosefsky. "Islamic Mobilization and Political Change: The Islamist Trend in Egypt's Professional Associations." In *Political Islam: Essays from Middle East Report.* Edited by Joel Beinin and Joe Stork. Berkeley: University of California Press, 1997.

Wiktorowicz, Quintan. *Islamic Activism: A Social Movement Theory Approach.* Indiana Series in Middle East Studies. Bloomington: Indiana University Press, 2004.

Wilson, Patrick C. "Neoliberalism, Indigeneity, and Social Engineering in Ecuador's Amazon." *Critique of Anthropology* 28, no. 2 (June 1, 2008): 127–44.

Wilson, Rodney. "Arab Government Responses to Islamic Finance: The Case of Egypt and Saudi Arabia." *Mediterranean Politics* 7, no. 3 (Autumn 2002): 143–63.

———. "Islam and Business." *Thunderbird International Business Review* 48, no. 1 (2006): 109–23.

Wilson, Willow G. The Show-Me Sheikh. *Atlantic Monthly,* July–August 2005.

Winchester, H. P. M. "Qualitative Research and Its Place in Human Geography." In *Qualitative Research Methods in Human Geography.* Edited by Iain Hay. Oxford: Oxford University Press, 2000.

Wise, Lindsay. "'Words from the Heart': New Forms of Islamic Preaching in Egypt." MSc, St. Anthony's College, Oxford University, 2003.

Wolch, J. R. *The Shadow State: Government and Voluntary Sector in Transition.* New York: The Foundation Center, 1990.

World Bank Group. *Egypt, Arab Republic Data Profile,* 2007.

Yoon, In-Jon. "The Changing Significance of Ethnic and Class Resources in Immigrant Businesses: The Case of Korean Immigrant Businesses in Chicago." *International Migration Review* 25, no. 2 (1991): 303–33.

Yusuf, Ibrahim Imam. "Dawr al-ittihad al-ʿamm li-l-gamʿiyyat wa-l-muʾassasat al-ahliyya fi-l-tadamun al-igtimaʿi." *Nadwat dawr al-munazzamat ghayr al-hukumiyya fi al-tadamun al-igtimaʿi,* May 31, 2006. Cairo: Markaz Salah Abdullah Kamel li-l-Iqtisad al-Islami. Gamaiʿat al-Azhar.

Yusuf, Nabil Muhammad. "Al-taqyim al-iqtisadi wa-l-igtimaʿi li-l gamʿiyyat al-ahliyya li-muhafazat al-Qahira." *Nadwat al-taqyim al-ʾiqtisadiyya wa-l-igtimaʿiyya li-l gamʿiyyat al-khayriyya al-ahliyya fi Gumhuriyyat Misr al-ʿArabiyya,* vol. 1, October 29–30, 1997. Cairo: Markaz Salah Abdullah Kamel li-l-Iqtisad al-Islami. Gamaiʿat al-Azhar.

Zaied, Al-Sayed. "Daʿwa for Dollars: A New Wave of Muslim Televangelists." *Arab Insight: Emerging Social and Religious Trends* 21 (Winter 2008): 21–27.

Zain, Maria. "Adnan Durrani's Saffraon Road and Ethic Consumerism." *Dinar Standard,* May 19, 2011. http://dinarstandard.com/adnan-durrani%E2%80%99s-saffron-road-and-ethical-consumerism/.

Index

Page numbers in italics indicate figures or tables. Page numbers in bold indicate location of definitions in glossary.

MONA ATIA is assistant professor of geography and international affairs at George Washington University.